BUCKET
~ TO ~
GREECE

Volume 14

V.D. BUCKET

Copyright © 2021 V.D. Bucket
All rights reserved.

No part of this publication may be reproduced, distributed, or transmitted in any form or by any means, including photocopying, recording, or other electronic or mechanical methods, without the prior written permission of the publisher, except in the case of brief quotations embodied in critical reviews and certain other noncommercial uses permitted by copyright law.

All names have been changed to spare my wife embarrassment.

Editor: James Scraper

Proofreader: Alan Wood

Cover: German Creative

Interior Format: The Book Khaleesi

Other Books in the Bucket to Greece Series

Bucket to Greece Volume 1
Bucket to Greece Volume 2
Bucket to Greece Volume 3
Bucket to Greece Volume 4
Bucket to Greece Volume 5
Bucket to Greece Volume 6
Bucket to Greece Volume 7
Bucket to Greece Volume 8
Bucket to Greece Volume 9
Bucket to Greece Volume 10
Bucket to Greece Volume 11
Bucket to Greece Volume 12
Bucket to Greece Volume 13
Bucket to Greece Collection Vols 1-3
Bucket to Greece Collection Vols 4-6
Bucket to Greece Collection Vols 7-9
Bucket to Greece Collection Vols 10-12

Chapter 1

A Monastic Meander

"Botheration, that's all I need. It's only gone and erupted." Calling out to Benjamin in a weary tone, I could almost visualise the mist of exhaustion exhaled along with my words, vaporising under the sun.

Coming to a reluctant halt, my son swivelled around to face me, shuffling impatiently as he waited for me to catch up with him; no easy feat since my steps were hampered by a limp. Reaching his side, I grasped my aching ribs and groaned. Rolling his eyes, Benjamin exclaimed, "Could you be any more melodramatic, Dad?"

V.D. BUCKET

"I can feel the gunk suppurating out of the wound? I'll have a heck of a job prising my sock away from my heel...it will end up encrusted on unless we take a breather so I can apply some rudimentary first aid. I don't fancy asking your mum to tweeze wool fibres out of the oozing crater if I leave it to fester. You know how squeamish she gets."

"You do realise that you're beginning to sound just like granny?" Benjamin scoffed.

"Perish the thought. I haven't said a single word about the likelihood of my swollen feet exploding." Admittedly, the thought had crossed my mind even though I hadn't actually verbalised it. Assuming a lofty tone, I added, "I can't say that I appreciate any comparison between Violet Burke's feet and my own."

"I doubt it's heredity," Benjamin opined in a jocular manner. "I rather suspect that granny's life-long love affair with artery-clogging chip shop fat has contributed to her bloated appendages. I suspect you're only suffering because you didn't invest in a pair of sturdy walking shoes."

"It wouldn't kill you to throw a little sympathy in my direction, you know. A burst blister is no laughing matter considering we've still got to trek all the way back. At least I didn't scream like a banshee, the way you did when you came off your bicycle."

BUCKET TO GREECE (VOL.14)

"In my defence, I was only six at the time. Even so, I can still recall the excruciating pain when my trapped thumb nail turned purple and dropped off. It was hardly comparable to a tiny blister on your heel," Benjamin said dismissively.

"Tiny?" Before I felt it erupt inside my sock, I had visions of the pustule being bigger than my actual foot. "Now that it's popped, it could develop into a nasty fungal infection if I don't attend to it pretty sharpish."

"For goodness' sake. Park your old carcass on that rock and sort it out."

Sinking down wearily, I began to unlace my shoe. "Have a good rummage through that backpack of yours, Ben. I threw some plasters and a bottle of hand sanitiser in before we left this morning."

"What on earth possessed you to cart a bottle of hand sanitiser to a monastery?" Benjamin asked incredulously.

"Well, I wasn't sure how basic it would be, or how well up the monks might be on personal hygiene…it's a good job that I threw it in. I can use it to disinfect the popped blister before sticking a plaster on."

Perching on the sun-warmed rock to remove my damp, sweaty socks, brought instant relief. Whilst Benjamin searched through the backpack, I took a moment to appreciate the sheer majesty of our surroundings. In such an idyllic spot, I felt as though we were worlds away from the hustle and bustle of regular life, almost as though we had been dropped into an isolated paradise of outstanding natural beauty. Verdant green oak, pine, and fir trees lined the narrow path, stretching out over the horizon as far as the eye could see. Hidden amongst the greenery, wild herbs released their intoxicating scent into the air.

The tangible silence of the gorge served to magnify the babble of the river Lousios below, along with the piping notes of an eagle soaring over our heads. The barely discernible breeze carried the melodic chime of bells plinking gently in the distance. Benjamin and I paused to exchange a smile before gazing upwards towards the source of the mellifluous tintinnabulation.

The sight of Prodromos Monastery, also known as The Holy Monastery of Timios Prodromos of Arcadia, clinging precariously to the vertical cliff face was beyond impressive, appearing as though miraculously suspended. Although it gave the impression it could come tumbling precipitously down into the gorge at any moment, it had held its grip on the rocky cliff for five centuries. It crossed my mind that if I ever penned an account about our trek to the monastery and its magnificent environs, any descriptions would be worthy of a dozen or so of

BUCKET TO GREECE (VOL.14)

Marigold's beloved plings. The stunning setting was certainly worth exclaiming over.

"I've got to say that Mum pulled a blinder choosing Arcadia for this trip," Benjamin said.

"Her choice of destination was certainly the last place I would have expected," I said.

Marigold had planned to surprise Benjamin and Adam by inviting them along on our second honeymoon, a trip that I knew nothing about until she sprang it on me after our vow renewal service two days earlier. Knowing that one of the must-do items on the boys' bucket list was a visit to a traditional Greek working monastery, she had selflessly chosen an area where they could tick said item off their list. Although the monasteries of Mount Athos were top of the boys' wish list, Marigold had ruled the famous site out, claiming the monks there were obviously sexist since they excluded women from visiting their male-only community. As it turned out, unfortunately, Adam couldn't prolong his stay in Greece due to work commitments, thus Benjamin had to make do with my company for the trek up to the shadowed cloisters.

Marigold had booked a couple of rooms at a traditional guesthouse in the charming village of Stemnitsa, located high above sea level in the heart of lush Arcadia, within trekking distance of the Monastery of Prodromos. Even though our particular monastic destination didn't bar women from entering as long as they didn't turn up in trousers and covered their cleavage, Marigold had cried off at the last moment, claiming she hadn't packed any suitable shoes for walking the gorge. Moreover, she insisted someone had to stay behind to keep Violet Burke company, the latter having invited herself along on the honeymoon trip to spare Benjamin the embarrassment of being a gooseberry.

Marigold was adamant that someone had to keep an eye on my mother to ensure that she didn't make an exhibition of herself if left to her own devices. Naturally, my mother put her foot down, refusing to accompany us to the monastery, convinced that her feet would explode if she attempted to tackle the trek. I was relieved to leave her behind; she would have been sure to show us up by blurting out blunt and derogatory comments about bearded monks wearing frocks.

"It's a good job that Uncle Barry didn't join us on this honeymoon, what with his vertigo. Can you imagine?"

"I rather think that Barry has what is known as selective vertigo. It never seems to impede him when there's a job to be done that involves scaling some dodgy scaffolding. He clambers up with nary a worry, yet if we'd suggested scaling this cliff to the monastery, he'd have gone to pieces," I sniggered.

BUCKET TO GREECE (VOL.14)

"In truth, I'm quite impressed with my own efforts. This cliff face is pretty steep. I wasn't sure we'd manage it without going to extremes and clamping crampons onto a rope to scale it."

"Crampons go on boots not ropes and are used on icy ascents," Benjamin corrected me, handing over the bottle of hand sanitiser. "It's not as though we were scaling the Khumbu Icefall at Everest. This meandering track isn't exactly vertical."

As the sound of the bells washed over us, I reflected on the unique experience the two of us had just shared. Benjamin and I had set off from Stemnitsa on the first stage of the Menalon Trail, early that morning. Taking the cobbled path out of the village which led to an old mule track, we followed the serpentine route meandering up to the monastery. In retrospect, it probably wasn't the wisest move on my part to think that covering nine kilometres would be a bit of a doddle, particularly now that we had only just begun the hike back. Moreover, when we had started out, Benjamin had insisted on no dawdling since neither of us fancied traipsing uphill in the hot midday sun, not to mention that the monastery closed to visitors at one o'clock. No doubt the monks were as keen to grab a siesta as the rest of the Greek population.

The Menalon Trail actually covered a whopping seventy-five kilometres in total. I imagined

V.D. BUCKET

that if Adam rather than I, had accompanied Benjamin, the pair of them may well have ventured further. Ben had been keen to explore the picturesque village of Dimitsana with its abandoned water mills, but there was no way my swollen feet would make the distance; it was twelve and a half kilometres each way. As much as I thought that my regular strolls around Meli had kept me in shape, I still found the distance we had covered a challenge, even before factoring in the festering blister.

It was only to be expected that Benjamin found it easier than I. Not only is my son still on the right side of forty whilst I have now passed into my sixth decade, he wasn't suffering the lingering pain of cracked ribs. Perchance the trek up to Dimitsana may have been doable in the cooler temperatures of spring but it was way too hot to contemplate in June, particularly in light of the fact that we were overdressed for the walk.

Considering our final destination had involved dropping in on a religious order, I had stressed that it was only fitting that we dress accordingly to avoid risking disrespecting the monks. Grouching when I pointed out that shorts and short-sleeved shirts would be inappropriate attire to wear, Benjamin had reluctantly joined me in donning long trousers and long sleeves, arguing there was nothing unseemly about displaying his calves. My son had scoffed at the sight of my tie, claiming it was more than a tad over the top; heeding his advice, I had shoved it into the backpack, only slipping it around my neck when we eventually reached the sixteenth-century monastery.

Entering through an ancient wooden door set into an arch, we had discovered it was delightfully cool inside. The old door was peppered with bullet holes from the Turkish occupation; steeped in history, the monastery had been used as a hospital for local fighters during the rebellion. Climbing the wide, white-washed stairs between cave-like white walls huddled beneath low wooden ceilings, we appreciated how atmospheric and timeless it felt, flickering candles illuminating the fascinating wall frescoes.

Hospitable monks greeted us, inviting us to explore. A grey- bearded monk in black vestments and a pill box hat invited us to step out onto a tiled balcony suspended over the sheer drop, only flimsy looking wooden railings preventing us from hurtling into the gorge. To our amazement, the monk treated us to a personal performance in the art of monastic bell-ringing. Beginning by striking a wooden semantron with a mallet, the presentation culminated in the monk striking metal bells tied onto the wooden railings. It was almost worth the blister.

Applying the bacteria killing ethyl alcohol to my now deflated blister, I squirmed in pain. I considered that it was no great surprise that my poor foot had developed such a pressure sore since we had been on the go for hours.

"Will an ordinary plaster do or will you be insisting on a blue catering one?"

"That sarcastic tone of yours reminds me of your mum," I snapped. "An ordinary plaster will do just fine. I can't envisage any circumstance where I'm likely to dangle my foot over a pan of food."

"Speaking of food, do you fancy some of that Turkish delight that the monks gave us? I saw you sneaking some of it into the backpack."

"To bring back for your mum. You know how her sweet tooth loves *loukoumi*."

"I thought it was quite extraordinary that the monks greeted us so hospitably and plied us with refreshments," Benjamin said, referencing the *loukoumi*, coffee and water that the monks had offered us.

"I thought it was a stroke of luck that they spoke English. I would have hated for you to feel excluded if I'd been forced to chat away to them in Greek."

"I don't know. If you'd been forced to speak in Greek, it might have spared the monks your long-winded advice on dumb waiters," Benjamin retorted. "If you'd struggled to come up with the necessary Greek words, we may have enjoyed some blissful monastic silence. I can't believe that monk didn't tell you to stick your ridiculous advice where the sun doesn't shine."

"Well, really," I spluttered.

I had suggested to the monk who served us with refreshments that they may find it handy to adopt my original version of a dumb waiter. Going into great detail which I had gleaned from personal experience, I had explained that attaching a bucket to a rope would spare any monks the bother of lugging carrier bags of shopping up to the monastery, though admittedly it would require an awfully long skein of rope, not to mention a fair bit of welly on the pulling end. It has to be said that they didn't appear too impressed with my words of wisdom about dangling buckets. Benjamin was under the impression that the order was more or less self-sufficient and unlikely to make a weekly trek to Lidl.

"All done," I announced, slipping my soggy sock back onto my now plastered foot. "Is there any water left?"

"Just a drop but it doesn't look very tempting. It's close to boiling point after being carted around in the sun. We could fill up the bottle from the river," Benjamin suggested.

V.D. BUCKET

"The same river that any passing animals may have used as their personal toilet," I snorted. "Unless you threw some water purifying tablets into the backpack, I wouldn't advise drinking untreated river water. I don't want to risk us coming down with a nasty case of leptospirosis."

"Fair point," Benjamin conceded with a cheery grin, offering me a hand up from the rock. I felt a rush of affection for my son. Of all my family members, he was the only one to take my dire warnings about bacteria seriously, rather than with a pinch of salt.

Chapter 2

A Gem in the Heart of Arcadia

It was late afternoon when we finally made it back to the village of Stemnitsa. I resisted the temptation to go full-on Greek and indulge in a spot of genuflection by making the sign of the cross, in gratitude for getting back under my own steam. I had declined Benjamin's grudging offer to give his old dad a piggy-back, preferring to suffer the torments of my feet than risk being spotted making such an ignominious entrance to the village.

Stemnitsa was a gem in the heart of Arcadia, a haven of shadowy, stone cobbled alleyways and old stone houses nestling in the timeless shade of cherry, acacia, plane, walnut, and chestnut trees. It would certainly be worth a return visit in spring when the cherry trees would be glorious in full blossom, or in autumn when the chestnut trees would be laden with nuts.

On our arrival the previous day, I had taken the time to read up on Stemnitsa, fascinated to discover it was known as the Goldsmith's village, having been a centre for silver and goldsmiths since Byzantium times. Marigold had listened with half an ear as I shared snippets of interesting facts from my newly acquired guide book.

Clearly disinterested when I told her that craftsmen had fashioned crosses, icons and candlesticks in the area for centuries, her ears perked up when I added that they also created brooches and rings. When I mentioned that the village even boasted its own smithery, the Gold and Silversmithing Workshop School of Stemnitsa, where students studied the art of creating handmade jewellery, Marigold practically snatched the credit card out of my wallet, saying she may well throw caution to the wind and treat herself to a little retail therapy whilst I was off gadding at the monastery with Benjamin.

After such an arduous trek, I was keen to get back to our lodgings and soak my aching body in a luxurious bubble bath. Marigold, knowing how

BUCKET TO GREECE (VOL.14)

much I missed a tub since our home in Meli only featured a shower, had thoughtfully chosen accommodation with a bath to indulge me. However, I had yet to enjoy a good soak as Marigold had claimed first dibs on the tub. I had been unable to drag her out of it the previous evening. Unfortunately, or fortunately from Marigold's perspective, there wasn't enough room for me to join her, the tub not as large as the one that Harold and Joan had wallowed in together back in Meli and which now adorns my garden.

Our route back to the guest house passed through the lively village square, bustling with tourists and locals. Traversing the cobbled square lined with coffee shops and tavernas, the dulcet tones of my wife caught my attention as she called out for us to join her for a spot of afternoon tea. Looking around, I spotted Marigold and my mother relaxing in the outdoor seating area of a *kafenio*. Although I wanted nothing more than to indulge my whim to soak in the tub, I recognised that Marigold had been stuck with Violet Burke all day and it was my husbandly duty to share the burden. Spotting the name of the café, Gerousia, I realised it was the historical place I had read about the previous evening. Since it came highly recommended, I jumped at the opportunity to introduce its famous pastries to my son.

V.D. BUCKET

"You must try the *galaktoboureko*. It's really quite superb," Marigold urged as we sat down to join them.

"What's that?" Benjamin asked.

"It's a Greek pastry soaked in syrup and filled with decadently rich milk custard," Marigold said.

"I've had two slices," Vi volunteered, though she needn't have bothered since the tell-tale traces of syrup that had dribbled down her chin were a bit of a giveaway. "I'm not much of a one for sweet stuff, but knowing that I'm right partial to a dollop of tinned custard, Marigold twisted my arm. Why the Greeks have to go making such a tongue twister of its name, I'll never know."

"It's simply a combination of the Greek word for milk, *gala*, and *boureko*, which is derived from the Turkish word for pastry," I explained.

"It's still a right gob full," Vi complained. "I don't know why they can't keep it simple. It's right easy to remember words like *krema* for cream because the Greeks just put a bit of a twist on the English word."

Since I was clueless if the word *krema* was borrowed from cream or if it was the other way round, I didn't argue the point. No doubt Spiros would insist that cream came from *krema* since he was generally resolute in his opinion that the Ancient Greeks invented everything. I thought I had trumped him with my claim to have invented my own innovative dumb waiter, but Spiros bested me by boasting that the ancients had employed the same method to hoist heavy loads upwards. When I challenged him to confirm if they'd actually used buckets and rope, Spiros retorted that the ancients attached much grander contraptions to their winches. I still recall the slight at his implication that there is nothing remotely sophisticated about my own bucket on a rope.

"You look a bit tired, darling," Marigold observed. In contrast to my own fatigued appearance, my wife looked chic and relaxed. Still carrying the bridal glow from our recent ceremony, she struck me as quite lovely, the afternoon sun highlighting her Titian locks.

"He's done nothing but complain about his feet all day," Benjamin joshed.

"'Appen they've caught up with you, lad. I did warn you that you'd likely inherit my swollen Blossom feet," Vi cackled with obvious glee at the notion that I had inherited something from her beyond our mutual obsession with hygiene.

"Nonsense. I just selected unsuitable shoes for such a trek and developed a painful blister or two." The blister which I had treated with hand sanitiser earlier had since bred, producing a number of offspring inside my socks.

V.D. BUCKET

After asking his mum to order him a coffee and a slice of the orange pie, *portokalopita*, which he'd spied a couple polishing off with relish at the next table, Benjamin excused himself to pop inside to the loo. Whilst he was gone, the waitress came for our order. I opted for a savoury cheese pie, *tyropita*, to go with my coffee. There was nothing discreet about the way Violet Burke blatantly unbuttoned her waistband before deciding she might as well force a third slice of *galaktoboureko* down her gullet.

"Wow, this place is really something," Benjamin said on his return.

"Indeed, Gerousia has been serving coffee since 1870," I said.

"That means it's been going for longer than you, Gran," Benjamin quipped.

"You cheeky 'apeth. Considering the place has been going so long, it's amazing that their custard pastries aren't riddled with mould."

"It's not as though the pastries have been hanging around since the nineteenth century," I pointed out, wondering if a third piece of *galaktoboureko* might finish Violet Burke off and spare us her company over dinner later.

"It's quite impressive inside," Ben said. "It's got a lovely wooden ceiling and one of those traditional wood-burners for the winter."

"They call them *sombas* over here," Violet Burke

BUCKET TO GREECE (VOL.14)

enlightened him.

"You've taken to speaking Greek like a duck to water, Granny," Benjamin flattered her.

"I was thinking it might be romantic if the two of us returned on our own for a winter mini-break," Marigold suggested, reaching across for my hand and giving it a squeeze. I could discern from her tone that she was keen to be shot of her mother-in-law. To be fair, when my wife planned this second honeymoon, she had no idea that Violet Burke would invite herself along or that she would be stuck with her whilst I disappeared for the day with our son. Rather, she had envisaged that Benjamin and his life-partner, Adam, would be off doing their own thing, traipsing around monasteries, giving us some alone time.

"This place has a fascinating history," I told my family. "This *kafenio* takes its name, Gerousia, from the Peloponnese Senate founded in the early days of the Greek War of Independence. You may recall that the Maniots led the uprising against the Turkish occupiers in 1821..."

"I don't know how Marigold puts up with all your waffling on about boring facts," Violet Burke chimed in.

Ignoring her interruption, I continued. "The Senate moved its seat to the Chrysopege Monastery in Stemnitsa..."

"You seem to be well up on the local history," Benjamin interrupted.

"Well, you know me. I like to familiarise myself with the history of the area…"

"Your dad had his nose buried in a book about the area last night," Marigold interjected. "I told him this was meant to be a second honeymoon and spending his time reading up on boring old wars was hardly romantic."

"This second honeymoon never had any chance of being romantic once you turned it into a family holiday," I pointed out.

"Victor has a point," Vi piped up. "I'm hardly going to get any romantic offers when any likely candidates find out I'm bunking in with my grandson."

Marigold, taking Vi's words at face value, looked quite horrified at the prospect of her mother-in-law spending the evening accosting strange men with her non-existent charms. My wife's features only relaxed when she realised that Vi was pulling her leg when Benjamin winked at Vi, proclaiming, "You are a scream, Granny."

"Eh, Ben, 'appen someone will mistake you for my toy boy."

"I don't mind playing along," Ben chortled, always happy to oblige his granny.

"Anyway, you're a fine one to complain about

BUCKET TO GREECE (VOL.14)

Victor having his nose stuck in a guide book. You've done the same for the last hour," Vi accused Marigold.

"Well, I had intended that we move on to Tripoli tomorrow but I was chatting to a couple of locals and they were surprised that I'd chosen Tripoli as a honeymoon destination," Marigold said. "They told me that Tripoli isn't at all a romantic city. They recommended that we stay in the Hanging Village of Lagadia which is only a short drive from here. Apparently, it is quite charming and very picturesque."

Marigold passed the guide book to me, the page conveniently open to Lagadia.

"It says that Lagadia dates back to probably the 13th century and that two prime ministers of Greece were born there," I said, my interest apparent.

"And were they particularly handsome?" Marigold asked. Noticing Marigold's eyes twinkling with amusement as she teased me about my apparent obsession with the handsomeness of the Albanian Prime Minister, Fatos Nano, I realised she'd set me up, knowing I would pick up on the reference to the birthplace of the two former premiers as soon as I got my hands on the guide book. I rather selfishly hoped that Fatos Nano would lose his position as prime minister in next month's Albanian parliamentary election as it might put an end to the teasing once and for all. The only reason I reluctantly followed Albanian politics was to keep one step ahead if any of the locals brought up Fatos' name.

"I have to say I like the sound of that Hanging Village," Vi piped up. "'Appen it's where the Greeks sorted out their witches, like that Pendle place back home."

"Actually, the Pendle witches weren't hanged at Pendle. They met their end at Gallows Hill in Lancaster," I said.

"You and your facts..." Vi grumbled.

"Anyway, it says in the guide book that Lagadia is known as the Hanging Village because it hangs over the gorge. It has nothing to do with hanging witches or anyone else. Perhaps it's rather similar to the way the monastery we visited was suspended from the cliff," I suggested.

"So, no witches," Vi said in a deflated tone. "Now, I quite fancied Tripoli because Marigold read that it's famous for having the best spuds in Greece. I wouldn't say no to a taste of the chips they make from them."

"It's all in the same area, Vi. I'm sure we'll be able to find you a plate of chips in Lagadia that are made out of Tripoli potatoes," Marigold said.

"I will leave it up to you, darling, to choose between Tripoli and the Hanging Village. I don't mind where we go as long as we're together," I assured Marigold.

"I can't decide," Marigold dithered.

"Well, I must say that I'm enjoying the quiet pace of Arcadia," I said. "The thought of exploring another charming village holds more appeal than the bustle of a city."

"I'm with dad," Benjamin agreed.

"It's decided then. Tomorrow we'll drive over to Lagadia and find a guest house there," Marigold said.

Tuning out as the three of them chatted, I reflected on our journey to this historic café. After bidding goodbye to our English guests, Douglas and Elaine, Adam, and Geraldine, who were flying back home via Athens, we had set off for Arcadia on the afternoon following our vow renewal service. Due to the lingering pain from my ribs, Benjamin and Marigold took turns behind the wheel of the Punto, my mother hogging the passenger seat.

Despite the short notice, Nikos and Dina had given Violet Burke their blessing to take some time off from peeling potatoes and slopping her mop around the taverna. Vi's expat clients proved more of a challenge, selfishly demanding to know how she expected them to manage without her and complaining about the lack of notice. Vi had responded by pointing out that they could always get off their lazy backsides and do their own scrubbing and squirt some bleach down their lavs, a response that didn't go down too well. I considered their attitude a tad churlish, begrudging a break to a poor, overworked pensioner who had worked tirelessly ever since landing in Greece.

Vi's arrival in Meli had turned our expat neighbours soft. They were loath to resume their own cleaning, a condition shared by my wife. Violet Burke spent the first hour in the Punto calculating how much she could up her hourly rate on her return, since the expat contingent were so reliant on her to keep their homes sparkling. It has to be said, Violet Burke does a sterling job. I would challenge any char to best her when it comes to a good bottoming.

A thoughtless nudge in my still aching ribs by my wife, brought me back to the present and I took a sip of my aromatic coffee.

"It's still not sitting well with me at all, Victor," Marigold complained.

Not wanting my wife to realise that I hadn't been paying attention to whatever she'd been chuntering on about, I adopted a thoughtful look in the hope that she would elaborate.

"You must have been out of your mind." Marigold's scathing tone pretty much convinced me that the subject of the Albanian shed dweller must have reared its ugly head again, a guess that was confirmed when she continued, "I will never understand what on earth possessed you to give Guzim a key to the house. You must have taken leave of your senses. I dread to think what he's up to in there."

"How else could Guzim feed your precious felines if I hadn't given him a key? It's not as if the coddled creatures are in the habit of venturing outdoors and down to the garden to catch their own meals. I hate to think how you would have reacted if I'd chucked the cats in his shed. I thought you'd prefer me to give Guzim a key than have your precious felines slumming it in the pink palace of love."

"There's no need to resort to sarcasm, dear. You know that I would never countenance Guzim looking after the cats in his shed. Being in a strange place would have upset Clawsome and Catastrophe. Goodness only knows if they'll take to Guzim and I don't know how you expect them to understand him if he tries to communicate with them in Albanian. You should have just given a key to Doreen."

"And risk her using our home as a love nest whilst we're away. I don't think it would have done our standing amongst the villagers any good to be seen condoning Doreen carrying on with that Texan whilst she's still married to Norman."

"I suppose you have a point," Marigold reluctantly admitted. "But surely anyone would have

V.D. BUCKET

been better than Guzim..."

"He hasn't killed off any of my chickens yet. Not to mention that he's always very diligent in making sure Kyria Maria doesn't chuck Doruntina in her cooking pot," I retorted. "If you hadn't sprung this second honeymoon on me without a moment's notice, there may have been time to sort out other arrangements."

As it was, Barry had been too swamped with work to pop in and feed the cats twice a day, and Cynthia was run off her feet at the tourist office, hence my handing over the key to the Bucket house to the Albanian shed dweller.

"Everything was in hand, Victor. I had already asked your mother to see to the cats as she would have been popping up to clean anyway."

"Well, I could hardly have been in two places at once, lass," Vi interrupted. "I'd have happily looked after them cats of yours if you hadn't insisted that I come along on your second honeymoon."

Marigold fired a withering look at Violet Burke. "I think it was more a case of you inviting yourself..."

"How about if I take Granny out for dinner this evening so you two lovebirds can have a romantic evening alone?" Benjamin offered, sensing the growing tension between his mum and his grandma.

BUCKET TO GREECE (VOL.14)

"Are you sure, lad? 'Appen Victor and Marigold might fancy a bit of company. I can't imagine they've much to talk about after being married so long."

"Did you have company on your honeymoon?" Marigold snapped, even though she'd been the one to make secret arrangements to include Benjamin and Adam in our trip, thus inadvertently lumping us with my mother.

"I can't rightly say that I ever went on a proper honeymoon, never mind a second one," Vi said.

"But you tied the knot four times." Marigold's obvious irritation with my mother switched to sympathy. With her obsession with mini-breaks, my wife was clearly aghast at the thought of Violet Burke being deprived of the traditional post wedding holiday, not only once, but four times.

"That trip to Blackpool what I took with my first husband, Ernest, back in 49, was the nearest I ever came to having a honeymoon jolly. Mind, I'm not sure it counts since it didn't happen until a couple of years after we wed, what with the dozy 'apeth going and getting himself drafted and sent overseas. Course, when we made it to Blackpool, Ernest wasn't able to do his bridegroom duty by me, if you get my drift, what with him having picked up that nasty dose of foreign mumps that left him with atrophied…"

"Yes, I remember you saying," I interrupted before my mother could embarrass us further by completing her sentence. It had not escaped my notice that the American couple on the next table were blatantly eavesdropping, their mouths gaping open as they hung on Vi's every word

"Testicles..." my mother completed her sentence to the great delight of the nosy Americans.

Spotting the gawking tourists, Marigold hastily changed the subject, belatedly deigning to enquire about our trip to the monastery.

"I do hope the local monastery wasn't a disappointment for you, Benjamin. Knowing how keen you were to visit the monastic communities of Mount Athos, I do hope that you didn't find the local one a bit of a let-down."

"I thoroughly enjoyed our visit to the Monastery of Prodromos," Benjamin assured his mum. "But if anything, it has only whetted my appetite to visit Mount Athos with Adam. The monasteries there are the oldest in the world; imagine, monks have populated the Mount since the fourth century."

"I wonder how a community made up of nowt but fellas goes about populating itself," Violet Burke posited.

Rolling her eyes dismissively, Marigold said, "Well, I just can't condone the attitude of such a

BUCKET TO GREECE (VOL.14)

blatantly sexist sect."

"Sexist?" Vi queried.

"They don't allow women in. No women at all. The Athos monks would have turned us away, Vi, if we'd turned up with Victor and Benjamin. At least the local monastery would have welcomed us."

Pointing out how illogical Marigold was being, Benjamin said, "But you and granny didn't want to come along to the monastery anyway. You said it would likely bore you rigid, especially since dad was sure to lecture you about every little detail that he'd gleaned from his guide books. You said you didn't want him lecturing you as though you were one of his tourist charges."

"I'm sure I never implied your dad was boring," Marigold said shamefacedly. "I didn't come along today because I forgot to pack any suitable shoes."

"Well, you missed out on a great experience," Benjamin said.

"I have a taste of the monastery for you," I told my wife, presenting her with the Turkish Delight we'd brought back.

"Oh, you are good to me, darling. You know how I love my *loukoumi*," Marigold simpered.

"Nearly as much as that sickly *halva* that gets stuck in my teeth."

V.D. BUCKET

"So, did the pair of you manage to get any dirt out of them fellas up at that monastery?" Vi demanded.

"No chance of that," Benjamin replied. "Can you believe that dad only carted a bottle of hand sanitiser up there?"

"Technically you were the one to cart it up there since it was in your backpack," I chortled, relieved that Benjamin had been the one to assume the role of a packhorse. The backpack weighed a ton since I had laden it with something for every conceivable emergency eventuality.

"Stop being flip, lad. You know what I mean. Did you get any dirt on the monks?" Vi pressed.

"Dirt on the monks. Have you lost the plot, Vi?" Marigold queried.

"What on earth sort of dirt were you expecting us to uncover, Granny? It's a very small community with only a handful of monks. The hospitable welcome they gave us went above and beyond. They even endured dad banging on about his bucket on a rope and advising them how to set one up."

"If you're going to disparage my bucket, at least refer to it by its proper name of a dumb waiter," I scolded my son.

Ignoring my correction, Benjamin continued, "Anyway, Gran, have you forgotten that dad has been retired off? I don't think it would have gone down too well if he'd started poking about in the monastery kitchen looking for dirt and doling out hygiene advice."

"I'm on about dirt as in goings on what shouldn't be, you muppet." Vi seemed unaware that the Americans were by now glued to her every word.

"You've lost me, Gran."

"For heaven's sake. Do I have to spell it out, lad? I didn't think you were that naïve. Were the monks romping around in pink panties?" Vi blurted.

Catching her drift, I couldn't resist a quiet chortle. "You mean red panties, Mother."

Chapter 3

Salacious Scandals

"Pink panties at a monastery!" Benjamin exclaimed. "Have you finally lost the plot, Granny?"

"Red panties," I corrected again, my words drowned out by Violet Burke tittering, "'Appen I forgot you might not be up on the juicy scandal, lad, what with you living in England..."

"Scandal, what scandal?" Benjamin asked. My son's ears weren't the only ones to visibly prick up. Noticing the American pair at the next table shifting their chairs ever closer, seemingly determined not to miss a word of our apparently gripping conversation, I was tempted to extend a sarcastic invitation for them to join us.

"Your dad and granny were fascinated by some clerical scandal that hit the Greek press earlier this year," Marigold volunteered, her tone implying she was above sullying her pure mind with such grubby matters. In truth, she'd been as riveted by the scandal as the rest of the population of Meli.

"Come now, Marigold, be fair. I was simply translating the news for Vi. In her defence, Vi wasn't the only one greedily devouring the news and lapping up every sordid titbit that was splashed in the papers," I pointed out, referencing the deplorable clerical behaviour that kept everyone in the village agog back in February.

"So, where do red panties come into it?" Benjamin asked.

"They don't, they're old hat. Your gran is confusing the monastic orgies that apparently made the headlines back in 1996, with this year's shocking exposé which didn't involve any pants," I explained.

"That's because the trollop was cavorting without any knickers on," Vi guffawed.

"When the nonagenarian bishop scandal broke this February, all the villagers were keen to dredge all the unrelated monastic skeletons out of the cupboard, regaling us with all the details to bring us up to date," I told Ben. "Admittedly, your gran did encourage them to fill us in on the sordid story of what went on in Kithira, long before we even moved to Greece, a shocking story that the villagers labelled the red panty scandal."

"I can't think why I got it in my head that it was pink underwear. Are you sure it was red, Victor?" Vi questioned.

"Most definitely," I confirmed, wishing I'd never bothered correcting her in the first place. The colour of the panties involved was really neither here nor there in the scheme of things.

"You might as well spill the beans, Victor, and put the lad out of his misery. I can see that Benjamin's dying to know what the monks got up to," Vi prompted.

"Apparently the monks at the remote monastery of Osios Theodoros on the Island of Kithira were engaging in homosexual orgies…"

"In their red panties," my mother added rather loudly, attracting a few more curious stares. "And tarting themselves up in revealing frocks for beauty contests."

"Quite ironic when you consider that if word of their shenanigans got out, they risked being defrocked," I quipped.

"Celibate monks engaging in gay orgies give homosexuals a bad name. They're supposed to be cloistered, not closeted," Benjamin opined in a disapproving tone. My son may be out and proud, but he frowns on in-your-face promiscuity and has never been one to mince or flaunt his gayness.

"It certainly isn't on when the official face of the Orthodox Church declares homosexuality an abomination whilst their monks are frolicking with one another behind closed doors," I agreed.

"And this was the scandal from 96?" Benjamin queried.

"That's right, lad. You don't want to go confusing it with what went on this February when that ninety-one-year-old bishop was caught on camera in bed with a naked young floozy. It was a sight filthier than anything they ever showed on 'Candid Camera.' I fair cringed at the right horrible images of the mucky buggers plastered all over the newspapers."

Although she professed to cringe, Violet Burke had greedily devoured the news, voraciously lapping up every salacious titbit that had been splashed all over the Greek newspapers. Not only did Nikos prove a willing accomplice to Vi by translating everything in the press for her benefit, he had made Kostis cart the old television down from upstairs so that all the taverna customers would be sure not to miss a morsel of the addictive carryings-on. Even our most devout orthodox neighbours piled into the taverna, crowding around the television and hanging on every word. Whilst our neighbour, Papas Andreas, acted outraged that such goings on should be associated with the church, most of the villagers made no secret of rejoicing in seeing their moral masters get their comeuppance.

Violet Burke delighted in filling her grandson in on what he'd missed. Having no time for organised religion since being disowned by the Methodist Blossoms, she liked nothing more than seeing anyone ostensibly holy being brought down a peg or two.

"It turned out that the cavorting nonagenarian wasn't the only bit of church dirt that the press was eager to report on." Vi paused for dramatic effect before continuing. "Even while tales of homosexual clerical sex were unfolding, one of them higher up bigwigs was caught out doing something right lewd with a young fella. As if all the mucky sex details weren't enough, there were them senior clerics caught out dealing drugs...and I don't mean aspirin."

"Allegedly," I reminded her. "The revelation which really fired up the local villagers was that of a cleric embezzling a couple of million to stash aside for his old age."

"Not that the orthodox church is hardly likely to miss the odd million. Nikos says it's worth billions," Vi practically spat in contempt.

"Naturally the Greeks were outraged to hear about a cleric dipping his hands in the till, so to speak. After all, it is ordinary taxpayers that end up footing the wages bill for the clerics, not to mention they pay the pensions of the clergy," I said.

"Victor, I seem to remember you saying something about the government abolishing tax on the revenues of the Orthodox Church?" Marigold prompted.

"Indeed, it was stopped in 2004."

"So, just last year," Benjamin clarified.

"Your dad had plenty to say about that at the time. He was forever griping that it wasn't right that he was paying tax on his meagre repping wages but the vast wealth of the church was left untaxed."

"I wasn't alone in making my displeasure felt," I assured them. "Whilst most of the Meli villagers profess to be good Christian churchgoers, they certainly resent the way that the god squad lives off the taxpayer dime when the church is worth billions. I have a theory that if the Greek populace had the choice of supporting the church through their taxes by declaring themselves orthodox, or of pronouncing themselves atheists with the option of holding onto the money that goes to the church, the entire populace would be turning out to profess they'd turned atheist overnight."

"So, that religious lot get taxpayer cash but don't pay tax?" Vi queried.

"A bit like you with your cash-in-hand cleaning jobs," Marigold reminded her.

"Aye, but I don't go getting any taxpayer handouts and I don't have the odd million stuffed down the side of my sofa," Vi retorted. "Give me a taste of that orange pie, Ben. 'Appen something a bit sharp might get rid of this sickly feeling that's come over me."

"I'm not surprised you feel sick with all this scandalous talk about clerical sex," Marigold sympathised.

"It's not that, lass. I reckon I shouldn't have had that last custard pastry. I can guarantee my stomach will be fair roiling later."

I was relieved that it was Benjamin rather than I, that would be sharing an en-suite bathroom with Violet Burke at the guest house.

"I've always said that the church lot are nothing but a bunch of hypocrites," Vi pontificated. "They do nowt but preach about morals, all the while trying to keep a lid on the lurid details of gay goings on between clerics, clerics what are meant to be chaste."

"I thought Greek priests could marry and procreate," Benjamin said, clearly confused by Vi's reference to chastity.

"The clergy is divided between those that are married and those that have taken a vow of chastity," I enlightened my son. "They can get married if they do it before they are ordained, but not after. I believe most of them are married, but of course the monks are meant to be celibate."

"What about Maria's son what lives next door? Is he supposed to be one of them celibates?" Vi asked.

"Yes, although I've never come right out and asked him, I imagine Andreas must live a celibate life since he never married before he was ordained. And being ordained, he isn't allowed to marry now," I replied.

"Then how come I clocked him canoodling with that daft Geraldine, only a couple of days ago?"

"Oh, no. Don't say that Geraldine has had her head turned by Andreas again," Marigold groaned. "I don't know how many times I've told her that he's a most unsuitable suitor. She's wasting her time carrying a torch for Andreas. It can never go anywhere."

I shared my wife's apprehension at the thought of Geraldine once again sneaking off to meet Andreas. She certainly hadn't wasted any time; she'd only flown over for a couple of days to celebrate our vow renewal. Perchance if the electric sparks were still flying between the couple that had no business being a couple, Andreas might one day unfrock himself and make an honest woman of Geraldine.

I recalled the sparks flying between them when they had initially met at Marigold's dinner party, a dinner she had thrown to dangle eligible bachelors in front of her best friend. Ignoring the eligible selection of Panos, Spiros and Dimitris, Geraldine had clearly been attracted to the uninvited Papas Andreas who had failed to meet the cut as an actual guest on account of him being a celibate cleric. It was obvious to me that there had been an instant attraction between them, Andreas even going so far as demanding I give him English lessons so he could telephone Geraldine on her return to Manchester and coo sweet nothings down the phone line.

Whatever sparks were between them seemed to fizzle out due to the physical distance between them and their inability to communicate with any comprehension over the phone. The next time Geraldine landed in Meli, she had the nylon haired Ashley in tow, who analysed sexually infected samples for a living. With Ashley now consigned to the dustbin of broken relationships, it seemed that the spark between Geraldine and Andreas may have been reignited on her most recent visit, if Violet

Burke was a reliable witness.

"Marigold, do you really think something is going on between Geraldine and Andreas?" I asked.

"I reckon Maria wouldn't mind if there was. She quite fancies Andreas making her a granny," Vi revealed.

"For goodness' sake, Mother, get a grip on reality. Even if Geraldine and Andreas are carrying on, Geraldine's a bit past it to be getting pregnant. She's getting on for sixty."

"So, did they get defrocked in the end?" Vi asked, deftly changing the subject.

"Did who get defrocked?" I was beginning to lose the plot.

"The red panty monks."

"I have no idea."

"'Appen if Andreas lost his frock and had a bit of a shave, he might look halfway decent," Vi opined. "If he could find himself a wife, he might move out and give Maria a bit of peace from his sermonising."

"Or he might move his wife in with his mother," Benjamin suggested.

"It's a common practice over here. Kostis moved poor Eleni in with his parents as an unpaid drudge," I said. "But I can't see anyone willingly taking on Kyria Maria."

Spotting the spark of interest in Marigold's

eyes, I sighed inwardly. I would hazard a guess that Violet Burke's talk of unfrocking Andreas had unleashed Marigold's irrepressible urge to matchmake.

"I've always said Papas Andreas might look half-way handsome without that unruly beard," Marigold concurred. "You should pop round when we get back to Meli, darling, and give him another English lesson."

Chapter 4

Marigold's Romantic Overtures

Sinking onto the bed and peeling my socks off, I gazed around our room in the charming guesthouse, borrowing inspiration from some of the unique decorative touches to apply to the old ruin that Barry and I planned to turn into tourist accommodation. The exposed stone wall behind the bed added a traditional touch and the wooden beams gave the ceiling old world charm. Although it was surplus to requirements in the warmth of June, the *somba* set into a recessed archway would be a big draw out of season.

Of course, the stunning view of the verdant

green mountain from the balcony could not be replicated. It was hardly surprising that the view was so spectacular, since Stemnitsa is one of the highest villages in Greece at 1080 metres above sea level. Still, I reflected, the views from the old house in Meli held their own distinct charm.

"We really should come back for a winter mini-break," I said, echoing Marigold's earlier suggestion. "Can you imagine how magnificent it would be with snow covering the mountain."

"It's not like you to suggest a mini-break," Marigold pointed out, her eyes widening. "You usually take quite a bit of persuasion."

"Perchance I am coming round to your way of thinking. Of late, life has been rather hectic. Considering that I am technically retired, I seem to have a lot going on, what with my repping job and supervising the renovation of that old property."

"Not to mention penning a book, tending your chickens and supervising Guzim."

"Despite working with Barry on our joint project, we rarely seem to have the chance to spend any quality time together like we used to," I lamented. "I don't mind admitting that I really miss his company sometimes…"

"I know what you mean. He's harder to pin down since he married Cynthia."

"No, it's not because he's married. We're both

so busy that when we are together, we spend all our time talking about the work that needs doing on the old ruin rather than falling into our usual relaxed banter."

"We must arrange a proper get together when we get back to Meli. You know that it has always made me so happy that you look on Barry as a brother; not everyone gets on so well with their in-laws," Marigold said.

I certainly admired Marigold for accepting the in-laws she'd known nothing about when we first wed, thinking she was tying the knot with an abandoned orphan. Clueless that decades later she would be confronted with a harridan of a mother-in-law crawling out of the woodwork, it was a testament to my wife's good nature that she hadn't filed for divorce when Violet Burke first arrived on our doorstep. Marigold had gone above and beyond, even encouraging my mother to move over to Greece and live right under our feet. She had also taken a shine to my half-brother Douglas and his family, welcoming them as guests in our home. She had yet to have the displeasure of meeting my other two half-brothers spawned by Vic, the limping soap salesman and all-round reprobate. Hopefully, they would remain anonymous figures in the family background.

"I did think you were taking too much on, dear,

when you volunteered to help Takis with his Sunday lunches. You don't want to spread yourself too thin," Marigold warned. I couldn't win; if I had allowed myself to sink into an idle retirement, it would have driven Marigold to distraction to have me getting under her feet.

"Well, that's after the tourist season finishes, so I won't be repping by then. Perhaps the winter would be an opportune moment to consider taking a bit more time to explore our adopted country," I suggested, thinking Marigold had excelled by choosing Stemnitsa as the first port of call on our second honeymoon. Thus far, I had found Arcadia to be quite idyllic. Renowned as a mythical destination, I found it certainly lived up to its reputation. I was definitely keen to explore more of the area.

"Just as long as we can do it alone. Fond as I have grown of your mother, in small doses…"

"That goes without saying…"

"I'd rather we left her behind in Meli on any future travels."

"We will have to try and persuade her that we couldn't possibly trust anyone else to look after the cats," I said.

"That would mean ignoring the fact that the last time we left the cats in Violet Burke's charge, we returned to find them bordering on the obese due to your mother's strange ideas of what constitutes an adequate feline diet."

Engrossed in examining the unsightly mix of swollen and exploded blisters on my feet, I didn't notice Marigold disappearing into the ensuite bathroom until I heard the tell-tale sound of the bath taps running. I cursed my wife under my breath for her selfishness in claiming first dibs on the bath yet again. I could hardly credit that she could be so self-absorbed that she failed to appreciate I was deserving of a long and luxuriant soak in bubbles, considering the long trek I had endured on blistered feet. In contrast, Marigold had spent the day doing nothing more taxing than relaxing.

Emerging from the bathroom, Marigold cooed, "I've drawn you a lovely hot bath full of soothing bubbles. Go and jump in it now and I'll bring you a glass of wine."

I flushed with guilt for jumping to the wrong conclusion and being mentally unappreciative of my wonderful, thoughtful, considerate wife. Even after thirty-eight years of marriage, Marigold was still able to surprise me. I didn't need telling twice. In two shakes of a lamb's tail, I stripped off my clothes and lowered myself into the bath, sighing in pleasure as the hot water eased my aching muscles.

Marigold breezed into the bathroom carrying two glasses of white wine. Passing me a glass, she perched on the side of the bath to keep me company.

V.D. BUCKET

Sympathising with me over my blisters, she told me she was not unaccustomed to the condition, having experienced the agony of high heels.

"That nasty discolouration on your ribs is beginning to fade. You must be careful not to overexert yourself, darling. I don't want you having a relapse."

"I should be fine as long as my mother doesn't try out her brutal version of the Heimlich Manoeuvre on me again."

"I'm so looking forward to a romantic candlelit dinner alone with you this evening." With Marigold making such obviously romantic overtures, I couldn't help but wonder if she had an ulterior motive. Perchance, she had her eye on some handcrafted jewellery produced in the Goldsmith's village.

"It was marvellous of you to put up with my mother all day," I told her, thinking perhaps I should treat my wife to a local trinket for enduring a full day with her mother-in-law, with nary a complaint.

"It certainly wasn't what I had in mind when I booked this second honeymoon. Still, I'm glad that Benjamin came along and you got the chance to have a boys' day out together. I do miss Ben when he's in England. I don't suppose we could start dropping a few hints that he and Adam should move over here. Imagine if we had all the family together in Meli."

"Much as I'd like it, I think we need to let the boys chart their own course in life. They both have careers that are based in England and they seem quite keen to make the move and flit up north. They've been spending most of their free time house hunting in the moors; it will be a handy base for us if we ever fly back to England. We should be thankful that at least the boys are always keen to fly over to stay with us. I don't believe that Doreen and Norman's offspring have ever visited, even though they have a standing invitation for a free holiday."

"Would you want to use up your precious holiday entitlement on Norman?" I didn't bother to respond. Marigold's question was evidently rhetorical.

"Speaking of Doreen, we were having a chat earlier...don't look at me like that, Victor, I didn't run my credit down. Doreen rang my mobile. She's managed to organise the jumble sale for next week. Nikos has agreed to let us use the tables in the courtyard as long as we've cleared everything away before they open in the evening."

"The jumble sale?" I parroted, thinking this was the first I'd heard of it.

"Sometimes I think you never listen to a word that I say, Victor. We've been talking about organizing jumble for months."

Deftly deflecting the accusation that I didn't listen, I countered, "Well, at least it will give you a chance to finally get shot of all those surplus old curtains and sheets that you dragged over from England. Not to mention, we've still got a pile of useless junk stored in Barry's shed."

"You must sort through it and see if there's anything salvageable that can be used in your renovation projection. I know how keen you are to keep costs down," Marigold said.

"You'll need to go through it with me, since you want to take charge of the interior decorating."

"I'm not going anywhere near the stuff in Barry's shed, it's likely overrun with frogs," Marigold protested. "Can you believe that Nikos had never heard of a jumble or even a car boot sale?"

"What's Doreen planning to flog?"

Instead of replying, Marigold blushed, refusing to catch my eye. Something was most definitely afoot.

I had a lightbulb moment when it suddenly dawned on me. "Don't say she's going to try and flog Norman's collection of traffic cones behind his back."

"I never said that." Marigold continued to avoid my eye.

"She is, isn't she. She's planning to take her

revenge on Norman by selling off his precious collection of traffic cones. From the look on your face, I would surmise that Doreen has dragged you into it as her co-conspirator."

"Well, what if she is? Norman is being so stubborn, refusing to move out of the marital home…"

"Not that I'm siding with Norman, perish the thought, but one could say that Doreen is being equally stubborn in refusing to move out of the marital home."

"Norman is the one who put no effort into repairing the breakdown of their marriage. At least Doreen tried," Marigold said in defence of her friend.

"She tried to make Norman jealous by draping herself all over that slimy Christos, and now, if she does manage to eject Norman from the house, we both know that she'll move Manolis in with her. I can see why Norman is refusing to leave…"

"So, surely it's self-explanatory why she wants rid of his traffic cones."

"There's just one fly in the ointment, darling, which you don't seem to have considered," I teased.

"What's that?"

"Who in their right mind would shell out good money for Norman's traffic cones?"

Chapter 5

The Bill

It was quite late when we eventually headed out to dine, the last of the daylight already faded. We had lingered on the balcony in companionable silence as the sun treated us to a captivating display; setting over the mountains, it painted the sky with glorious reddish hues casting a magical glow over the greenery before eventually losing lustre.

Since Stemnitsa is so high above sea level, the evening was beginning to turn a touch chilly as we strolled through the village, prompting Marigold to suggest finding a taverna with indoor seating. I suspect vanity may be at play as she didn't want to hide her lovely floral frock under a cardigan. Selecting a restaurant that Marigold deemed to have a suitably romantic atmosphere, we peered discreetly inside, ensuring it was a Violet Burke free zone before we entered.

The lighting inside the taverna was subdued, thus meeting Marigold's criteria of romantic even though it lacked candles. Personally, I found the dim lighting a dratted nuisance since it made it a tad tricky to decipher the menu unless I held it directly under my nose. Sampling a local wine that I had read up about in the guide book, we perused the menu, looking for dishes promising a flavour of Arcadia.

"This white wine you ordered is delicious," Marigold said, savouring the taste. "What did you say it was?"

"It is a *moschofilero krasi* made from local *moschofilero* grapes. It has quite a refreshing floral aroma." Whenever the opportunity arose, we both liked to make a point of sampling food and drink local to the area, made with fresh local ingredients.

Surreptitiously giving my shin a sharp kick under the table, Marigold hissed, "Have you noticed the way that couple keep staring at us?"

Covertly looking over in the direction Marigold indicated, I noticed a couple that appeared somewhat familiar, but I couldn't place them.

"I think they're waving at us," Marigold said. "Shall I wave back?"

"I wouldn't. I expect they've confused us with someone else," I replied.

Glancing over in a guarded manner, I avoided their eyes. It slowly dawned on me why they appeared familiar. "It's that pair of American tourists that made no attempt to be discreet about eavesdropping our conversation in the *kafenio* earlier. Whatever you do, don't encourage them. They strike me as the over familiar type that would have no qualms about breezing over and initiating a conversation about atrophied testicles."

"Oh, goodness, no. I don't want our romantic dinner interrupted with talk of such things."

Ignoring the pair, we concentrated on the menu. "Oh, this sounds interesting," I said. "They have a starter of *manitari keftedes*. It's the first time I've seen the traditional dish of meatballs made from mushrooms."

"Let's share that and choose another starter to compliment it," Marigold suggested.

"Do you fancy trying the *tiganopsomo*? I asked.

"What's that?"

"It says it's a local dish of fried round bread stuffed with *feta* cheese and an array of herbs."

"Fried bread will play havoc with your cholesterol, darling."

"I doubt it bears any resemblance to the type of fried bread one finds in a full English."

Spotting my deflated look, Marigold changed her tune. "I suppose we could throw caution to the wind and try it. We are on holiday, after all."

"Our second honeymoon," I corrected, hoping the allusion would earn me some brownie points. The tender smile I received indicated I was most definitely in my wife's good graces. Perchance Marigold's tolerance for the fried appetiser would extend to my ordering a full English breakfast the next morning, if such a thing was to be found in Stemnitsa. She may well approve it since it wouldn't be our kitchen where the smell of fried food lingered.

Catching the waiter's eye, Marigold used her Greek to ask about a main course. "*Signomi, ti einai to kontosouvli.*"

"He is the crispy pork on the skewer with the tomato, pepper and onion," the waiter replied in English.

"So, it's like *souvlaki*?"

Kissing his fingers to make his point, the waiter assured Marigold, "He is the tastier than the usual *souvlaki*."

"I'll try it," Marigold said enthusiastically, no doubt won over by the young man's charm.

Placing our order for appetisers and mains, I

didn't bother using my Greek since the waiter was clearly keen to try out his excellent English, a point Marigold took up as the waiter headed off to the kitchen.

"It's no wonder my Greek comprehension is coming along so slowly. Half the time, when I use my Greek, the Greeks respond in English. I wonder how the waiter realised I am English? Did you think my pronunciation was wildly off, Victor? I thought I had it down pat."

"Your pronunciation was perfect," I fibbed, not wishing to ruin the romantic atmosphere by bursting Marigold's vanity. "I imagine he thought you were English because one doesn't see many Greek redheads."

My words seemed to satisfy Marigold. Referencing the local dish of rooster in red sauce with noodles that I had ordered, Marigold quipped, "If you wanted to eat rooster, you should have just slung that noisy cockerel of yours into the oven at home."

"I think it might be a bit stringy and tough," I protested. I thought that Marigold had finally accepted my refusal to murder my pets and bung them in a hot oven, but apparently her acceptance only extended to the hens. She harboured a particular dislike of my rooster because it had the temerity to often disturb her frequent lie-ins.

BUCKET TO GREECE (VOL.14)

The *manitari keftedes* and the *tiganopsomo* proved quite delicious, surpassing our expectations. The combination of sage, rosemary, and mint, not only offered a tantalising aroma, but also a touch of green to the fried bread dish. Our main courses were equally tasty, the rooster not at all leathery or stringy; perchance the victim had been a tad younger than the old bird ruling the roost in my hen house.

Marigold enjoyed the wine so much that we ordered a second bottle. I would hazard a guess that the *moschofilero* contributed to Marigold's euphoric mood which I found quite contagious. I reflected that she really was the most delightful companion. Despite my mother's concerns that after being married so long, we ought to find each other tedious company, there was no one else I would rather choose to spend my evening with.

We had just finished our meal when I noticed a middle-aged man enter the taverna, checking out each of the patrons with a piercing stare as though on the hunt for someone. Clean shaven and dressed in an immaculate suit and tie, he carried himself with a distinctive air of authority. The way in which he scanned each of the diners with an intense look made me wonder if perchance he was a plain clothes detective in pursuit of some criminal type. As his gaze settled on me with a particular focus, I could feel myself becoming so hot and bothered under the collar that I was tempted to loosen my tie. To my consternation, the man approached me directly.

Assuming he represented some kind of authority, I stood up as he reached our table, taking me completely by surprise when he pronounced my name. "Victor Bucket?"

"Yes, I am Victor Bucket," I replied warily, hoping my first instinct that he was a policeman was wrong. Racking my brains, I pondered the remote possibility that I had inadvertently broken some obscure Greek law. Ever law-abiding, I worried that I had perhaps parked the Punto in a no-parking zone, thus incurring a sizeable fine. It would certainly put a spoke in our plans if my number plates were confiscated.

Having confirmed my name, the stranger's stern expression relaxed. Breaking into a wide smile, he fairly dazzled me with an impeccable set of gleaming white teeth, something that neither the British or Greeks are renowned for in general. I was taken completely by surprise when the stranger enfolded me in a hearty hug. Assailing me with the strong smell of garlic, the force of his embrace exacerbated the lingering pain in my ribs.

"I think yes, it must be the you. I spend the last many hour to look you. I have to go all over the

Stemnitsa for to find you. All I go on is that you are the tall English man with the attractive red hair wife."

"Do I know you?" Glancing at Marigold, she shrugged, indicating she was equally as clueless as I was to the identity of this stranger.

"The Spiros is the brother," the man announced.

"Your brother...are you speaking about Spiros the undertaker?"

"*Nai*," he confirmed with a yes. "The Spiros from the Meli."

"I never knew that Spiros had a brother." Taking a closer look, I observed that this strange chap bore not even the merest hint of a physical resemblance to my good friend.

"The, how you say, the blood brother? The *koumparos*."

"Ah, you're Spiros' *koumparos*?" I parroted, reflecting that the Greek word for best man was often used in a wider context, occasionally used to indicate a close relationship that wasn't familial. This chap wasn't an actual brother of my friend.

"The Spiros and me, we like this." Gesticulating, he laced two fingers together to symbolise a close bond. "The Spiros' uncle, the Petros, was the *koumparos* with my father and the *nonos* to the me, and my the father was the *nonos* to the Spiros. You know the *nonos*?"

"The godfather."

"*Nai, nai*, the godfather."

"This is all very fascinating, but I'm at a loss as to how you knew we were in Arcadia, or how you even know my name."

Slapping his brow as though belatedly realising that he had taken the Buckets by complete surprise, leaving us somewhat befuddled, he said, "I am the Vasilis, but everyone he to call me the Bill…"

I suppressed a chuckle. Before he had introduced himself, I had made a wild guess from his demeanour that he was a policeman and here he was calling himself the Bill.

"This is my wife, Marigold." Grasping her hand, Bill raised it to his lips, kissing it with old-fashioned gallantry and blasting her with his garlic breath.

"When I speak the telephone with the Spiros, he tell to me, 'Vasili, my the very good friend, the Victor Bucket, he to holiday near to your the home. You must to meet and say the hello.'"

As it all began to belatedly make sense, I invited Bill to sit down and join us, Marigold nodding her encouragement. Signalling for the waiter to bring another glass, I poured Bill a glass of the excellent local wine and settled back in my seat, interested to hear about his friendship with the undertaker.

BUCKET TO GREECE (VOL.14)

"The Spiros and the me, we like the brother..." Bill said.

"So, are you from Meli?" Marigold asked, equally as intrigued by this well-dressed stranger with the dazzling smile.

"From the Nektar. The Spiros and the me go the school together from this high..." Bill extended his arm, indicating a level barely above the floor. Either they had been very short children or they had started school as toddlers.

"Fancy you being at school with Spiros." Even though Marigold recoiled from the blast of garlic that Bill emitted, she was clearly warming to him.

"I was the seventeen-year-old when my the family leave the Nektar and move to the Patras. It was the wrench to leave the Spiros but *ti tha borousa na kano?*" Shrugging, Bill finished his sentence with the typical Greek saying 'what could I do?' "I to finish the school there and then go to the, how to say, the Patras *panepistimio?*"

"The university..."

"*Nai*, the university. There, I to meet my wife. He is from the Arcadia and when we to marry, we come back to live in her the village."

I suppressed a chuckle. I was used to the locals confusing their English genders but it seemed that even those with a university education were not exempt from making the same blooper.

"Do you ever make it back to Meli?" Marigold asked.

"The life he is the too busy to come much the often." Sighing heavily, regret suffused his tone. "The last time I go the Meli was for the Petros funeral. It was so the tragic...so the terrible. He to fell from the roof of the house and make the splat." Illustrating his point, Bill clapped his hands together with a sharp slap. The sound reverberated around the taverna, attracting curious glances.

Marigold and I exchanged a questioning look, wondering if it would be tasteless to admit that we now lived in the house where Bill's godfather had plummeted to his death. Neither of us volunteered the information, thinking it prudent to keep schtum. I reflected how strange it was the way things had turned out. If we had accepted Spiros' invitation to attend his uncle's funeral on the occasion of our very first meeting, we might well have met this blood brother of Spiros back in 2002.

"When the Spiros to marry, I go the Meli to stand as his the *koumparos*."

Once again, I shared a look of confusion with Marigold. After telling us that the last time he had visited Meli was for Petros' funeral, Bill now claimed to have been Spiros' best man at his wedding. Just as it belatedly dawned on me that Spiros had tied the knot with Sampaguita in the Philippines rather than Meli, Bill clarified his remark by adding, "When the Spiros to marry the Charoula."

"Ah, his first wife. Have you had the pleasure of meeting his new wife, Sampaguita?" Marigold asked. "She's quite delightful."

"I regret the not. The Spiros have the plan to come to the Lagadia with his the wife last the winter, but he must to cancel. Too many the body need bury."

"So, you said Spiros planned to visit you in Lagadia. Funnily enough, we are planning to go there tomorrow. Is that where you live?"

"I to live near to the Lagadia…"

"And you came all the way over here to look for us?"

"He is no more than the twenty-five minute in the car. I spend the longer the time to look in all the shop and taverna to find the you. It was not the easy because some the women to keep the sunhat on to cover the hair."

I surmised from Bill's reference to sunhats that he must have been searching for a redhead for several hours. Surely no fashionable woman would be seen out in a sunhat after sundown.

"Did you approach many couples?" Marigold asked curiously.

"A little the few. I go up the one red hair woman but she tell me to, how to say, to sling my hook…I not to understand because I have no the hook…" His words tailed off in confusion.

I couldn't help wondering if perchance Bill had approached Violet Burke; my mother was after all a redhead. Telling a stranger to sling their hook sounded like the sort of brusque response she delighted in lobbing. I surmised the same notion may have crossed Marigold's mind when she turned on the charm, deftly sidestepping any embarrassment by saying, "Well, Bill, I'm glad that you found us. You must tell us all about growing up with Spiros."

The wine and the conversation flowed as Bill regaled us with tales of his and Spiros' school days, filled with mischievous antics when they attended the primary school in Meli before travelling further afield for their secondary education. Bill spoke with regret of the sad moment when Spiros called him with the news that the school in Meli was closing down as there were no more than a handful of children left in the village.

"There's only one school-age child in the village these days," I told him. "Poor Tonibler has to spend close to two hours travelling each day to reach the nearest school."

Bill spoke with regret about not being able to get together with Spiros as much as they would both like. In addition to the physical distance between Meli and Arcadia, each man had work

BUCKET TO GREECE (VOL.14)

commitments to shuffle.

"My life is much blessed with the good luck. The best luck in the world was meeting the Vasiliki, my wife. His family is the very rich, much the money which to make our life run the smooth," Bill confided. "But more important than money, the Vasiliki is the beautiful soul mate. When we to marry, we to move to the Arcadia and I to join the family business of my the wife. I must to work many the hour to prove my worth and demonstrate I am the success in my own the right, not because I am the husband of the Vasiliki. Now the father of the wife to retire and I to run all the business. We much the expand and now all the son to work in the business too."

"What sort of business is it?" I enquired.

"It is the business with the finger in, how you to say, the many property pie. We to run the holiday rental and have the shops. When the first son to finish the *panepistimio* and qualify as the architect, we expanded into the building the houses."

"How many sons do you have?" Marigold asked.

"The four. In my house, my wife, the Vasiliki, he is the queen." When Bill referred to his wife by name, I could understand why he went by Bill rather than Vasilis; it must have been verbally confusing when Vasilis married Vasiliki. "She make four the boy to carry the name. Always we to want the girl and it take many the year, but then my wife to make the Rothopi."

"Rothopi?" I questioned. Unfamiliar with the word, I wondered if perhaps it was Greek for fertility treatment.

"*To koritsaki mou, i prinkipissa mou.*" Bill lapsed into to Greek as he gushed about his baby girl, his princess. I felt relieved that I hadn't gone and put my foot in it by verbalising my thoughts that his daughter's name was a conception aid. "All four the son work in the business after they to finish the *panepistimio*. The Rothopi, she just the six year. She is our the miracle baby."

"How gratifying it must be to have all your sons working alongside you in the family business," Marigold cooed

Slapping his forehead again, Bill said. "I forget to say to you, the congratulation."

"Congratulations?" I queried.

"The Spiros tell to me, you just the remarry…"

"Actually…"

"I tell to the Spiros that it is good that he marry the new woman so he cannot to remarry the Charoula." I nodded my agreement, recalling my meeting with Charoula and how she had spitefully made off with Spiros' furniture. "I think the Charoula, he was not the good woman for the

BUCKET TO GREECE (VOL.14)

Spiros."

"Actually, we didn't remarry," I blurted, finally managing to get a word in edgeways. "Marigold and I have been happily married for thirty-eight years and have just renewed our vows."

It was Bill's turn to look confused. I suppose it was only to be expected; not one of our Greek friends had grasped the alien concept of trothing our commitment to each other for a second time.

"So, you to make the wedding vow for the second time without the divorce, *nai*? He is the *romantikos* gesture?"

"Exactly, you've hit the nail on the head. We did it to show to the world that after so many years of marriage, we are still in love and committed to spending the rest of our days together," Marigold explained.

"I am the big *romantikos* and very much like the idea of the, how you to say, vow renew? I could to steal your the idea, *nai*, and surprise my wife?"

"We can't take credit for the idea of renewing one's vows," Marigold reluctantly admitted. "The concept first became popular in Italy and then spread to America and Britain…"

"The Italian invent it? I think the not," Bill said sceptically. "It is usually we the Greek that are first…the Italian like to pretend they invent the pizza but the ancients were first. The Greek invent the democracy, the philosophy, the pies, the *romantikos*..."

"I believe the notion of romantic love originated in France," I interjected, thinking that Bill clearly shared Spiros' way of thinking in insisting the Greeks invented everything.

"But the Greeks, he is the best lovers in the world," Bill proclaimed, determined to give the last word to Greek superiority. I chuckled, recollecting his view was a popular one amongst the men of Meli. Even the garlic eating octogenarians that hadn't made successful *kamaki* for years, knocked back in all their attempts at chatting up women, still professed their prowess with the ladies, even if it was only in their reminiscing or imaginations.

Reverting to the subject of renewing one's vows, Bill said, "I think to renew the vow would to make the Vasiliki very happy."

"I'm sure she'd love it. I was over the moon when Victor suggested it," Marigold said, conveniently forgetting that my suggestion had been born out of my desperate need to convince Sherry that I wasn't an available object of fancy.

"You tell to me that tomorrow you come the Lagadia, *nai*? You must to come to stay at my house. You can tell the Vasiliki all about the vow renewal and how to make it."

"Oh, we couldn't possibly impose," Marigold

said.

"It is no the impose. We have the big house with many the room. You must to stay…"

"But it isn't just the two of us," I interrupted. "We have my mother and our son with us."

"No problem, the more the merry, *nai*. I write you the direct to the house," Bill said, scribbling a map on a paper napkin. "Come the seven tomorrow…"

"That's a bit early," I interjected, thinking Marigold would never forgive me if I dragged her out of bed at dawn on her second honeymoon."

"The seven the afternoon," Bill clarified. "I will be the home then to introduce you to the Vasiliki and the children. The Vasiliki cook the big food and we enjoy much the company. You must to talk the *romantikos* vow renewal with the Vasiliki."

"It's very generous of you to invite…"

Interrupting me before I could complete my sentence, Bill said, "You find the Papas to make it?"

"Didn't Spiros tell you? He actually officiated at our ceremony on the beach," I said.

"The Spiros to marry you?"

"He presided over the ceremony," I confirmed.

"So, the Spiros can to marry me too." Bill's booming declaration attracted so many open-mouthed stares that I was tempted to make an announcement that the Greeks invented homosexuality.

Chapter 6

A Quintessentially Greek Setting

The enclosed courtyard of the guest house in Stemnitsa offered an idyllic, quintessentially Greek setting for a relaxing al fresco breakfast. The courtyard was a riot of clashing yet cheerful colours; red, pink, and purple bougainvillea climbed the whitewashed walls creating shady arbours, the scent of their delicate perfume suffusing the clear mountain air. Typical wooden chairs painted in classic Greek blue with scratchy rattan seats, surrounded tables laid with white cloths. Each table featured a basket brim-full with nectarines and apricots, so delightfully fresh that their skins still bore the traces of early morning dew, the trees they were plucked from offering yet more courtyard shade.

Steering Marigold away from the fruit trees to avoid any falling juicy missiles splattering our breakfast, I selected a table for four, my wife pulling a face at the sight of the rattan seating. Since she was breakfasting in shorts, the weaved wicker was sure to leave unsightly lines on the back of her legs unless I could save the day by getting my hands on a cushion.

Even though there was no sign yet of Benjamin or my mother, we expected them to join us shortly. Ekaterina, the guest house owner, immediately greeted us with a cheery *kalimera*, bustling over with Greek coffee, soon followed by a sumptuous platter piled high with olives, sliced tomatoes and cucumbers, cold hard-boiled eggs, and freshly baked *spanakopites*, spinach pies. Rustic bread and *koulouri* were accompanied with kumquat and cherry spoon fruits. We both accepted the offer of yoghurt and honey with sliced bananas and strawberries, eager to sample the local fir honey produced from the nectar of the Arcadian pine forests.

Sipping my coffee, I greeted Benjamin as he joined us, noting that he didn't look very rested.

"It's difficult to manage any sleep in the same room as granny. She snores like a freight train."

V.D. BUCKET

Benjamin winced as he spoke.

"Is she up yet?" Marigold asked, her eyes scanning the courtyard.

"Yes, she's up but still in that grotesque candlewick thing. I left her putting some slap on her face."

"I hope she won't embarrass us by breakfasting in her candlewick," Marigold sighed.

"I wouldn't worry. She usually makes a point of dressing before showing her face," I reassured my wife.

"At least we can have our breakfast in peace then," Marigold said, dipping her spoon in the yoghurt and honey.

We had barely made inroads into the delicious spread when Violet Burke made her entrance. As I'd predicted, the candlewick dressing gown had been discarded in favour of normal apparel, even though the apparel wasn't my mother's usual typically tweed style. The three of us gawped in wonder at the sight of a casual tee-shirt straining at the seams over Violet Burke's ample bosom, said tee-shirt paired with denim shorts finishing in a frayed hemline just above her knees.

Spotting our somewhat gormless expressions, Vi announced, "Benjamin said he fancied the four of us climbing up to some castle this morning. I can't be doing a hill in a skirt with no give."

"You might have asked me, Granny, before

helping yourself to my tee-shirt. It's going to end up all shapeless now," Benjamin complained. His words struck me as a bit of an understatement. His garment would only be fit for the bin after being stretched out of shape over his granny's sizeable chest.

"I've never seen you in shorts before, Vi," Marigold commented, trying not to stare at Vi's pallid legs, only the visible hairs adding a splotch of colour to their whiteness.

"I cut down the jeans that I wear when I bicycle around Meli. It'll likely get too hot for legs full of denim," Vi said.

"You won't be able to call them bell-bottoms anymore, now you've gone and sheared the bottoms off," I quipped.

"Granny, are those my trainers you've got on your feet?" Benjamin snapped.

"Don't worry, lad, it's not as though I've got any of them horrible contagious verrucas."

"You can't just go helping yourself to my wardrobe," Benjamin objected peevishly. Usually, Benjamin was nothing but indulgent when it came to his granny's quirks. It seemed that after two nights of sharing a bedroom with Violet Burke, he was beginning to rapidly lose patience with her.

Changing the subject, I asked Benjamin which castle he had earmarked for us to visit that morning.

"It's Karytaina Castle. I read about it in the guidebook; it's on our way to Lagadia. I don't think the three of you will find the walk too strenuous," Benjamin said.

"There's no need to make us sound like a bunch of feeble geriatrics," Marigold scolded.

"Seeing as I'm the only one who puts in a full day of physical graft, I reckon I'm fitter than the lot of you," Vi opined. "It's hardly a picnic wielding a mop and all that scrubbing hasn't half built up my stamina."

"I work as well," I pointed out.

"Is that what you call swanning around on a yacht with my old mucker, Vasos?"

Ignoring her put down, I declared, "I'm up for visiting the castle as long as it doesn't exacerbate my blisters."

"You can be a right big girl's blouse, lad," Vi scoffed. "Your poxy blisters have got nowt on my swollen feet and I'm up for it."

"You spent yesterday sitting on your backside while I limped up to a monastery." It felt very satisfying to have the last word, until Benjamin went and spoilt it by coming over all pernickety.

"Technically you only limped down from the monastery…"

His tone indicated he was finding my odd grumble tiresome. "So, are you all up for exploring

BUCKET TO GREECE (VOL.14)

Karytaina Castle or will it just be me and granny?"

"Yes, let's all go," Marigold said with surprising enthusiasm. "I anticipated stretching our legs this morning. Victor and I need to walk off some of the calories we put away over dinner last night. I don't want Victor getting a paunch with all that lying around in bed he did before the vow renewal service."

"You make it sound as though I was deliberately idle rather than following doctor's orders to get some bed rest," I sniffed.

"Excellent," Benjamin smiled indulgently at his mum. "The guidebook says the castle is known as the Greek Toledo."

"What's a Toledo when it's at home?" Vi questioned.

"Don't go setting Victor off, Vi," Marigold warned. "Can we at least enjoy our breakfast in peace before he sticks his tour rep cap on and starts lecturing us on local sites?"

"At least he didn't sneak his whistle in my backpack," Benjamin said.

Ekaterina reappeared bearing cushions to protect the back of the ladies' legs from rattan markings, and Greek coffee for Vi and Benjamin. Vi immediately demanded a teapot of hot water to pour over the English teabags she always carried on her person when out and about. Ekaterina looked somewhat taken aback to have one of her guests thrusting a teabag in her face.

"I always come prepared in case the only tea on the go has them nasty twigs in it," Vi barked, before demanding, "I'll have a full English fry up with my tea. You'd have to be daft in the head to eat olives and yoghurt for breakfast."

Cringing in embarrassment at my mother's dismissive tone, I was relieved when Ekaterina, after admitting she didn't have the fixings for a full English, somewhat appeased Vi by offering to fry her a couple of eggs.

"'Appen if she plonks them on top of a couple of slices of fried bread it'll set me up until we stop for elevenses."

"We enjoyed an appetiser of fried bread yesterday evening," Marigold said. "What was it in Greek again, Victor?"

"*Tiganopsomo*," I said, thinking it would hardly be Violet Burke's cup of tea. She wasn't a great fan of things stuffed with anything green unless it happened to be mushy peas.

"I'm developing quite a taste for *koulouri*," Benjamin said, breaking a piece from the circle of sesame seeded crispy bread with a hollow centre and piling it high with the kumquat preserve.

"I can't be doing with it, lad. It looks harmless enough but it's nigh on impossible to get them seeds out of your teeth."

"I've never taken to *koulouri*," Marigold said, for once in solidarity with her mother-in-law. "All the sesame seeds remind me too much of taste-testing bird food."

"I thought you were winding me up, lass, the first time you told me about that daft job of yours. Taste-testing pet food...potty it is."

"There is nothing daft about it, Mother. Someone has to check the food to ensure it is safe for animal consumption..."

"They should just get a dog to taste it," Vi countered.

"You can't go around having dogs taste testing cat food..." Benjamin proclaimed at the same moment that I retorted, "Dogs are unable to verbalise their opinion."

"I reckon an empty bowl is a vote of confidence," Vi proclaimed.

"But an empty bowl doesn't give any insight into the nutritional value of the food," Marigold explained, reminding Vi that, "Pet food tasters are required to have a degree in food science."

Ekaterina deposited a couple of fried eggs in front of my mother, prompting Vi to opine, "'Appen Marigold should taste test these eggs. I don't like the look of that green stuff sprinkled all over them. It could be owt."

V.D. BUCKET

"For goodness' sake, Mother. It's just a smidgen of oregano…"

"Who in their right mind wants oregano messing up their eggs?"

"That cat, by the look of things," Benjamin said with a laugh, pointing to the black and white feline that was eagerly straining to get at Vi's plate.

Muttering under her breath, Vi scraped the offending oregano off her eggs before flicking it into my now almost empty bowl of yoghurt. Grabbing the bowl, she offered it to the cat in an effort to detract its attention from her food.

"Really, Mother. It's hardly hygienic to have the cat eat out of the crockery intended for human guests."

"Stop your fussing, Victor. We're only here for the one night so you won't have to eat out of that bowl again tomorrow morning."

I tuned out, determined not to allow my mother's grumbles to spoil my breakfast. After over indulging in rooster and *tiganopsomo* the previous evening, I was quite content to enjoy a light breakfast of yoghurt, Greek olives and fruit. I was looking forward to a day out with my family, exploring a castle before moving on to the Hanging Village. I was grateful that Marigold had made some changes to our original itinerary of spending the day in Tripoli. Of all the myriad treasures that Greece offers, I most enjoy exploring small villages populated with the type of genuine Greeks that remind me of the Meli villagers. I suppose it is rather akin to tourists searching out what they refer to as the real Greece, as though anything that attracts tourists must lack Greek authenticity.

Marigold kicked my shin, bringing an end to my reflections. Having attracted my attention, she rolled her eyes in my mother's direction. Violet Burke was spouting her mouth off again.

"Some young whipper snapper tried to chat me up last night. I told him straight, sling your hook. I've never trusted a fellow done up in a suit and tie since that fourth husband of mine, Arthur Burke."

"The philandering serial bigamist that came to an untimely end under the wheels of the number 47 bus," Benjamin said in a questioning tone.

Recalling that Bill had mentioned approaching a red-headed woman who told him to sling his hook, I surmised that my initial hunch that he had perchance encountered Violet Burke the previous evening, was spot on. I interpreted Marigold's meaningful glance as a warning to keep quiet about their likely run-in. There would be time enough to consider the matter if Bill remembered their brief encounter when we turned up at his house later with Vi in tow. Fortunately, I also recalled that Bill had been baffled by the English idiom: blissfully unaware of its meaning, he hadn't actually twigged that he'd been insulted. I reflected that my mother must have been tone deaf to the situation, jumping to the assumption that Bill had been trying to chat her up. I could only hope that she wouldn't go accusing him of all sorts in front of his wife.

Ignoring Vi's remark, Marigold asked Benjamin and Vi whether they'd enjoyed a pleasant evening.

"We ate early in a lovely outdoor taverna..." Benjamin began.

"Cracking chips they had. I told them straight, I wanted chips from them famous Tripoli spuds. Course I couldn't get Benjamin to try them. I just can't fathom his fear of chips, it's unnatural..."

"It wouldn't be unnatural to you if you'd grown up listening to dad describing the grossly insanitary habits of some reprehensible restaurant owners. Some of them had a very lax interpretation of hygienic food standards and used to pick the uneaten chips off customers' plates and then refry them ready to serve up to the next sucker that walked in." Benjamin visibly shuddered as he spoke.

"Cor, I never heard the like. With all my years working in chippies, I never saw nowt of that skanky practise," Vi stated.

"You weren't above marrying the contents of

the sauce bottles though, Mother, another deplorable habit which I despise."

"I sometimes think you forget that you've been pensioned off from the Food Standards Agency. Why don't you fill Vi and Ben in on our plans for this evening, dear?" Marigold urged.

"Well, we met a fellow called Bill last night who is a very good friend of Spiros and excellent company. We've accepted an invitation for the four of us to dine at Bill's house and then stay overnight."

"When you insisted on me coming along on this second honeymoon of yours, I thought we'd be living it up in posh hotels, not roughing it in some stranger's house. 'Appen they'll likely serve nowt but that disgusting twig tea," Vi grumped.

"You'll be more likely to spend the night in the doghouse if Bill recognises you as the stroppy redhead that told him to sling his hook," I taunted, omitting to mention that Bill had failed to grasp her meaning.

For once Violet Burke was lost for words. I gave myself a mental tap on the shoulder, satisfied that I had bested her with the last word.

Chapter 7

No Gift Shop or Public Lavs

"You could show a bit more interest," I lectured my disinterested family. Having parked up the Punto in view of the famous stone bridge crossing the River Alpheus on the outskirts of Karytaina, I was less than impressed with their lacklustre reaction.

"It's a bridge, Victor." Marigold is an expert in stating the blatantly obvious.

"I'll have you know that it's not just any old bridge. It was constructed in the thirteenth century and is of great historic significance. Moreover, Karytaina Bridge is well-known throughout Greece as it used to be pictured on the 5,000 Drachma note. If you look closely, you will see that each of its five arches is finished to a different height," I said, summarising the description I had read in the guide book.

"People seriously pay good money to listen to tedious tripe like that? Remind me not to sign up to one of your tours," Violet Burke scoffed.

"It's not my fault that you are too much of a Philistine to appreciate historical landmarks, Mother."

"It's nowt but a dirty old bridge. Them stones could do with a right good polishing. I thought we were supposed to be doing a castle before we stop for our elevenses."

"Fine," I snapped, muttering under my breath as I ushered my completely underwhelmed family back in the Punto to resume our journey to the village of Karytaina.

"Well, I thought the bridge was interesting, Dad. I'm glad you parked up for a look-see." Since Benjamin was seated behind the driver's seat, I couldn't tell if he was being sarcastic or simply humouring me. If I had to take a wild stab, I would plump for sarcasm. Spending so much time with his mum was clearly rubbing off on our son.

"Oh, look. This looks delightful, what a hidden gem," Marigold cooed as I drove into the village, passing the beautiful vaulted stone fountain that marked the entrance.

Built on the slopes of a hill topped by the castle, Karytaina comprised aged Byzantine churches set amidst cobbled streets and traditional stone houses with red tiled roofs, either huddled together or seemingly scattered at random, clinging to the hill and nestled amongst the trees. From its lofty perch, the village offered spectacular views over the lush green valley.

"So, what's first on everyone's agenda?" I asked. "Shall we make a start by trooping up to the castle?"

"I reckon we should stop for elevenses before owt else," Vi piped up.

"It's not even ten o'clock, Vi. You only finished your breakfast an hour ago," Marigold said impatiently. Despite Vi complaining about the Greek victuals on offer rather than her longed-for full English fry up, she had polished off a huge chunk of village bread, two hard boiled eggs and half-a-dozen *spanakopita*, on top of the oregano polluted fried eggs. I reflected that it would be on her own head if she ended up egg-bound later: she needn't expect any sympathy from me. To be honest, I was amazed that my mother had actually chomped her way through so many spinach pies. She had shot down my sarcastic comment apprising her that the green stuffing didn't comprise mushy peas by countering, "'Appen if I eats me spinach, I'll end up as strong as Popeye."

"The guide book mentioned there are the remains of some old Turkish baths in the village that we might fancy exploring…"

"It's too hot to be doing with all that steam," Vi interrupted.

"I said 'remains.' The baths are no longer functional," I clarified.

"'Appen they'll be full of frogs like Cynthia's mucky pond…"

"It's ecological, not mucky…"

"But you can't deny it's full of frogs," Marigold interjected, once again siding with her mother-in-law. "We never had to put up with all that croaking when the pond was a swimming pool."

"No, but we had to take evasive action to avoid being dragged to one of Harold and Joan's pool parties," I reminded my wife. "Since none of you appear interested in the Turkish baths, we may as well head straight up to the castle."

"Straight up sounds about right. That hill is practically vertical," Vi griped.

"Definitely the castle first," Marigold decided, staring at the hill with obvious misgivings. "It will be too hot to tackle that climb if we wait any longer."

"The castle it is then. Let's put our best feet forward," I encouraged. My attempt to rally my family was put on hold when Vi demanded the keys to the Punto.

"I'm going to need some sort of walking stick if you expect me to make it to the top," Vi explained.

"Well, you won't find a walking stick in the car," I told her.

"'Appen not, but have you never heard of improvising, lad?"

"Improvising with what exactly?"

"I chucked a mop in the boot just in case the bedrooms in one of them posh hotels was a bit mucky and needed a good bottoming. You can't be too careful. I didn't want to risk picking up some unhygienic nasty."

"So, you plan to put your weight on a mop…"

"Aye, lad. I can balance the mop head under my armpit for a bit of support." Sometimes I truly question how it is possible that I am the spawn of Violet Burke.

Trekking up the well-worn stony path, I began to wish I'd made first dibs on the mop. With my blistered feet to contend with, the route was not exactly a walk in the park but rather an arduous challenge. Still, at least my party of four had taken the necessary precautions, slapping on the sun screen and donning suitable hats. My blisters were well plastered up beneath my socks and Benjamin's backpack practically groaned under the weight of bottled water sloshing around.

As a feat of endurance, climbing the hill gave yesterday's excursion to the monastery a run for its money. Although the distance to the top was shorter than the route which we had taken the day before, it was steeper. Fortunately, Vi's swollen feet slowed us down so much that there were plenty of opportunities to stop for a breather whilst I waited for her to catch up, without looking like a wimp.

"I feel as though we are heading into the clouds," Marigold said as the two of us stopped, her voice tinkling with laughter as we watched Benjamin give his granny a helpful shove from behind. Marigold called down, "Are you sure you can make the distance, Vi?"

"I've started so I'll finish…" Vi bellowed in a passable imitation of Magnus Magnusson. I chortled at the thought of Violet Burke glued to 'Mastermind' and yelling the answers at the telly. I amused myself by wondering if she would opt for chips or a good bottoming as her specialist subject.

Thinking of my mother watching television, I felt a touch of nostalgia as I recalled how she and Panos had snuggled up on the sofa to enjoy Corrie together. It saddened me to think that Panos' death had deprived my mother of the chance of

V.D. BUCKET

experiencing a happy marriage rather than the disastrous pairings she had known before the welly wearing farmer erupted on the scene. I would have been very content to have welcomed Panos into the family as my father-in-law. Thinking about the stoic way in which my mother had dealt with his loss, I felt a rush of affection for Violet Burke.

As Benjamin and Vi caught up with us, I threw my arm around my mother's shoulder, giving her a spontaneous hug,

"Get off, you soppy beggar," she joshed, her voice choked with emotion. "Pass me one of them bottles of water, Ben."

Grabbing the bottle, Vi glugged some water before making a beeline towards a clump of rather majestic wild flowers next to a rock.

"Marigold, do you reckon if I shove this flower in the bottle of water, it will keep it alive until we get back to Meli. 'Appen it'd look right nice planted in my window box."

"Keep your hands off that flower, Vi," Marigold warned in a steely voice. "The Madonna lily is a protected species. If you go picking it, you're liable to get us all arrested."

"All right, keep your hair on, who appointed you as the flower police? There's no need to start bleating like one of them goats," Vi grumbled, her swollen feet stomping the coveted lily to the ground as she re-joined us.

Vi's reference to goats proved quite timely as the gentle tinkle of bells alerted us to the presence of a herd grazing nearby. The sight of a bedraggled, dirty brown creature boasting an impressive set of curved horns prompted me to enlighten my family about the Greek god, Pan.

"Did you know that the Greek god, Pan, is the patron god of Arcadia?"

"Isn't he the one that is depicted as half-man, half-goat?" Benjamin queried.

"Indeed," I confirmed.

"If I had to be half-goat, I reckon I'd go with my bottom half," Vi mused.

"Because of their nimble feet," I guessed. Glancing up and seeing how far we still had to go to the top of the hill, I thought I wouldn't mind swapping my own feet for those of a sprightly goat.

"No, because I wouldn't fancy having nowt but weeds and bark to eat," Vi replied.

"Well, their diet must be healthy. You never see an overweight goat," Marigold chimed in.

"An interesting fact related to Pan is that the word panic is derived from his name," I said.

"In Greek or English?" Marigold asked.

"Both of course. The Greek word for panic is *panikos*."

"I'll be panicking, lad, if we don't stop for some

elevenses soon," Vi said before resuming the trek uphill with a determined step.

There was a collective sigh of relief as the four of us arrived at Karytaina Castle. Majestically perched at the summit of the hill, it struck me that it could be considered the poor man's imitation of the Acropolis. Amazingly we had the place to ourselves. Fortunately, there was a refreshing mountain breeze to somewhat revive us after our strenuous climb.

The outer walls of the castle appeared to be in pretty good condition considering they had been standing around exposed to the elements for more than seven centuries. The stone walls surrounded a ruined interior where nature had taken its course, leaving it to the imagination to conjure up an image of the castle fortress in its heyday.

"I can't believe we trailed all the way up here for some bloomin' dilapidated ruin," Vi carped. "There isn't even a café for our elevenses."

"Not even a gift shop," Marigold complained.

"Not to mention no public lavs," Vi grumbled.

"I did mention it was a ruined castle when I suggested it," Benjamin said defensively. "Surely you can appreciate the magnificent view instead of grousing. The way it's positioned at the top of the hill puts me in mind of the Acropolis and we have it all to ourselves."

BUCKET TO GREECE (VOL.14)

As Benjamin's words echoed my thoughts, I felt proud to consider he was a chip off the old block.

Not used to being on the receiving end of Benjamin's harsh words, Marigold and Vi shuffled uncomfortably, before practically launching into competition with one another to see who could make the most impressive display of oohing and aahing over the 360-degree panoramic view. Thinking to cash in on their enthusiasm, I launched into my prepared spiel about the castle.

"This may be a ruin now but it has an incredible history. It is quite fascinating to think that when this Frankish castle was constructed in the thirteenth century, it was built on top of the ruins of an ancient city."

"It's hardly surprising that the city fell to rack and ruin, plonked on top of this great big hill," Vi observed. "It's hardly what you'd call practical to get up here, unless them ancients had one of them nifty mopeds. I'd never have made it on Cynthia's bicycle."

"Donkeys were more in vogue at the time," I pointed out. "Many ancient towns were built on high as a defensive measure against marauding invaders..."

"Aye, I suppose that olive oil had its uses then..."

"You've lost me, Mother."

"They could boil it up and have a bit of fun pouring it over any enemies trying to scale that bloody great hill."

"Remind me not to get on the wrong side of you when you're wielding the chip pan, Granny, if you think lobbing hot oil is a fun activity."

"Am I the only one interested in the history of the castle?" I asked. Ignoring their silence, I continued, "Back in 1485, the village of Karytaina fell to the Ottomans…"

"'Appen it was a bad year for olives…a shortage of boiling oil."

"But the castle is historically significant as it was one of the first to be liberated during the 1821 War of Independence…"

"Who won that one then?" Vi demanded.

"The Greeks of course. They finally achieved independence from the Ottomans by defeating them in the Battle of Karytaina."

"'Appen it's as well that the Greeks saw the likes of them Ottomans off, otherwise we'd be stuck eating Turkish food."

"Well, since the Ottomans held the fort here for so long, naturally quite a lot of Greek dishes have a Turkish influence."

"Nikos would be having none of that. He spits on Turkish food," Vi said.

"It's just as well that he doesn't serve it up in

the taverna then. It's completely unhygienic to go around spitting on food," I quipped.

"He reckons the Ancient Greeks came up with all the recipes for Greek food and the Turks had nowt to do with it."

"In this instance Nikos is wrong. There are many similarities between the foods of both cultures, although arguments abound over whether *baklava* was invented by the Greeks or the Turks. The Greek word for meatballs, *keftethes*, is derived from the Turkish word for meatballs, koftes. Also, it is pretty well documented that Turkish sis kebabs were around before Greek *souvlaki*."

"Not according to Spiros," Marigold teased, her eyes full of amusement.

"It is a well-known fact that Spiros believes the Greeks invented everything. He is hardly what one could describe as a reliably impartial source."

"All this yabbering on about food is doing my stomach no good. I need my elevenses."

Chapter 8

Too Much of a Coincidence

I must confess to feeling a tad queasy watching Violet Burke shovel two large *milopites* down her gullet, leaving her with a ridiculous icing sugar moustache. It struck me that nurture over nature must have resulted in my own more cultured bent, my mother seemingly devoid of a single refined bone. I dread to think how uncouth I may have turned out if I'd been dragged up by my mother: there was no denying she had a tendency towards the vulgar.

After making our descent from the castle, we had made good time on the drive to the charming village of Lagadia. The Hanging Village, suspended from the slopes of the mountain, proving to be as wonderfully picturesque as the guide book had promised, but my mother remained miffed that the village had no actual history of hanging. She even went so far as voicing her disappointment that the village lacked even so much as a pillory designed for the public humiliation of criminals; for once, she didn't accuse me of boring her with dull facts when I revealed that the Ancient Athenians had been big on wooden stocks. I could certainly picture Violet Burke being the first one to lob a tomato at some reprobate's head wedged in the stocks or to take a front row seat with her knitting at a public guillotining.

Before we had the opportunity to explore the village, my mother insisted on stopping for her elevenses. Even though the rest of us were still perfectly satiated from our delicious breakfast, we gave in to her relentless demands, if only to shut her up. Choosing the first café we spotted, we relaxed in the shade of the plane trees, sipping our coffees whilst my mother grumbled between mouthfuls of pie.

"I don't know why you're all complaining about stopping for a bite to eat. Victor never stops harping on about how we ought to eat locally grown stuff. I'll have you know that these apple pies are made out of genuine authentic Arcadian pilaf apples."

"I think you'll find that's *pilafa* apples, Mother," I corrected. "Pilaf is a rice dish."

"'Appen I could manage a nice bowl of rice pudding if you twist my arm." Vi appeared impervious to the rankled look that Marigold fired in her direction. My wife, being keen to start hitting the gift shops, was rapidly losing patience as evidenced by her failure to point out Vi's sugared moustache, a petty yet telling omission.

Marigold fidgeted in her seat, clearly loathe to risk losing any precious retail therapy time in case the shops shuttered up for the afternoon siesta. Sensing his mum's frustration, Benjamin offered, "Why don't you and mum take a wander around the village and catch up with me and gran later. After all, you are on your second honeymoon and deserve some time alone."

"They had dinner on their own last night…" Vi piped up.

Ignoring her, I mouthed a thank you at Benjamin, suggesting, "Let's all meet back at the car in two hours

"Make it three," Marigold contradicted.

"I'll flick through the guide book and find a local attraction for us to while away the rest of the afternoon when we meet back up," Benjamin offered.

Dropping an appreciative kiss on Benjamin's

head, Marigold practically legged it out of the café, oblivious to whatever objections Violet Burke was attempting to voice through another mouthful of *milopita*.

"I think my mother fancied wandering around the gift shops too," I said, feeling just a tad guilty that I had lumbered my son with Violet Burke yet again. "She mentioned buying gifts for Maria and Dina."

"Then we must be sure to avoid her…I've had as much of your mother as I can stomach. I didn't know where to look when she asked for an apple pie with a side of chips; she can be such an embarrassment."

"Well, we have some time alone now," I said. Marigold linked her arm through mine, her tender smile showing that she didn't hold me personally responsible for my mother's often cringeworthy behaviour.

"This village is certainly beautiful," Marigold said.

"I read in the guide book that Lagadia is famous for the unique stone work crafted by local stonemasons. They made quite a name for themselves," I said, appreciating the style of the houses we passed. "You can see how the craftsmen deliberately selected stones of different hues. See how the sun brings out the blue in that archway."

"I love the way that the wooden doors are surrounded by stone arches and there's such a variety of colour in the wood…"

"One certainly never encounters a boring front door in Greece. Each one is something special," I concurred.

"If you ever get around to publishing that book of yours, you should use a Greek door for the cover art. They certainly draw the eye and are so quintessentially Hellenic that readers would know at a glance that your book is set in Greece," Marigold suggested.

I had to admit that her idea had legs. An old wooden Greek door would be far more appealing to readers with an interest in our adopted country than the image of a galvanised bucket plonked on a taverna table that I had mentally envisaged adorning the cover of 'Bucket to Greece', my tentative title. I could even chuck in the odd cat for good measure.

Despite having already trooped up a steep incline to stop at Karytaina Castle, we once again trekked upwards, negotiating the cobbled steps and winding streets that took us from the lower part of the village, Kato Mahala, to the upper level, Pano Mahala. Seemingly the caffeine shot we had imbibed during our coffee break had revived us enough to tackle the upwards climb. Pausing at regular intervals to admire the stunning view prevented us from becoming overly winded.

"Let's take a breather on that bench," Marigold suggested, pointing to a convenient seat in the shade. She didn't need to twist my arm; I would much rather relax and drink in the stupendous views than follow Marigold around like some gormless idiot as she mooched around the gift shops. Perish the thought that Lagadia might be home to a dress shop where Marigold would relegate me to hanging around outside the changing room. I had suffered quite enough of that on our infrequent trips to Athens where Marigold invariably made a beeline for Marks and Spencer. Even though I in no way resemble a pervert, there have been enough occasions when I have been on the receiving end of scathing looks whilst lurking outside the women's changing rooms, to ensure it is an experience that I tend to dread.

"This is so romantic, dear. The vista is breathtaking," Marigold whispered. I know my wife well enough to realise that if she starts getting mushy before noon, she is clearly buttering me up.

Resigned to the inevitable hit on my credit card, I played along with my wife. "Indeed. I wish I could bottle that view."

"Lovely though it is, it doesn't have the sea view that we enjoy in Meli," Marigold observed.

V.D. BUCKET

"What on earth?" My question was prompted by a sudden surge of mangy cats hot-footing it past our feet.

"That couple of hikers over there are putting food out for the cats," Marigold said, pointing towards a row of village bins overflowing with rubbish. Instead of putting their rubbish directly in the bins, the couple were unwrapping various parcels retrieved from their backpacks, placing the contents on the ground next to the metal waste receptacles.

"I do despair of such unhygienic practices," I complained, thinking that after making merry in the communal bins, the grungy looking strays would likely head off to the nearest taverna at lunch time, full of wide-eyed innocence as they cosied up to any tourists to beg for scraps. Said gullible tourists would undoubtedly take pity on the cats, stroking and petting the creatures, completely oblivious the felines were likely flea ridden or riddled with a nasty dose of roundworm or worse, picked up from rummaging around in the bins. Of late, if I have call to drop in on Milton and Edna, I take the precaution of discreetly dropping off a box of anti-flea powder due to the sheer preponderance of strays that Edna adopts from the bins. Whenever I take a seat on their sofa, I suffer an acute case of phantom itching and I have to get Marigold to disinfect my clothing when I get home.

BUCKET TO GREECE (VOL.14)

"Oh dear, it looks as though our romantic alone time is about to be disturbed," Marigold sighed.

Revelling in the peace of the moment, I was rather put out when the littering hikers headed towards the bench.

"Hey, folks. How y'all doing? We've howdy-ed but we ain't shook," the man greeted us, the southern twang in his drawl much more pronounced than that of Doreen's Texan beau. Manolis spoke with some weird kind of hybrid mix of Texan and Greek.

"Any room for two little ones?" Glancing up, I thought the woman must be deluded if she really considered the word little to be apt, the American pair being decidedly on the chunky side. Nevertheless, we obligingly nudged up to make room for the couple, their wide beamed smiles rather disarmingly giving the impression that they were our long-lost friends.

Finding their genial grins a tad disconcerting, I belatedly recognised them as the couple that had been blatantly eavesdropping over our afternoon tea in Stemnitsa, seemingly fascinated as my mother regaled Benjamin with all the sordid details of the monastery scandal. To top it all, they had waved at us in the taverna the previous evening. Were it not for Bill's timely arrival, they may well have attempted to join us.

"Y'all having a dandy vacation?" the American woman piped up.

"Yes, indeed," I responded, my tone rather curt since I had no desire to encourage them. I certainly had no inclination to let them know that we were European citizens with Greek residency. We might never get shut of them if they realised that we lived in Greece.

"We're on our second honeymoon," Marigold volunteered. My wife is incorrigible when it comes to striking up conversations with any random strangers that happen along. "Have you come all the way over from America?"

"Sure have. Visiting Greece has always been number one on our bucket list," the woman replied. "We've always said, one of these fine days, we're gonna treat ourselves to a whole month exploring the Peloponnese."

I tuned out as my wife and the couple chatted away, feeling rather peevishly aggrieved that they had interrupted our precious time alone. Whilst not exactly unsociable, I more easily tire of tourists since I endure quite enough of them during my job as a rep; at least in my work capacity, I am paid to make small talk with them. Having more time on her hands, Marigold is far more tolerant. Since retiring to Greece, her only job description is that of housewife; she has even managed to wriggle out of that one by employing Violet Burke as our char.

It suddenly occurred to me that this was the third time in two days that these seemingly innocuous American tourists had turned up in the same place as the Buckets; it struck me as just a tad too coincidental. To turn up in the same place twice might be considered accidental but there was something suspicious about a third occasion. The hairs on the back of my neck stood on end and my thoughts wandered off on a tangent, wondering if perhaps they were spying on us for some obscure reason that I couldn't quite put my finger on. Nevertheless, the thought unnerved me enough to want to put some distance between them and us.

Before I could suggest to Marigold that we make tracks, the feral felines turned their attention to us in the hope of soliciting more food, having devoured whatever leftovers the possibly spying hikers had deposited by the bins. Cooing over the cats, the American woman made a grab for one, cradling it and depositing sloppy kisses on its likely flea ridden fur. Marigold shot up from the bench, distancing herself. Whilst my wife is soppy in the extreme when it comes to her own pampered felines, she is naturally more cautious when it comes to cats that she has personally observed ferreting about in the bins. Ever since we first landed in Meli, she has treated the numerous strays with caution, alert to the possibility they may harbour something unhygienic that could be passed onto Clawsome and Catastrophe.

Joining Marigold, I warned the tourist woman to show some restraint. "It's not a good idea to cuddle a feral that's been in the bins. It's most unhygienic. That cat could well have contracted Bartonella Henselae…"

"Say what?" the man stuttered.

"It's something felines carry which manifests as cat scratch disease in humans," I explained.

The man's face contorted with alarm. "That sounds dang nasty. You might wanna put the cat down, Karen."

"I would recommend a good scrub with antiseptic soap if you come down with a nasty itch. It is never a good idea to get too close to a strange cat when you don't know where it's been," I advised.

Stating the patently obvious, Marigold said, "It's been in the bins."

"But it's sure cute," we heard Karen object as we made our escape, Marigold waving at the couple.

As soon as we were out of earshot, I raised my concerns with Marigold. "Don't you think it was a bit odd, that pair turning up in the same place as us for a third time?"

"Odd? It was just a coincidence."

BUCKET TO GREECE (VOL.14)

"I think it was more than that. They may have been following us."

"Why on earth would anyone want to follow us, Victor?"

"I don't know. Perhaps they are undercover agents from the tax office."

"Have you any idea how paranoid you sound, Victor? Undercover agents indeed." Marigold rolled her eyes. "You've clearly been spending far too much time with Spiros."

Realising that Marigold had hit the nail on the head, I reddened. My good friend, the undertaker, loves nothing more than a juicy conspiracy theory; of late he was forever harping on about his worries that the tax office might engage clandestine agents to be on the lookout for tax avoiders.

"I thought you had more sense than listening to any of Spiros' harebrained conspiracy theories," Marigold scoffed. "Why on earth would the tax office be interested in you. Your wages from the tourist company are taxed at source."

"But I rent out the *apothiki*…"

"To your mother who doesn't pay any rent…"

"But the taxman might not know that."

"Victor, if that couple were following us, can you explain why they're now heading in the opposite direction?"

Even though Marigold's logic exposed the utter

fallacy of my suspicions, I was determined to have the last word.

"I expect that they're legging it to the nearest pharmacy in search of a good antiseptic soap."

Chapter 9

Trading Marigold in for a Bunny Girl

"Are you having a laugh? In my considered opinion, Guzim will want nothing to do with anything featuring pompoms. He's bound to think they are much too girly," I protested.

"How can you say such a thing, Victor?" Waving a pair of rather flimsy, imitation *tsarouchia* under my nose, Marigold nearly had my eye out with a pompom adorning the upturned toe. "There's nothing at all effeminate about those Greek Evzones guarding the Tomb of the Unknown Soldier in Athens, and they wear these shoes."

"The Evzones wear traditional *tsarouchia* made out of leather. Those shoddy knock-offs look more like fluffy slippers. I suppose you are expecting Guzim to pair them with *periskelides* and a *fustanella*…"

"If you're going to argue, at least do it in English. It's very patronising of you to throw your superior Greek into an argument…"

"I was referencing the woollen stockings and the pleated skirts that the Evzones wear…I thought you would be familiar with the terms since that photo of you cosying up to a Greek presidential guard takes pride of place on our mantelpiece."

"It's a pity you cut his head off…he was dashingly handsome."

"In my defence, he was exceptionally tall. Anyway, it's a very good shot of you."

Although Marigold visibly preened at my compliment, she still argued the point, reverting to flaunting the disputed gaudy shoes under my nose for a second time. "I think that Guzim will love them. The least we can do is get him a gift for looking after the cats while we're away; better these than Amstel."

"Wouldn't you rather wait to ensure he hasn't lost the cats or killed them off, before showering him with gifts?"

"How can you even joke about such a thing?

BUCKET TO GREECE (VOL.14)

You're the one who keeps pointing out that he hasn't managed to kill off any of your precious chickens. I think Guzim will appreciate these *tsarouchia*. He'll find them more comfortable than his flip flops to wear in the evening when he's relaxing in his shed."

"Perhaps you could persuade Doreen to run up a pleated *fustanella* in case the shoes put Guzim in the mood for marching," I quipped.

Since Marigold seemed to be weighing up my ridiculous idea, I sarcastically suggested that she plump for a pair of *tsarouchia* with pink pompoms, pointing out that they would match the décor in the pink palace of love. Marigold's sarcasm detector was clearly off beam since she immediately scooped up the pink ones.

Arriving at the gift shops, Marigold had been tempted to go on a buying frenzy until I cautioned her that we would need to physically carry whatever she splurged on all the way back to the car. Initially showing remarkable restraint, Marigold told me that she would concentrate on finding a gift for Anastasia. To my surprise, moseying around the shops together turned into a pleasant experience, the gift shops stocking an interesting and eclectic mix of the usual tourist paraphernalia, locally produced products and some rather unique craft items. Fortunately, the apparent lack of a dress shop spared me the ordeal of hanging around outside a changing room and being mistaken for a pervert.

Marigold pounced on some rather quaint wooden spoons featuring hand painted images of olives and flowers, declaring she would buy them for Violet Burke to gift to Maria and Dina in case my mother didn't spot anything suitable. I was touched by her gesture; clearly her irritation with Vi had been short lived. Even though my wife was squandering my cash on unnecessary kitchen implements, her heart was in the right place.

Almost tripping over a selection of brightly coloured metal buckets fashioned into hanging plant pots, the two of us shared a tender moment as we reminisced about our very first meeting in the bucket aisle of B&Q. Since said buckets appeared too clumsy to cart back to the car, I thought I had managed to persuade Marigold to resist an impulse purchase until she insisted on buying just one. She pointed out that whenever the subject of my being abandoned in a bucket came up in Violet Burke's hearing, my mother continued to lament the loss of the good sturdy bucket she had dumped me in. "I suppose it just might shut her up," I reluctantly concurred.

I rather lost patience when Marigold started oohing and aahing over a display of white window hangings embellished with exquisite embroidery, the type of which can often be seen adorning the wooden windows in traditional Greek houses.

"Don't you have enough curtains already?" I asked in exasperation. "For goodness' sake, you were only just talking about donating some of those drapes that you dragged over from Manchester to the jumble sale that Doreen is organising."

"These aren't curtains in the British sense of drapes," Marigold argued. "They are known as traditional cutwork curtains and they simply hang in place. They aren't meant to be drawn like curtains back in England. I suppose they are the Greek equivalent of net curtains, designed to prevent prying eyes from seeing in."

"But as our house is sited on the second storey, we don't have a problem with people peering in," I pointed out, neglecting to mention the moment the lapsed Jehovah Witness had frightened the life out of Marigold when he scaled his ladder to clean our bedroom window.

"I think they would be perfect for the *apothiki*," Marigold said.

"Surely my mother is capable of choosing her own curtains."

"Don't be such a grump, Victor. I'm sure Vi will appreciate them. They're so much nicer than the ones already there. Perhaps I should buy a second set for that old wreck that you're renovating…

tourists will love the traditional touch."

"We haven't even installed the new windows yet," I remonstrated as Marigold rather sulkily restrained herself, only shelling out for new cutwork curtains for the living room window in the *apothiki*.

"I must get something for Doreen. She needs cheering up. The poor thing is a bit down in the dumps over Norman refusing to move out of the house. How about a bar of this olive oil soap?"

"That's rather like taking coal to Newcastle. Tina sells olive oil soap in the village."

"But that's just unhewn lumps of the stuff; it's very unwieldy in the shower and positively dangerous if you drop it on your toes. This one is infused with pomegranate and comes in a fancy decorative box."

And so, it had continued, Marigold making merry with my credit card, until inevitably, I ended up traipsing back to the Punto in her wake, burdened down with carrier bags of superfluous tat.

"Good grief. What on earth are you doing with that ginormous stuffed rabbit? It's almost bigger than mum," Benjamin chortled as I staggered towards the Punto, weighed down with Marigold's purchases.

"'Appen he's traded Marigold in for a bunny girl," Violet Burke cackled.

"It's a gift for Anastasia," I snapped, having

encountered enough sidelong glances and outright sniggers, carting the grotesque, oversized stuffed creature all through the village. It wasn't an exaggeration to say it was life-size: human, not bunny, that is.

"'Appen it'll give the little dumpling nightmares. It's four times the size of the nipper."

"I told you it was too big," I chided Marigold.

"Nonsense, Anastasia will love it," my wife retorted, demonstrating an appalling lack of taste.

"There's no way you're going to be able to fit it into the Punto?" Benjamin observed. "We'll have to tie it onto the roof."

"I'm having nothing to do with it," I said churlishly.

"What have you two been up to?" Marigold asked Benjamin as he busied himself securing the stuffed monstrosity to the roof of the Punto.

"Granny wanted lunch..."

Marigold rolled her eyes dramatically. "But she was still tucking into her elevenses when we left you."

"If that guest house had served up some decent bangers for breakfast, 'appen I wouldn't have been left starving. We found some half-way decent Greek sausages, a local speciality..."

Fine praise indeed from Violet Burke. "Would that be the local *splenandero*?" I asked, referencing a popular local sausage I had read about that was made from mutton and grilled over a charcoal fire.

"Aye, that's the one. 'Appen they could have done with a good battering and deep frying." I swear I could almost feel my arteries contracting at the thought, even though Marigold and I had foregone lunch in favour of moseying around the shops.

"Did you find somewhere for us to explore this afternoon?" I asked Benjamin, since we had several hours to kill before we landed on Bill.

"A couple of places jumped out at me," Benjamin said. "We could drive to the ski resort of Mainalo. Granted there isn't likely to be much snow in June but Granny thought you might be keen to take a look in case you fancy returning for a skiing break in the winter."

I could only think of one possible self-serving motive for Violet Burke being of the opinion that we might be interested in a skiing break, the word 'break' featuring heavily in her motivation. No doubt she had calculated that with the odd broken leg or two, we might be persuaded to install an outside stairlift up to the house. Ever since Milton had installed one in his home, Vi was forever nagging me to follow suit, convinced such an unnecessary, not to mention unsightly contraption, would spare her swollen feet.

BUCKET TO GREECE (VOL.14)

"We aren't the slightest bit tempted to risk life and limb by skiing," Marigold shot Vi down.

"'Appen you could have a go at snowboarding," Vi suggested.

"Neither of us are in any hurry to contemplate hip replacements just yet..."

"All right, keep your hair on. It was just an idea."

"I told you that a ski resort was a non-starter, Gran," Benjamin sighed. "The river Ladon sounds as though it's worth exploring. It's supposed to be a very scenic spot. The construction of a hydroelectric dam created an artificial lake surrounded by an ecological park."

"A pleasant stroll around a lake sounds more the ticket," I enthused as the four of us piled into the Punto. Not only would it allow Violet Burke to walk off the *splenandero* sausages, it would keep Marigold well away from the temptation of any more gift shops.

Presented with the leisurely options of gliding across the lake's calm and glassy surface in a boat or a kayak, I mentally debated the risks before ruling out both activities. Our lack of swimming cossies was the deciding factor. Since Violet Burke was incapable of squeezing her sizeable bulk into the narrow confines of a kayak, and one clumsy move on her part would likely result in a capsized rowing boat, I had no desire to take an impromptu dip in my clothes. It would hardly make a good impression if we turned up at Bill's place in sopping wet clothes. Instead, we settled for a pleasant afternoon stroll through the ecological park surrounding the artificial lake of Ladonas.

Arm in arm, Benjamin and Marigold sauntered ahead. I delighted in the sound of my wife's tinkling laughter as she enjoyed some time with our son, making the most of their last full day together before Benjamin returned home to Adam. Even Violet Burke appeared to appreciate the beauty of the setting, grudgingly admitting that it beat the Manchester ship canal.

"That Cynthia would love it here, what with her ecological obsession."

"Don't go putting any ideas in her head," I warned. "I need Barry to crack on with renovating that old ruin so we can rent it out. There's no time for Cynthia to be whisking him away on romantic mini-breaks."

The lake reflected the clear blue sky, the water subtly changing shade as it edged towards the greenery of overhanging trees. After walking a while, the path narrowed, forcing us to troop along in single file, nature's silence only broken by the sound of leaves crunching underfoot and the whispery whistle of reeds rustling, disturbed by a sudden gust of wind as the four of us reached a clearing and gathered together. The wind surprised us, presaging the disappearance of the sun as it drifted behind the clouds. The temperature dropped, offering a welcome break from the heat. The sight of the natural reeds flourishing in the ecological park inspired me to regale my family with the tale of the wood nymph, Syrinx: legend had it that Syrinx turned into a hollow reed to escape the unwanted, amorous attentions of the Greek god, Pan.

"I read about that in the guide book," Benjamin piped up. "That's how panpipes were created, by Pan blowing into the reeds."

"That's right. Pan is often depicted playing his syrinx…"

"You don't half spout some right old cobblers," Vi mocked. "If some nymph had turned into a reed, you can bet that the horny old goat would have polished her off for his lunch…"

The rest of her waffle was drowned out by an enormous clap of thunder. The sky darkened ominously. With no warning, the heavens opened, unleashing a torrential downpour of biblical proportions. Within seconds we were all totally drenched, utterly thrashed by a wall of rain.

"I haven't experienced bucketing rain like this

since Adam and I took a mini-break in Braga," Benjamin said through shivering teeth.

"Summer downpours like this are rare and usually short lived," I said. "It's a good job that we didn't take a boat out."

"'Appen we'd have had to bail out..."

"We couldn't be any wetter if we were in the lake," Marigold complained.

Within minutes, the downpour abruptly ended as quickly as it had begun. The sun reappeared, its welcoming rays somewhat alleviating the misery of being soaked to the skin.

"Here, Granny. I've got a spare tee-shirt in my backpack," Benjamin offered. "Slip behind that tree and change before you catch your death of cold."

With her lips curling in annoyance that Benjamin had put his aged grandma's needs before hers, Marigold made a song and dance about wringing out her own clothes whilst admonishing me for not having predicted the sudden downpour and failing to equip our son's backpack with a brolly. Even as I took the blame for the unacceptable turn of the weather, the sun's warming rays soon helped to dry us out, leaving the four of us looking decidedly crumpled and dishevelled.

Picking our way back to the Punto, we carefully avoided the puddles. Reaching a particularly muddy spot on the path, I jumped clear across, extending a helping hand to my wife who was rather reluctant to muddy her shoes. As Marigold placed her hand in mine, preparing to step forward, something suspiciously snake like slithered through the reeds. Squealing in alarm, Marigold pulled back, her hand still tight in mine. Yanking me forwards, I landed face first in the mud.

Chapter 10

Palatial Luxury

"I dread to think what sort of first impression you're going to make, Victor," Marigold carped. "Turning up as a guest at Bill's house while covered in mud is hardly a respectable look."

"How many times? I was not going to strip down to change on that car park in full view of all those tourists," I retorted, thinking Marigold certainly had a cheek: she knows that I am just a tad too prudish to even wriggle out of my damp swim shorts under a towel on the beach. Moreover, a bit of sympathy from my wife wouldn't be misplaced considering I wouldn't be in this muddy mess if I

BUCKET TO GREECE (VOL.14)

hadn't extended a helping hand to her so she could avoid the muddy patch at the lake. "Why don't you just concentrate on reading the map?"

After driving around in circles for the last forty minutes, I was beginning to doubt my wife's competence at map reading.

"It isn't a proper map," Marigold snapped, waving the paper napkin adorned with Bill's scrawled map under my nose. "How am I supposed to identify which forest track we need when they all look the same?"

"Didn't he draw any identifying landmarks?" I asked.

"Only a tree." The exasperation was evident in Marigold's tone, hardly surprising since the roads we'd been driving on were all tree-lined. Whilst aesthetically pleasing to the eye, it was certainly confusing when our only directional landmark was a tree of no particular descriptive species.

"Back up, Dad," Benjamin barked. Slamming the brakes on, I reversed the Punto. Benjamin leaned over my shoulder, pointing towards some lights at the end of a track we had just passed. "That might be it."

"Cor, I wouldn't fancy their leccy bill. 'Appen they forgot to take down their Christmas lights," Vi tittered, her rather gauche observation putting me in mind of Norman's illuminated traffic cones.

"It looks more like a stately pile than someone's house," Benjamin openly gasped. He certainly had a point. The track appeared to lead to an enormous place, flooded with lights.

"Perhaps it's a hotel. We could at least drive up and ask for directions," Marigold suggested.

Snatching the napkin from Marigold's hand, I tried to make sense of Bill's childlike attempt at cartography.

"I think this could be it," I mused. "Bill did say that he'd married into money…"

"I don't recall him saying that his wife's last name was Rockefeller." Marigold sighed, her worries about my turning up covered in mud dwarfed by the realisation that she might not make the best impression turning up in shorts rather than some posh frock. Clearly, only the latest fashion from Marks and Sparks would do in order to make a suitable entrance at such a swanky residence.

"'Appen he married one of them Onassis shipping billionaires," Violet Burke quipped. At least my mother wasn't fussing about being caught out in cut down shorts. She was more than capable of staring down anyone who dared to have the audacity to challenge her style. She may have only been a Greek resident for less than a year but she had already mastered the evil eye.

"I wish Athena was here to do something with

my hair. It's gone all frizzy from the rain," Marigold grumbled.

"You and your vanity, lass. The way you carry on anyone would think you had your hair done in some posh salon, not the builder's kitchen."

Taking the rough forest track, I aimed the Punto towards the lights. Thankfully the track soon morphed into a cemented, pothole-free lane framed with colourful oleander shrubs, the clusters of flowers quite glorious in captivating hues of white, pink and red. The track led towards a pair of ornate iron gates set into a stone wall surrounding the property. Luckily the gates were open. All doubts that we were at the right place were dispelled when the suited figure of Bill rushed out of the grand residence.

"Welcome, welcome. I think you not to come," Bill greeted us.

"Sorry we're late. We had a bit of a problem finding the place," I said.

"No the matter. You are the here now."

Offering Marigold a hand in a gentlemanly gesture, Bill's forehead creased in a frown as Violet Burke's bulk alighted from the Punto. I could practically see the cogs of his brain churning as he said to Vi, "I think I to know you?"

"'Appen I just have one of them faces," Vi said, visibly reddening as I hurriedly introduced Bill to my mother.

"You look very the familiar...perhaps it will to come to me," Bill persisted, before turning his attention to Benjamin and greeting him with a hearty handshake.

Joining the dots, I hissed at Vi, "You told him to sling his hook last night, didn't you, Mother?"

"How was I to know he wasn't one of them peculiar sex pests with a fetish for redheads?" Vi attempted to cover her embarrassment that her loose tongue had caught up with her.

With the introductions dispensed with, Bill said, "Come in and meet the Vasiliki. We will to have the drink and then to show you to your room." Looking at me pointedly, he added, "You can to change the dress before we eat."

As the four of us trailed behind Bill, Marigold whispered in my ear, "He said room. I'm not staying here if they expect me to share a bedroom with your mother."

"I'm sure that 'room' was just a Greekism," I assured her. "And it's not as though I'm wearing an actual dress."

My eyes nearly popped out of my head as I took in the sea of polished marble stretching out endlessly before me. The house was positively palatial, practically a mansion, obviously worth millions; when I say millions, I mean euros rather than

BUCKET TO GREECE (VOL.14)

drachmas which became obsolete back in 2002. When Bill had told us the previous evening that he'd married into money, he hadn't revealed that he'd hit the jackpot. From a cursory glance at his home, I surmised this was no ordinary wealth, it was huge piles of the stuff; yet the place struck me as tasteful rather than ostentatious.

Leading us past an ornate curved staircase spiralling to the upper levels, Bill ushered us into a vast living room overly stuffed with furniture. Despite the house being home to Bill and his four grown up sons, everything in the living room was pink: pink sofas, pink easy chairs, pink drapes. Even the intricate teardrop lights dangling from the elaborate chandelier, cast a pink glow.

"Ah, here is my wife, the Vasiliki," Bill gushed. Turning to the woman who entered the room carrying a tray of glasses, he dazzled her with a display of his perfect white teeth. Switching to Greek, he said, "*Ela, agapi mou. Elate na gnorisete tous kouvades*," meaning, 'Come, my love. Come and meet the Buckets."

"How lovely to meet you all. Bill tells me that you are good friends of Spiros," Vasiliki said in perfect English, smiling tenderly at her husband. Rushing forward, she embraced Marigold and my mother, bestowing double kisses on the pair of them.

V.D. BUCKET

Even though I could feel my mouth gaping open, I remained unable to prevent my jaw from dropping. Curvaceous, with an hourglass figure, Vasiliki was without doubt the most beautiful woman that I had ever clapped eyes on. Short, dark wavy hair framed the most perfect face complete with chiselled cheekbones, but it was the warmth of her deep brown eyes, flecked with gold, that was truly captivating. It seemed that Bill had lucked out with not only a rich wife but a stunning one who was clearly devoted to him. After double kissing Benjamin on both cheeks, Vasiliki turned to me, stopping short of embracing me when she spotted that I was covered in dried on mud.

"As it is such a lovely evening, perhaps you would prefer to enjoy your drinks in the garden." Even though her invitation encompassed all of us, I could understand her particular reluctance for my muddy clothes to come into contact with her impeccable frock or the plush, pink soft furnishings. "It is too stuffy to be indoors."

"I reckon this air conditioning is better than sweltering in the heat outside," Vi griped as we followed Vasiliki through the French windows onto a floodlit patio. Relieving his wife of the tray, Bill trailed behind, a bottle of wine clutched under his arm.

The marble patio was dominated by a huge

dining table, the table and chairs positively littered with enough sprawled out cats to give Milton and Edna a run for their money. Confronted with such an unhygienic display, I could only hope that Vasiliki would give the table a good scrubbing down if she expected us to eat from it.

Beautiful red flower drops added a splash of colour to the trees casting shade over the wide marble steps leading down from the patio to a large garden pond set in a well maintained, mature garden that boasted carefully cultivated flowers and shrubs. The area was mercifully free from the blight of a shed inhabited by an Albanian and not a whiff of chicken poop contaminated the scented air, redolent with the smell of fresh herbs planted adjacent to the patio.

"What lovely trees," Benjamin commented.

"They are the *rothia*, how to say in the English?"

"Pomegranate," I translated.

"*Nai*, the pomenrabbit," Bill said, fluffing his English pronunciation. "He is the ancient Greek fruit."

"Pomegranates symbolise prosperity and fertility in Greek culture," Vasiliki added, blushing slightly. Considering that she and Bill had produced five offspring, perhaps the association between the luscious red fruit and fertility wasn't so far-fetched. "We have the New Year tradition of

V.D. BUCKET

throwing the pomegranates at the front door. The scattered seeds represent good luck."

"I bet it takes a lot of scrubbing to clean that sticky mess up," Violet Burke muttered under her breath.

Ornamental rocks and weatherworn Greek urns brim full of vibrant floral displays framed the garden pond, the surface of the water rippling imperceptibly as a gulp of swallows scooped down, their wings just tipping the water. Noticing the birds had caught my eye, Vasiliki said, "You must pay us a visit at the end of September. The swallows are quite something to see when thousands of them start to migrate. They put on such a wonderful display."

Four life-size statues standing sentinel around the pond caught my interest. I immediately recognised the figure of the Water Goddess, Dione, balancing an urn on her shoulder, and the figure of Hercules.

"That fella over there puts me in mind of Guzim," Violet Burke said, pointing at the statuesque figure of Hercules. Her remark struck me as bizarre in the extreme since the mighty warrior bore not the slightest resemblance to the weedy Albanian shed dweller.

"Guzim?" Vasiliki questioned.

"The fella what mucks out Victor's chickens…"

BUCKET TO GREECE (VOL.14)

"I fail to see how a statue of a Greek god reminds you of Guzim," I said in exasperation.

"Well, he flashes his bits under the hosepipe. Just because that fella is made of stone doesn't mean he wouldn't be a sight improved with some undies on."

"It's culturally acceptable for classic Greek males to be depicted nude," I told my mother, hoping our hosts didn't interpret her prudish streak as a disparagement of Greek culture.

Sipping our wine, we made small talk and admired the stately grounds. Excusing herself, Vasiliki disappeared, saying she must put the finishing touches to dinner. Considering the size of the place, I would have expected the couple to have an army of servants preparing dinner rather than Vasiliki slipping a pinny over her posh frock and getting hands on in the kitchen.

There were sighs of relief all round when Bill offered to show us to our 'room' so we could have a quick wash and brush up before dinner. The four of us trailed silently after our host as he led the way upstairs, giving us a hand with our luggage. Gasps of astonishment escaped our lips as we stared wide-eyed at the palatial majesty of his home, feeling rather out of place amongst such grandeur in our noticeably scruffy state.

To Marigold's great joy, Bill showed Violet

Burke into a room of her own. Marigold's evident euphoria was surpassed by Benjamin's delight when he realised that a room of his own represented a reprieve from the horror of sharing another night in the same bedroom as his snoring granny.

"Come the down to eat when you have to change the dress," Bill invited, leaving us at the door to our room.

"Heavens!" Marigold exclaimed when Bill was out of earshot. "Do you suppose that Bill and Vasiliki have given us their bedroom. It's more luxurious than a five-star hotel."

"There's no personal effects lying around to indicate it is more than a spare room," I observed.

"Such opulence for a guest room. Can you imagine how many rooms there must be in this house?"

"Well, if each of the children have a room, plus our hosts, that's six. Then, of course, we've taken up another three, so that's at least nine bedrooms."

"And to think that we're reduced to offering our overseas visitors the sofa bed in your office."

"We haven't had any complaints so far," I parried, ignoring the odd gripe about the lumpy sofa bed. "There's no point in making comparisons. Just think, it would cost us a small fortune if we had to pay my mother to clean nine bedrooms."

The guest room was exquisite in every detail,

BUCKET TO GREECE (VOL.14)

Greek blue accents complementing the expensive and tasteful white décor. The mosquito net suspended from the white wooden beams above the king size bed was big enough to double up as a tent. Floor to ceiling windows offered a stunning view over Bill's immaculate garden, French windows leading to our own private balcony hosting miniature lemon trees in yet more earthenware pots.

"Oh, my goodness, just look at the size of this ensuite bathroom," Marigold called out.

Dragging myself away from the intoxicating scent of lemons on the balcony, I headed into the marble bathroom. Clear glass enclosed the largest shower cubicle I had ever encountered. I gazed in wonder at the multiple shower heads, hoping I could fathom out how to make them work. I had only read about the wonders of shower heads offering massaging jets and rainforest rainfall settings. Wondering if I could sweet talk Marigold into showering with me since the cubicle was bigger than the entirety of Guzim's shed, I decided to ease into it after gauging her mood. "I hope the water pressure can do justice to that shower. Can you imagine anything more annoying than having to shower from a bottle of water when that magnificent contraption is at our disposal?"

"It certainly makes our shower at home look rather pathetic," Marigold said. "We really ought to think about getting an ensuite. It's always such a palaver getting a turn in the bathroom whenever we have guests to stay."

Whilst I was naturally uneasy that Marigold was getting ideas to make merry with my credit card, I had to admit that sharing our bathroom with houseguests was a pain in the proverbial. At least she hadn't started making noises about littering our garden with marble statues of naked men.

Stepping back into the bedroom, Marigold scolded, "Honestly, Victor, I didn't know where to put myself. The embarrassment of turning up here with you covered in mud, not to mention that I look like a wrung-out dish rag."

For once, I didn't attempt to reassure my wife that she looked lovely. After her impromptu drenching, Marigold's Titan locks resembled a mop head that had been used as a lavatory plunger and her casual clothes were still slightly soggy and wrinkled.

"If I'd realised what sort of place Bill lived in, I would have insisted we drove over to Tripoli to find a decent dress shop."

I offered a silent thank you that Bill hadn't boasted about the grandeur of his home the previous evening, thus sparing my credit card from Marigold splurging on a new frock.

Opening the suitcase, Marigold inspected the

contents dismissively. "I was going to wear this but it just won't do for such luxurious settings," she said despairingly, holding up a perfectly presentable frock.

"What about this one?" I suggested, pointing to a cheery floral number. "I'm sure you'll look lovely in that."

"Really, Victor. In case it escaped your notice, I wore that one last night. Bill has already seen me in it."

"I hate to break it to you, Marigold, but with Bill being a man, he probably never even noticed your frock. Us men don't always notice the finer details of what you women wear…"

"I distinctly recall you telling me that I looked quite glamorous last night…"

"You did, darling…"

"I don't know why I bother to make the effort when you've just admitted you never pay any attention to what I wear. I may as well go down to dinner in a paper bag. You'd never notice the difference."

"Of course, I would…" I protested as Marigold stalked off, shutting herself in the bathroom and dashing my hopes of indulging in the luxury of the magnificent shower with my wife.

Chapter 11

The President Drops In

"Do go easy on the wine," I whispered in Marigold's ear. "You don't want to get squiffy, drinking on an empty stomach."

Although we had turned up a good forty-five minutes late, and another hour or two had passed since our arrival, there was still no sign of any food being served to soak up the copious amounts of alcohol. The Bucket clan, together with Bill but minus Violet Burke, were gathered around the enormous patio dining table under the stony gaze of statues of Greek gods and goddesses. I wasn't overly concerned about my mother's absence from our small gathering; presumably she was sleeping off the string of local sausages she had guzzled at lunch.

Bill and I had just returned to the patio. Bill had earlier dragged me off to the far side of the garden to show off a sandpit featuring sunken buckets. I had been completely clueless to its purpose, unable to fathom Bill's Greek description; moreover, Bill had made a total pig's ear of trying to grope for the necessary English vocabulary. I remained unconvinced that the pit was a goldmine, one of the English words Bill had thrown out. Bill had delighted in telling me that the sand had been filched from the nearest beach in the dead of night, saving him a small fortune on having commercial sand delivered. Our host might live in a palatial home but he didn't believe in throwing his money around. He could perhaps offer some tips to my spendthrift wife.

As the temperature dropped in the evening air, the myriad cats began to stir from their languid sprawling, impatiently rubbing their bodies against our legs as though it might speed up the advent of food. Rothopi, Bill's adorable, cute-as-a-button, six-year-old daughter, was running riot in the garden under the doting gaze of her father. Despite living amidst such splendour, the child lacked any pretensions, remaining sweet and innocently unspoilt. She had completely charmed us by chattering away in grammatically correct English.

Our host had apologetically announced that his four sons would not be joining us for dinner as they were attending a business dinner in Tripoli. Although his sons were all grown men, they still lived in the family home, Vasiliki no doubt catering to their every whim in the legendary tradition of all good mothers with a drop of Greek blood. I considered there could be little incentive for male offspring to flee the nest and set themselves up in some grubby bedsit when they were indulged in the parental home. Greek mothers positively encouraged them to stay, generally putting their sons on a pedestal and treating them like Greek gods.

In contrast, I recalled how James Scraper, my editor and erstwhile colleague at the Food Standards Agency, had reacted negatively when his grown-up offspring returned to the parental home following the breakdown of his marriage. The Scrapers were not amused by their thirty-year-old son's inability to operate the washing machine or muster up anything more taxing in the kitchen than a pot noodle; that's if the idle lummox could manage to tear himself away from the video games he played in his bedroom. I remember feeling quite smug, listening as old Scrapes bleated on about how they'd managed to raise a lazy bum with no noticeable life skills. Scraper's wife even went so far as going on laundry duty strike, instead packing their son's smelly socks into his suitcase, hoping he would take the subtle hint that it was time to move out and fend for himself. A court order to evict their son was only avoided when their daughter-in-law finally agreed to take her husband back. I rather suspected that Scrapes might have bribed her.

Marigold and I had never experienced anything but exemplary behaviour from Benjamin, our son keen to fend for himself in the kitchen from his teenage years. Benjamin had once confided to me that he had been inspired to master the basics of cooking at a young age as he didn't want to follow my example of the hapless male unable to manage anything more creative than slinging a tin of Fray Bentos in the oven. These days, Benjamin tells me he is very proud of the way I have excelled at cooking since my early retirement, taking to it like a duck to water. He even let slip that he is grateful to have a father with a newly developed culinary bent as it gives him a tasty alternative to Marigold's rather uninspired offerings when he visits us in Meli.

Fortunately, if Bill's four sons were to marry, the family home was palatial enough to accommodate four daughters-in-law. I mused that Vasiliki would no doubt delight in the advent of a *nyfi* or two since Bill had disclosed that his wife ran their home single-handed. In spite of the size of the place,

V.D. BUCKET

Vasiliki didn't even have the equivalent of a Violet Burke to step in and give the place a good bottoming. Bill assured us that his wife's greatest pleasure in life was looking after her family and their home; she flatly refused to employ any outside help. Vasiliki had already declined Marigold's offer to help in the kitchen, an offer my wife had made in the hope that it might speed up the arrival of dinner since the two of us hadn't eaten so much as a morsel since breakfast.

"Good grief. Why is Vi so red in the face? She looks as though she's about to have a heart attack," Marigold exclaimed, springing out of her seat to rush to Violet Burke's aid. My mother lumbered across the patio, sweat dripping from her crimson cheeks that clashed with the purple tweed number she'd squeezed her sizeable bulk into.

"Stop your fussing, lass," Vi insisted, batting Marigold away as though she was a pesky mosquito.

"But you're so red in the face. Is it your blood pressure?" Marigold's voice quivered with genuine worry.

"There's nowt wrong with my blood pressure, lass. I just got a bit overheated like, falling asleep in that sauna thing."

"That sauna thing?" I queried in confusion.

"Aye, that Vasiliki thought I might like to relax

for a bit in their home sauna. I felt like I was at some fancy spa, though I reckon I might have overdone it a bit. My feet won't stop sweating." As if to illustrate the point, Vi removed her lace-up flats, tipping out a puddle of sweat before grabbing a paper napkin to give the insides of her shoes a good drying. To my horror, two of the cats started vying to see which of them could assuage their thirst first by lapping their tongues in the pooled sweat. "I have to say I feel better for it. Vasiliki reckoned it would help to sweat out all the impurities that make my feet swell up."

Staring at Vi's ruddy complexion, I hazarded a guess that she had sweated out several pounds of liquefied lard.

"I wish I'd known there was a sauna." There was a trace of envy in Marigold's tone.

"'Appen Vasiliki reckoned it would have been too dangerous for a stick insect like you, lass. 'Appen you'd have sweated your way down the plug hole," Vi mooted. To my amazement, Marigold preened as though Vi had bestowed an enormous compliment on her. I made a mental note to compare my wife to a stick insect the next time I landed up in the doghouse.

Pouring my mother a glass of wine, Bill nearly dropped the bottle at the sound of ominous rumbling. "I hope we not to have the another summer storm when we to eat outside."

"That wasn't thunder, you daft 'apeth. It was my stomach rumbling. I've had nowt to eat since them sausages. I'm that starved, I could polish off a scabby horse on mouldy bread."

"Mouldy bread?" Bill repeated, his words exhaled on a cloud of garlicky breath.

"*Mouchliasmeno*," I translated.

Raising his eyebrows in confusion, Bill asserted, "We are just the waiting the President to arrive before the Vasiliki to bring out the food. I go to look if he on the way."

Excusing himself, Bill made his way down the driveway, leaving the four of us alone. Although it was clear that our host had riches far beyond the ordinary, I had no idea that he moved in such exalted circles.

"Did he say the President?" Marigold hissed, fluffing her hair and smoothing her skirt. "If I'd known that we were going to be joined by a dignitary, I would never have worn this old thing."

"Your frock looks lovely." My words lacked conviction. If Bill had warned us that we would be dining in such illustrious company, I would personally have dragged Marigold along to a designer dress shop. I certainly wished that I'd chosen a more elegant tie for the evening.

"'Appen he might have a fancy title but he uses

the lav just like everyone else," Violet Burke declared, indicating the eminent visitor could hardly expect any deferential treatment from my mother.

Firing a blistering look at her mother-in-law, Marigold's voice was shaky when she asked me, "Do you even know who the President is? I do hope he doesn't have one of those long unpronounceable names that I won't be able to get my tongue around. Can you imagine how embarrassing that would be?"

Racking my brain, I tried to recall any snippets of news relating to the recent election of the new Greek President, back in March. "His name is Karolos Papoulias. It was his predecessor, Konstantinos Stephanopoulos, that had one of those tongue twisters of a name."

"Papoulias. I should be able to remember that easily enough, it sounds a bit like the Greek word for grandfather, *pappous*," Marigold sighed in relief.

"As best as I can recall, Papoulias has a rather grandfatherly air about him," I said, my mind conjuring images from the television news of a pleasant looking chap with a balding white pate and bushy white eyebrows that would give Dennis Healey, the former Labour Chancellor, a run for his money.

Becoming flustered again, Marigold blurted, "But I've no clue what the Greek word for president is. I can't just call him *Kyrios* Papoulias. It would be terribly disrespectful."

"It is *proedros*. *Proedros* Papoulias," I told her.

"Well, whatever he calls himself, I hope he isn't going to sit around spouting politics all evening," Vi said. "I get enough of that from Nikos..."

I was rather taken aback by my mother's comment, clueless that she and Nikos discussed such contentious subjects over the potato peeler. "The president's role is primarily ceremonial, though I do believe that the current president has a political background. I'm pretty sure he was a government minister before he became president."

"Shush, I can hear Bill coming back...does he have the President with him?" Marigold asked, her voice a tad muffled as she slapped on a fresh layer of lipstick.

Craning my neck, I was surprised to see Bill, who isn't particularly tall, towering over a rather emaciated elderly gentleman. Leaning heavily on a stick, the president's gait appeared bent, his white hair hidden inside a rather dapper straw boater placed at a jaunty angle. I noticed the hat was a tad too big for his head, the brim concealing his features along with his signature eyebrows. Scanning the driveway, I couldn't see any sign of the bodyguards that would surely accompany the President of Greece.

Overcome with a racking cough, the shuffling

figure halted. As he lost his grip on the walking stick, Bill grabbed him by the elbow, shouting over to me, "Victor, come to take his the other the arm."

Before heeding Bill's call to action, I cautiously looked around to ensure any loitering bodyguards wouldn't get the wrong impression. If I made a sudden dash towards the president, I didn't fancy being tackled to the ground by a pair of muscled brutes jumping to the erroneous assumption that I was attempting to assassinate the elected head of state. Surveying the area, I concluded the president's protection squad must be either non-existent or proficiently skilled in making themselves invisible.

Dashing down the driveway, I ended up rather winded as I drew level with the honoured guest. Bill prompted me again. "Take the arm, Victor. Let me to introduce the Haralambos, but everyone to call him the Babis."

"It's an honour to meet you, Sir, I mean, Mr President..." My words faltered as I wondered if I ought to bow. It wouldn't look good if I didn't adhere to the correct Greek etiquette.

"There is no the need to stand on the ceremony," Bill assured me.

"Good to meet you, young man." As Babis spoke in confident English, he tipped his boater, revealing his features. If Bill's guest was the President of Greece, I would eat his hat, straw and all. He certainly bore no resemblance to the president that had been plastered all over the Greek news.

"The Babis is the good friend and the president of the village," Bill continued.

"The President of Lagadia?" I questioned, noticing that despite his rather cadaverous appearance, Babis certainly had a strong handshake, albeit a tad damp.

"No, the president of our little..." Bill referenced the name of the hamlet where his house was sited, a hamlet so small and seemingly inconsequential that it failed to feature on an actual map.

"I didn't realise that village presidents were actually a thing," I said. The nearest thing we had to a village president was the mayor, *o dimarchos*, of the small town where the town hall, *to Dimarcheio*, was based, the permanently scruffy chap who had officiated at Barry's wedding at lightning speed. Said mayor made a point of going out of his way to avoid me whenever I tipped up at the *Dimarcheio*, hoping to persuade someone in authority to implement my suggestions about improving hygiene conditions relating to the village bins. I had spent many an hour studying suitable cat deterrents to keep the village ferals out of the bins, only to have my efforts wasted by the elusive mayor refusing to give me the time of day.

BUCKET TO GREECE (VOL.14)

"Babis has been our president for over four decades," Bill declared.

"They tried to retire me off when the KEP was officially opened in Lagadia..." Babis volunteered.

"But we make the petition to keep him as our the president..."

"Alas, it is little more than a title and small stipend," Babis lamented. "I have no real power these days. The computer take over my role."

"It is the weeping shame," Bill groaned. "Before the computer, the Babis have much the influence. He could to arrange that the local child receive money to attend the university. Why, when I first meet the Vasiliki and we engage, the Babis secure me the money grant for the university, even though I not to live in this area. And he turn many the blind eye to the, how to say in English, the not quite the correct planning application?"

"Dodgy," I suggested, my thoughts immediately turning to the ubiquitous brown envelopes stuffed with cash bribes.

As if reading my mind, Bill declared, "The Babis never to take the *fakelaki*. He to help because he the people person. Everyone to love him."

Bill's kind words about his guest were affirmed when Vasiliki sauntered down the driveway, concern evident in her voice when she asked Babis why he was so late that evening, her question perchance indicating Babis was a regular guest.

Greeting Vasiliki fondly in familiar Greek, Babis said, "*Agapimeno mou koritsi,*" meaning 'my darling girl.'

"We must to speak the English tonight, Babi. We have the English guests," Bill said.

"I stopped off to translate a letter from Kyria Sophia's nephew. He send her the American dollars but write in English."

Walking towards the patio, the three of us adapted our pace to Babis' slower one, Vasiliki saying, "I will call in on Sophia tomorrow and clean out her chickens. She is finding things difficult now she is on her own. Come, Babi, take a seat. I have cooked your favourite *trahanas*."

My mind whirled like a washing machine on the spin cycle as I mentally groped for the translation of *trahanas*; although I was pretty sure it meant porridge, the notion was simply too ludicrous to contemplate. Since Vasiliki had been ensconced in the kitchen since our arrival, I had presumed that she was concocting an elaborate feast for dinner. I must confess that the thought of being served a bowl of porridge for my evening meal was a monumental let-down. As a mental image of Norman, who always reminded me of a bowl of congealed porridge, flooded my brain, I rather lost my appetite, even though the hunger pangs were beating a steady drum in my stomach. Perchance I could find an opportunity to sneak away at some point in the evening and raid Violet Burke's suitcase. It was unimaginable that my mother hadn't stocked her case with more edible victuals than porridge. Even a tin of Spam held more appeal.

Spotting the dejected look on my face, Vasiliki raised her perfectly arched eyebrows, prompting me to blurt, "*Trahanas*? Isn't that porridge?"

"It is not the porridge in your English way," Vasiliki said, indicating she was familiar with foreign food. A gentle laugh followed her words before she explained, "Because Babis has the problem with the teeth, I make my own *tarhana* pasta from semolina and yoghurt to make the porridge soup. I add a little chicken for flavour."

"Vasiliki is the goddess in the kitchen. How I miss the days when I could sink my teeth into one of her divine pork chops. *Poly nostimo*." Babis finished his sentence by describing Vasiliki's food as very delicious.

"Please, everyone take a seat and I will bring the food," Vasiliki said. Once again declining Marigold's offer of help, Vasiliki called out for Rothopi to help her carry the food to the table.

Watching as Bill busied himself introducing Babis to the rest of our party, I stifled a laugh at the fleeting look of disappointment when Marigold realised that the guest of honour wasn't in fact an esteemed dignitary. I was less successful in suppressing the snort that escaped me when the seemingly frail, old village president practically catapulted himself into the seat next to Violet Burke. If I wasn't mistaken, the twinkle in his eye indicated he wasn't too past it to be up for a bit of *kamaki*, the infamous Greek art of seductively reeling a woman in.

Chapter 12

Porridge, Garlic and Mucky Spoons

Delighted to be disillusioned of the notion that our evening meal would be nothing more than a bowl of unappetising porridge, I watched in amazement as Vasiliki and her young helper, Rothopi, piled the table with enough tempting dishes to feed an army. In no time at all, the table positively groaned under the weight of choice Greek favourites. I released a groan of my own when I spotted Rothopi sticking her fingers into one of the dips before licking them clean, her disgusting fingering failing to raise a single objection from her overindulgent parents. If they allowed their child such insanitary liberties at the table, I dreaded to think what unhygienic horrors went on in the kitchen. Catching my eye, Marigold mouthed 'Kyria Maria' across the table. I smiled at her obvious reference to our elderly neighbour's vile habit of sticking her grubby fingers in our condiments.

Vasiliki had laid on a sumptuous spread. The bread was accompanied by *skordalia* and *tzatziki* dips and an array of salads. Huge slices, or *fetes*, of oregano speckled feta cheese topped the traditional Greek salad, *horiatiki salata*, and a sprinkling of crushed walnuts glistened atop the fleshy red beets in the beetroot salad, *pantzarosalata*. Another two salads offered yet more variety; a platter of light summer *horta*, and a simple dish of shredded cabbage doused in olive oil and freshly squeezed lemon juice, *lahanosalata*.

Bringing yet more delicious dishes to the table, Vasiliki explained away the size of the lavish spread by confiding that her four sons may be feeling a bit peckish when they returned home from their business dinner.

"And if they not to eat at the midnight, they can to make the breakfast feast," Bill said, rubbing his hands in delight as Vasiliki placed a dish of oven baked feta with peppers and tomatoes on the table. An enormous platter of *briam* followed in close order, the dish of roasted vegetables incorporating courgettes, potatoes, tomatoes and red onions, glistening with extra virgin.

"I made two *stifados*," Vasiliki said when the final two dishes took pride of place on the table, served alongside a platter of garlic and lemon roasted potatoes.

"This one is *spetsofia*. It is made from local sausages cooked with green peppers in a red wine and tomato sauce."

Immediately leaning forward to spear a sausage, Violet Burke appeared to savour the flavour before pronouncing it, "Not half bad, lass. It's a sight better than them sausages I had for lunch."

"Oh, I wouldn't have cooked a sausage dish if I'd known you'd already had them today," Vasiliki said apologetically.

"Nay, lass. I could fill my boots with bangers," Vi reassured her, dismissively rejecting the salads that were being passed around the table. She demonstrated little tolerance for anything green unless it was her beloved mushy peas.

"I hunt the boar in this the *stifado*," Bill proudly announced, lifting the lid off a huge pot to release a deliciously intoxicating aroma of bay leaves, cardamom and wild game. "He is the *stifado agriourouno*."

"Here, pass it over," Vi demanded. "I'm right partial to a bit of pig. I hope you gave its trotters a good scrubbing to get the mud off. Pigs revel in mud."

"I don't believe that wild boar necessarily share the habits of pigs," I said in an attempt to deflect attention away from my mother putting her foot in her mouth yet again.

Hearing Bill boast that he had shot the main ingredient in the wild boar stew, I pondered the wisdom of asking Kostis to bag me a boar to turn into a tasty *stifado* during the next hunting season. The idea certainly posed a dilemma: whilst boars and their humbug offspring were becoming a dratted nuisance in the village, and goodness only knows how big the humbugs would be this coming winter, it may end up being a dangerous folly to encourage the pot-shot happy Kostis to be out and about in Meli with a lethal weapon. Marigold would be sure to be against it, considering the mess Kostis' bullet had made of Catastrophe's tail.

Tucking into a portion of *stifado agriourouno* and lemon roast potatoes, I appreciated the nutty flavour of the tender sweet meat. My only slight criticism of the food which Vasiliki had prepared was her noticeable tendency to be a tad heavy-handed in the garlic department, though it certainly explained Bill's overpoweringly garlicky breath. I was surprised when Vasiliki consulted her husband, asking him if he thought she had added enough garlic to the *stifado*. Addressing the group, Vasiliki shared, "Bill loves his garlic. If he had his way, he'd have me adding it to *bougatsa* and *baklava*."

Marigold visibly winced at the very suggestion of garlic infusing her favourite sweet *bougatsa* as Vasiliki continued, "My *yiayia* would turn in her grave if she knew how much garlic I add to her recipes, but I discovered years ago that a generous addition of garlic is the way to Bill's heart."

"I think the your *yiayia* would be the happy because the garlic is so the good at killing the germ," Bill said to his wife. Bringing the rest of us up to speed, Bill added, "The Vasiliki bring up the five child on the garlic to keep them safe from the germ. The garlic is the excellent disinfectant for the gut..."

"Disinfectant for the gut?" Benjamin queried, steepling his fingers under his chin and casting an askance look at his portion of boar. I could tell from my son's expression that he was pondering the likelihood of said boar having been marinated in bleach and herbs.

"Whilst not classified as a disinfectant, garlic has antiseptic and antibacterial properties," I confirmed, thinking Bill's theory wasn't too much of a stretch.

"The garlic teach the children, how you to say, the importance of the good *ygieni*?"

I nearly fell off my chair when Violet Burke

interjected to offer the English translation of *ygieni*. "Hygiene is the word you're after, lad." Spotting my mouth gaping open in wonder, she added, "You needn't act all surprised that I've picked up the Greek word for hygiene. I did birth a public health inspector."

I rolled my eyes at the ludicrous twist the conversation had taken. Whilst Vasiliki was clearly an excellent cook and mother, I had noticed her failure to scrub the dining table of cat hairs before serving dinner. Not only had she allowed her daughter to stick her fingers in the communal food, she had turned a further blind eye when Rothopi licked the *stifado* serving spoon before sticking it back in the stew. I had cringed inwardly when Marigold helped herself to some sausage *stifado* from the contaminated spoon, oblivious to Rothopi's potentially pestilent faux pas. Only my innate good manners preventing me from making a scene.

After witnessing such filthy goings on, it will come as no surprise to hear that I took Bill's words about Vasiliki's concern with hygiene with a pinch of salt. Although Bill had given us a tour of the house earlier, he had not only neglected to show us the kitchen, he had gone out of his way to avoid it. Perhaps Spiros had warned him that I could be tad exacting when it came to hygiene standards. I would put money on Vasiliki practising extremely lapse sponge hygiene.

Since I had expressed such an interest in *trahanas* earlier, Babis dangled a spoonful of the stuff under my nose, insisting I must try it. Reluctantly tasting a smidgeon of the dish that Vasiliki had lovingly prepared for the old fellow, I feigned enjoyment, politely pretending to find it palatable. In reality, I found the texture a sloppy turn off and the bland flavour could certainly have been improved with a hefty addition of garlic. I made a mental note to book an appointment for a dental check-up. It was imperative that I keep all my teeth in good order to avoid being reduced to suffering a diet of bland Greek porridge in my dotage. I wondered if Vasiliki's recipe might come in handy if my mother lost her teeth anytime soon. Somehow, I doubted *trahanas* would be my mother's cup of tea; a toothless Violet Burke would more likely subsist on a diet of liquidised Fray Bentos and mucky fat.

Whilst Babis monopolised Violet Burke's attention, thwarting my desire to learn more about his role as village president, Marigold told Bill about the old property that we were renovating to use as a tourist rental.

"As you're big in property, you may be able to give Victor some pointers," Marigold suggested.

"Oh, it's nothing on a grand scale," I modestly protested. "It's just one old house which we are turning into two apartments for tourist accommodation."

"If I can to take the time to visit the Spiros, I will to give you my the opinion on your the apartment," Bill offered. "It would be the good to get over to the Meli again..."

Bill's words tailed off as the familiar lyrics of 'Die for You', the 2001 Greek entry that had placed third in the Eurovision Song Contest, blasted out. It took a great deal of self-control to stop myself from involuntarily singing along. Fortunately, my feet were out of sight under the table as they danced to the beat. Ferreting around in his pocket, Bill produced his mobile phone. I chuckled at the cheesiness of Bill selecting 'Die for You' as his ringtone. Intercepting a warning look from his wife, Bill stepped away from the gathering to answer his telephone.

Whilst not ostensibly attempting to eavesdrop, snippets of Bill's animated conversation drifted over but it was indecipherable to my ears, the speed of the Greek dialogue way too fast for me to follow. My attention was distracted by Rothopi encouraging the cats to lick her plate clean of the last of her *stifado*, her indulgent Mama saying nothing to discourage the child from such deplorably unhygienic behaviour. Perhaps Vasiliki, like Spiros, used the cats as an alternative to a dishwasher.

BUCKET TO GREECE (VOL.14)

"*Ela*, Victor. It is the Spiros on the *kinito*," Bill called over, beckoning for me to join him. Handing over his mobile, Bill drifted back to the table whilst I chatted to the undertaker.

"I am the happy the Bill to find you. You to like the big house?" Spiros gushed. Giving me no opportunity to respond, he continued, "The Bill to say the President is all over the Violet like the rash."

"I wouldn't go that far," I said, straining my neck to see if there was any truth to it. Whilst it might appear that Babis was hanging on Violet Burke's every word, I would hazard a guess that he was simply concentrating on trying to make head or tail of her northern slang.

"Tell me, Spiro, why doesn't Meli have a village president?" I was keen to hear the answer. Perchance if I could get myself elected to such a prestigious position, assuming foreign residents were allowed to fill the role, the local mayor would have to sit up and take notice when I turned up at the *Dimarcheio* to bend his ear about the bins.

"We to have the president." Spiros' reply baffled me. I had been resident in Meli for almost three years without getting so much as a whiff of a village president. "He to live in the Nektar and is the president of three the local village."

"Three villages," I repeated, thinking he must spread himself thin. "How come I've never come across him?"

"He is the very old and lie in the bed all the day…"

"He doesn't sound up to the task…"

"That is the true, he do *tipota* for the village. But it is not the good to try to out him from the position. He need the stipend."

"So, he's paid to lie around in bed all day doing nothing useful?"

"I think I not to explain well. He is the *katakoitos*."

"Bedridden?"

"That's the word." I felt a tad guilty presuming the president was an idle layabout when it turned out he was physically incapacitated.

"The daughter think he not long for this world. You fancy the job when I to bury him? We could to have the election then."

"It doesn't seem fitting to discuss it whilst the poor chap is at death's door." Hastily changing the subject, I asked, "What news from Meli, my friend?"

"No one to die," Spiros confided, a heavy sigh following his words. "I get the call they have the drown tourist to bury and get the excite. I arrive too late. They had already to kiss him back to life on the beach."

"Oh, bad luck," I sympathised.

BUCKET TO GREECE (VOL.14)

Whilst my response may sound callow, I am intimately acquainted with Spiros' grumbles about failing to make any inroads into the business of laying dead tourists to rest. Since any holidaymakers that have the misfortune to drop dead on their vacation are invariably repatriated to their homeland for burial or cremation, Spiros constantly laments his failure to make inroads into this potential new market. He is convinced that if he could just establish a reputation for burying holidaymakers, his business would branch out in new directions. Personally, I think he is on a hiding to nothing. Nevertheless, I am always willing to give his business cards to any unhealthy-looking expats. Unfortunately, most of them are rather repelled by the notion of their bones being exhumed from the grave after three years.

Eager to change the subject, I assured Spiros that his good friend Bill was proving an excellent host.

"Did the Bill to show you his the, how to say, the *gipedo nkolf*?"

"His what?"

"The sand for the hit the balls. You must to wear the loud trouser when you to smack the balls," Spiros said.

"The golf course!" I exclaimed, the penny finally dropping. I suppose with a vivid imagination, the bucketed sandpit that Bill had shown me earlier might loosely resemble a children's miniature golf course. It was certainly a more plausible theory than a goldmine.

"Any other news from Meli?"

"The Guzim cry because he to lost the pet."

"It's sure to turn up, it always does," I said rather heartlessly. I was all too familiar with Guzim turning on the waterworks every time his pet rabbit, Doruntina, went on the missing list. It was after all a pretty regular occurrence, the rabbit invariably turning up in my vegetable patch.

"Come home soon, Victor. I miss you." Feeling a lump in my throat, I must admit that I felt quite touched that Spiros was able to express his feelings man to man. "Yesterday the only company in the taverna was the Norman and the Christos. The Giannis was with the Yiota but he tell me to sling the hook because he was to make the *romantikos*."

"Sling your hook. I think my mother's influence is rubbing off on you," I joshed.

"The Violet is to grow on me and the Sampaguita to adore her."

"Well, we'll both be home tomorrow," I promised my friend, feeling a wave of homesickness wash over me. Still, Marigold would be over the moon when I told her that Giannis had been spotted out and about making romantic overtures to Yiota.

BUCKET TO GREECE (VOL.14)

On my return to the table, snippets of conversation hit me from every direction. Marigold was holding court, regaling Vasiliki with every detail of our vow renewal service, our Greek hostess hanging on her every word.

Nudging me in the ribs, Bill encouraged me to try the local cheese. "He is the Arcadian *kefalotyri*. He is the little salty."

"Are you sure it's not made from potatoes. Marigold was banging on about Tripoli potatoes all afternoon," Vi chortled.

"I think you may be confusing your wine with your vodka, Granny," Benjamin quipped, topping up the glass of his apparently inebriated granny. By the time that Violet Burke had sat down for dinner, her face had lost the unnatural flush she had picked up in the sauna. I rather suspected that alcohol flush reaction was responsible for her current puce visage.

"Spiros say he can to marry us again, *agapi mou*," Bill called across to his wife. Vasiliki impressed me no end by being the first Greek of my acquaintance to get the concept of renewing one's vows without going through the pesky business of divorcing first. Her eyes only narrowed in confusion at Violet Burke's response when Bill extended a bowl of salad to my mother, encouraging Vi to take a helping.

V.D. BUCKET

"I'll give it a miss, lad. I've no truck with mucky spoons."

Chapter 13

A Catastrophe

It was early evening when we pulled into Meli. Fortunately, the drive home from Arcadia had been almost incident free. A bit of nifty steering on my part had prevented the Punto from ending up in a ditch when I was startled by the freakish rabbit's head flopping down in front of the windscreen, its overly large ears almost costing me a windscreen wiper. Ignoring my advice to sling the stuffed creature into the ditch, Benjamin had simply readjusted the rope securing it to the roof, thus ensuring the Punto was the subject of howls ribald laughter for the rest of the journey.

V.D. BUCKET

Driving down the deserted main street, an aura of peace pervaded the village, only the black clad figure of Litsa visible as she watered her pot plants with a hose. I felt a rush of affection for the village. Although we had enjoyed a wonderful break in Arcadia, there really is no place like home. Once again, I reflected that making the move from Manchester to the Greek Mani had been the best decision the Buckets had ever made.

"It's so good to be home," Marigold shouted over my shoulder, her words mirroring my thoughts. Since Violet Burke had claimed the passenger seat, my wife was stuck in the back of the Punto, forced to shout if she wished to make herself heard over her mother-in-law's snoring. Although neither of us had expressed much sympathy when Benjamin had complained of sleepless nights because his granny's snoring sounded like a freight train, we had learnt to our cost that he had been spot on. Fortunately, he had been spared Vi's day-snoring as we'd parted company in Tripoli, Benjamin picking up a hire car to head directly to the airport in Athens, leaving the two of us to endure the horrendous din of Violet Burke sawing logs.

Nudging my mother awake none too gently, I winced as she shifted her bulk in the seat. Snorting and dribbling, she dislodged a stream of pastry crumbs into the footwell. I would need to give the

BUCKET TO GREECE (VOL.14)

Punto a thorough vacuuming to remove all evidence of her constant snacking or it would attract every feral feline that fancied a more appetising option than the dregs and sludge of spoiled food on offer in the village bins.

Since Violet Burke was firmly wedged in the passenger seat, Marigold and I grabbed an elbow each to yank her out of the car. My mother had clearly used the excuse of our second honeymoon to gorge herself into a stupefied state. Apart from the trek to the castle and a gentle stroll around the lake, she hadn't expended any of her usual workday energy; as a consequence, her bulbous frame was beginning to look decidedly flabby around the edges.

Barry appeared at my side, breathless in his rush to greet us. "Here, let me give you a hand. Vi's too much of a weight for Marigold to be grappling with," Barry offered, ever considerate of his sister.

"I'd sooner have a bit of meat on my bones than be one of them stick insects like your Cynthia," Vi retorted. It was quite amazing how quickly she'd come out of her stupor, her razor-sharp repartee as quick as ever.

"I'll tell Cyn that you said that, Vi. She'll be tickled pink, for sure. She never stops fretting about the baby weight she gained with Anastasia, even though I keep telling her I like her a bit cuddly.

V.D. BUCKET

Now, how was the second honeymoon?"

"It was dead romantic having to listen to these two lovebirds bickering ever since breakfast," Vi retorted with a deadpan expression.

"We haven't been bickering, Vi," Marigold protested.

"Well, what was all that shouting about? I've barely had a second's peace since we left that Bill's house."

"I never knew snoring whilst awake was an actual thing," I snapped, deftly avoiding being handbagged by Violet Burke.

"I've been keeping an eye out for your return," Barry said. "Cynthia sent me over to say that you must come over and eat with us. She's knocking something up and I know that she needs to discuss the repping rotas with you, Victor."

Biting my tongue, I reflected that at least we had enjoyed some excellent food in Arcadia: it was certainly more than we could expect this evening with Cynthia in charge of the cooking. Despite attending my cookery classes over the winter, my sister-in-law remained as unimaginative as ever in the kitchen. Like Dina with her mop, Cynthia's heart just wasn't in it.

Spotting that his invitation hadn't exactly been received with enthusiasm, Barry hastened to add, "Don't worry. I'll be doing a barbecue and Cynthia is on salad duty."

"Since when did you invest in a barbecue?" Marigold asked. Barbecuing was most definitely not an approved pastime of the Buckets or our extended family due to my repeated warnings about the dangers of bacteria breeding in barbecue charred chicken with bloody raw innards. Although my family had once been sceptical about the risks and made fun of my warnings, they soon changed their tune when our neighbours in Manchester went down with a debilitating dose of salmonella after consuming undercooked barbecued bangers.

"I didn't invest in a barbie. We picked up a couple of disposable ones in Lidl. They look a doddle. All you have to do is rip the cellophane off and strike a match. No need to lug around bags of charcoal."

Barry looked so keen on the idea that I didn't have the heart to remind him about the dangers of undercooked meat and the sort of suspect bacteria that tended to breed when amateur chefs slapped their bangers on an outside grill. I made a mental note to stick to the salad and poke my food thermometer inside any suspect sausages that Marigold might have her eye on.

"I should give you fair warning, Victor. Cynthia has rostered you on for work tomorrow. I hope

V.D. BUCKET

your ribs are up for it."

"All recovered now," I assured him. Resigning myself to working the next day, I realised our holiday break was well and truly over. I'd enjoyed it so much that the next time Marigold started prattling on about us taking a luxury mini-break, I may perchance reward her with some hearty enthusiasm rather than hiding my credit card.

Adopting an atrocious imitation of an Australian accent, Barry pressed, "So, you're up for a barbie this evening?"

"Splashing out on a disposable barbecue in Lidl doesn't make you Australian," I scoffed pedantically.

"Just ignore Victor, Barry. We'd love to come. We are both dying to see little Anastasia."

"Wonderful. I'll set the barbie up near the pond."

I made a mental note to slather myself in plenty of Marmite and wrap the hem of my trousers in elasticated bands and tuck them into my socks. The ecological pond was a magnet for biting insects at sundown. I could only hope that any flying critters would fall prey to the frogs before they started sucking my blood.

"I'll have to shower and change before we come over for dinner," Marigold said.

"What about you, Vi? Do you fancy joining us

for a spot of food?" Barry invited, ignoring the withering look his sister fired in his direction. Marigold had rather been counting on parting ways with Violet Burke for the evening: one can, after all, have too much of a good thing.

"I can't, lad. I promised Dina that I'd get straight over to the taverna to give her a hand with the spuds. 'Appen the place will have got in a right filthy state while I've been honeymooning it up. Dina just doesn't have my touch when it comes to giving the place a right good mopping, her heart's not in it," Vi said. "And I'll be needing a right early start in the morning to catch up with all my clients in need of a right good bottoming. You can bet the lazy beggars have let the muck pile up and are expecting me to clean up their messes."

"Vi, I don't suppose that you can squeeze us in first thing?" Marigold cajoled in a honeyed tone. "The house is bound to have gathered dust while we were away."

"Go on then, lass. Seeing as it's you, I'll pop up first thing in the morning and give the place a good going over. Perish the thought that you'd have to get your own hands dirty." With that, Vi flounced into the *apothiki*, slamming the door in our faces.

"Did my ears deceive me or did Vi just come out with a Victorism?" Barry asked with a smirk, barely able to contain his mirth. "I never thought the day would come when Violet Burke would start peppering her chat with 'perish the thought.'"

"She's clearly been spending far too much time with Victor. They've started to rub off on one another." Marigold made a poor job of suppressing a titter.

"How you do exaggerate," I said.

"You were the one who wanted to stop at that petrol station on the way home to use the lav rather than the toilet."

"Well, the place looked too rough and ready to be graced by a sparkling clean water closet," I retorted, wincing as I recalled the stained and smelly outside facilities I had been reduced to using as a last resort when I'd been caught short on the drive home.

"We got a little something for our darling niece," Marigold said, her eyes flitting towards the ginormous rabbit tied to the roof of the Punto. I swear that every time I clapped eyes on the thing, it seemed to have grown, appearing more monstrous every time. In my opinion, the thing was downright creepy. Marigold couldn't have come up with a more freakish gift for Anastasia if she'd plumped for an inflatable clown.

"Oh, I reckoned you must have got that stuffed grotesquery for Guzim, what with him being rabbit mad," Barry snorted. My mind boggled at the thought of Guzim bedding down with the life-size bunny without provoking a jealous fit from Doruntina.

"You might as well take it over for Anastasia now, Barry," I suggested, hoping to spare myself the inevitable sniggering from any of the villagers who might clock me carting the freakish thing through the village.

"You bring the cases up, darling, and I'll head straight up to the shower...."

Marigold's words tailed off. Following her upward gaze, I spotted Guzim leaning over the balcony, waving frantically in our direction, a look of panic plastered on his face.

"What on earth is Guzim doing in our house?" Marigold demanded.

"I expect he's feeding the cats," I said.

"I still can't get over you giving him a key, Victor. You must want your head examining." Marigold's complaint was one that I had grown familiar with over the last few days since she'd never stopped harping on about it. In the course of our normal daily routine, we didn't grant access to the Albanian shed dweller, expecting him to know his place on the other side of the front door.

"How else would he be able to mind your precious felines if I hadn't given him a key?"

"Well, do go and get rid of him, darling. I'm in

no mood for any of Guzim's nonsense. I'm going to head straight to the shower…by the time I've finished, I expect our home to be a Guzim free zone. Oh, and don't forget to give him the gift we picked up for him in Lagadia."

"That will only delay his departure," I muttered under my breath as Marigold waltzed upstairs. Whenever I gave Guzim anything for free, I invariably had to endure the convoluted rigmarole of gushing thanks he proffered. By now, with so many cast-offs directed his way, I could predict the Albanian shed dweller's performance down to a tee. Guzim would likely take one look at the tourist tat that Marigold had selected for him and immediately prostrate himself on the floor. Gripping my shins, he would gush and grovel with over-the-top gratitude that I very much doubted was sincere. I had long suspected that he revelled in fake dramatic performances, under the delusion that his performance tugged at my heart strings as a prelude to loosening my purse strings.

Leaving Barry to grapple with the monstrously giant rabbit, I promised him that we'd be over shortly. I followed Marigold up to the house, dragging a suitcase and the bulging carrier bag of gifts up the stairs. I had no qualms about leaving the second suitcase on the street until I got my second wind: Meli is renowned as such a crime free zone that I knew no one would make off with it. I could perchance persuade Guzim to tootle down and collect it, thus sparing myself a hernia.

Entering the kitchen, I ran slap bang into the Albanian shed dweller. Lurking behind the door, he managed to simultaneously stand around like a spare part whilst looking as though he was up to no good. His hair stuck up in unruly clumps and his forehead shone with a sheen of sweat that threatened to drip onto Clawsome, the cat squirming uncomfortably as it tried to escape Guzim's clutches.

"*Kyrios Victor, einai mia katastrofi.*" Preceding my name with Mister alarmed me almost as much as Guzim declaring something was a catastrophe. My gardener usually dispenses with the formalities unless he's made some almighty cock-up that is likely to get him fired.

"*Iremise, Guzim.*" Instructing him to calm down, I asked him what was a catastrophe. "*Ti einai i katastrofi?*"

Glancing around, I couldn't see anything to indicate that anything remotely catastrophic had taken place; most likely, Guzim was simply engaging in a bout of his usual dramatic hyperbole. Admittedly, it struck me as odd that every cupboard door and drawer was wide open. Moreover, the debris of some sandwich makings left out on the kitchen table hinted that Guzim had been making himself at home and helping himself to our food, unless he'd been feeding the cats on sandwiches.

I considered that if I'd caught him out raiding our larder, whilst it was a bit of a cheek and most definitely not the sort of behaviour that I would choose to encourage, it didn't exactly warrant Guzim's doom laden words of catastrophe. Dropping the cat, Guzim put his hands together in a pleading gesture. I began to suspect there was more to it than Guzim simply being overcome with insatiable hunger whilst feeding the felines and failing to clean up the evidence before we returned.

"*I katastrofi,*" Guzim repeated, adding the words, she's missing. "*Afti leipei…*"

Remembering that Spiros had mentioned that Guzim had been crying over his lost pet, I told my gardener it was hardly a catastrophe since he was always losing his rabbit. "*Den einai katastrofi. Panta chaneis to kouneli sou.*"

"*I Doruntina einai sto spiti mou.*" As Guzim declared that Doruntina was in his house, I asked him what was missing.

"*I katastrofi.*" Guzim shouted 'the catastrophe' whilst nodding his head as though I was a simpleton.

The penny dropped. "Catastrophe."

"*Nai, katastrofi.*"

Belatedly twigging that Guzim was trying to

tell me that Marigold's precious cat was missing rather than something catastrophic had occurred in our absence, I gulped. I had rather naively assumed that Spiros was referring to Guzim's dratted rabbit when he referenced a lost pet; it had simply never occurred to me that Spiros had been referring to one of the three cats I had entrusted to the care of the feckless Albanian. This was serious. Gathering my thoughts, I realised that it wouldn't just be Guzim in the doghouse if Marigold discovered her pampered pet was on the missing list. I would be in for it too, having been the one to entrust the useless Albanian with the simple task of feeding a trio of cats.

Considering my wife's likely reaction, it was indeed an absolute catastrophe that Catastrophe was missing. Recalling Marigold's hysterical reaction when Clawsome had been on the missing list, I shuddered. Having been the one to inadvertently lock Clawsome out on the balcony overnight, I had argued that technically the cat hadn't been missing since it never left home. My argument had failed to sway Marigold who was forever dragging it up whenever the cats became a bone of contention between the two of us.

"*Prepei na einai sto spiti. Fovatai poly na vgei exo,*" I said, telling Guzim she must be in the house as she is too afraid to go outside. Ever since Kostis had taken a pot shot at Catastrophe, resulting in a partial amputation of her tail, the cat remained stubbornly housebound with no interest in the outside world.

"*Echo psaxei pantou sto spíti.*" I found Guzim's assurance that he had searched everywhere in the house rather perturbing.

"*Pantou?*" 'Everywhere?' I questioned, thinking that accounted for all the cupboards being open.

"*Nai, pantou.*"

Marigold would have kittens if she discovered that Guzim had been looking high and low for the cat, perchance rifling through her underwear drawer and rummaging around in my office. Realising that I had omitted to establish a pertinent fact, I asked Guzim how long Catastrophe had been missing. Unable to look me in the eye, Guzim shuffled shiftily, before admitting that he had no idea how long she'd been gone.

His face a picture of guilt, Guzim avoided my eye when he told me that all three cats had most definitely been present and correct when he'd fed them their breakfast the previous day. However, when he'd popped in the evening before to sort out their next meal, Catastrophe hadn't made her usual appearance. Guzim had commenced a rigorous search which had failed to uncover the cat.

When I exclaimed that we would both be dead men if Marigold discovered the cat had snuck out under his watch, Guzim's lower lip wobbled, a solitary tear tracking a visible path through the grime on his face. I tutted at the sight of a grown man turning on the waterworks; it was obviously a ploy to play on my good nature, the ploy being quite superfluous as it was Marigold's wrath he should fear, rather than mine. As the tear was joined by another, I realised I was in fact mistaken and Guzim wasn't crying; the tears were actually drops of sweat dripping down from his forehead.

"Min peis lexi se Kyria Bucket." I instructed Guzim not to say a word to Mrs Bucket. Although it wasn't much of a plan, I considered the best way for the two of us to avoid being skinned alive was to keep the truth from my wife for as long as possible. Informing Guzim that we would be out for the evening, I told him he must spend the time searching the village, stressing that nowhere was off limits. Ordering him to comb through the village bins and the neighbours' gardens, leaving no stone unturned, I arranged to meet Guzim at his shed on the stroke of ten. With a bit of luck, he would have found the feline by then: if not, we would conduct a further rigorous search together.

Hearing Marigold leave the bathroom, I slapped a finger over my lips, warning Guzim to keep quiet.

"Victor, a moment please," Marigold called out,

V.D. BUCKET

summoning me to join her.

Huddling together in the bathroom doorway, Marigold chided, "I could swear that I just heard Guzim. I thought I told you to get rid of him. I don't want him getting the idea that he can just pop in whenever the fancy takes him."

"I'm sure he wouldn't dream of overstepping the mark," I assured Marigold. "He only popped in to feed the cats. It's not as though he's been sleeping in our bed or soaping up in our shower."

"You're right, dear. Sorry, I was overreacting. But do get rid of him quickly so we can go over to Barry's. And do make sure you get the keys back." Marigold pecked me on the cheek before heading into the bedroom to dress for dinner. Changing her tune, she called back over her shoulder, "Don't forget to give Guzim that gift we got in Lagadia. It's the least we can do to thank him for looking after the cats."

Marigold wouldn't be so keen to thank Guzim if she knew that he'd managed to lose one of her pampered imported domestics. Still, on the bright side, he hadn't managed to lose Clawsome or Pickles. They were bound to be a huge comfort to Marigold if we failed to locate Catastrophe, though for now I preferred to keep her in the dark about the whole sorry business.

Joining Guzim in the kitchen, I dug through the

carrier bag of gifts, presenting him with the pompom adorned *tsarouhia*. As predicted, the Albanian shed dweller instantly prostrated himself on the kitchen floor and grabbed my shins in his usual grovelling manner upon being the recipient of the Buckets' munificence.

As I hoisted him up off the floor, reminding him that he had a cat to search for, Guzim gushed, "*Toso omorfa papoutsia,*" proclaiming 'such beautiful shoes.' Discarding his flip flops, he immediately stuck his grubby feet in the *tsarouchi*, declaring he would wear them everywhere and never take them off. He seemed so thrilled with the gift that I didn't have the heart to burst his bubble by pointing out that the gaudy shoes were actually slippers, especially when he went on to declare that all his Albanian compatriots would be jealous since none of them had such beautiful shoes.

Although I had argued with Marigold that the shoes were nothing more than a tacky knockoff version of the authentic *tsarouchi*, with girly pompoms to boot, I had failed to take into account Guzim's complete lack of good taste. He had certainly grovelled his thanks for receiving even more tasteless apparel in the past, Barry's jingle Christmas pullover being a prime example.

About to send Guzim on his way, he dug his feet in, insisting he had something important to tell me. I could barely keep a straight face when he told me that he'd had a run-in with Mrs Bucket's friend, Doreen. Apparently, Doreen had physically grappled with Guzim over the key to our house, insisting she would take over the cat feeding duties. Keenly aware that I had entrusted him with this great responsibility, he had fought Doreen off, refusing to grant her admittance. Confiding that he suspected Doreen wanted the keys so she could sneak her Texan paramour into the Bucket house while our backs were turned, Guzim assured me that he had been keeping a close watch on the place.

Inwardly cursing that I had missed the ludicrous spectacle of Guzim and Doreen engaging in a spot of public grappling, I looked forward to sharing this choice titbit with Marigold. I would put money on Marigold declaring, "Who does Guzim think he is? The morality police?"

Grasping his arm, I ushered Guzim out, reminding him of our ten o'clock rendezvous if the cat was still on the missing list. No sooner had I rid the Bucket household of Guzim, than Papas Andreas appeared on my doorstep, kindly delivering the suitcase I'd left on the street.

"Did you see the Guzim?" Andreas chortled with unbridled merriment. "He leave the here in his, how you say, the *pantoufles*?"

"Slippers," I translated. "Actually, Marigold

bought them for him in Arcadia as a thank you gift for feeding the cats whilst we were away. Mind you, he's only gone and lost one of the cats. Perhaps you'd better warn your mother that if she sees Guzim poking around in her garden, he's just out there looking for Catastrophe, rather than up to no good."

"I am to avoid the mother. She is in the terrible temper with me…"

"How so?"

"A poor Albanian family move to the Nektar and need the work…the man, Drin, he labour on the coast. His wife in the Albania not to trust him, she to think he play around with the women so she turn up in Greece. The Drin, he tell me the wife, Agnesa, need the work but difficult to find because she no speak the Greek, only the handful of word." Sighing heavily, Andreas continued. "I take the pity on them and pay the Agnesa to clean for my mother. I think this would to help the family and please my mother. But my mother the angry, she not to want the stranger in the house, looking through the things."

I suppressed a chortle at the irony of his words whilst simultaneously being impressed that the cleric had finally managed to get a grasp on his English genders, no longer referring to his mother as he. Marigold did everything she could to discourage

V.D. BUCKET

Maria from coming into our house, despising our elderly neighbour's proclivity for quite shamelessly poking through our things. Many a jar of condiment had ended up in the bin after being contaminated with one of Maria's probing fingers.

"If my mother finds out that you employed an Albanian woman to clean for Maria, instead of paying her to do it, you'll be on the receiving end of Violet Burke's temper too," I pointed out.

"I not to think of that." Finger combing his unruly beard with a contemplative air, a look of alarm crossed Andreas' face as it dawned on him that he might end up on the wrong side of the formidable Violet Burke. "I think to, how to say, kill two stone with one the bird; to help out the poor Agnesa and to do something the nice for my mother."

"A noble gesture on your part," I commended.

"The mother has to be the very demanding of late. Every day, she want me to make the bed with the blanket, exactly thirteen the blanket. It is not the good enough to make tidy the bed, she want I to take all the blanket off and put back the neat with, how you say, the hospital *gonies*?"

"Corners," I translated. "Thirteen blankets in summer seems a tad excessive."

"It make no difference, the summer, the winter. My mother must to have the thirteen blanket. I think the Albanian woman can to make the bed to spare me the job."

"It sounds to me as though Maria was very ungrateful for your kind gesture," I said.

"She think the Agnesa try to, how to say, swindle?"

"Swindle her. In what way?"

"Even though I pay the Albanian woman to clean, she still to make the demand on my mother. Agnesa tell to her that she is the poor woman and my mother must to give her things…"

"I thought you said she couldn't speak Greek."

"She know how to make the demand in our language."

"What did this Agnesa demand from Maria?"

"The blanket. She count the thirteen and say my mother show off her rich by having so many. She tell her it not right my mother so rich when she has no blanket…"

"But no one needs a blanket in June…"

"The Agnesa demand my mother give to her the blanket. Agnesa say it is her right. My mother to throw her…"

"I can't say I blame Maria. It's a bit of a cheek for the cleaner to start demanding the bedding off Maria's bed…"

"I feel in my water that the Agnesa will to make much the trouble in the Meli…I think I to make the big mistake in giving her the work…"

Andreas' words were interrupted by Marigold calling out, "Victor, have you still not got rid of Guzim?"

"Not a word to Marigold about the missing cat," I hissed to Andreas, shooing him back down the stairs.

Chapter 14

Charred Wieners

Waiting on the doorstep for Barry to let us in, Marigold and I exchanged worried glances, almost deafened by the heart-wrenching sound of Anastasia's relentless screams. As Cynthia threw the door open, Barry cradled his baby daughter in his arms, attempting to calm her.

"Shush, sweetie. Look, your favourite Aunty Marigold and Uncle Victor are here," Barry cooed, wiping the tears from her face with the hem of his tee-shirt.

"What on earth has upset Ana so much?"

Marigold's voice fairly quivered with concern.

Gulping and sobbing, Ana pointed at the giant stuffed rabbit propped up next to the staircase, stuttering, "Yucky." Now fifteen months old, my adorable niece was usually more articulate.

"Poor Ana has had a fit of the screaming abdabs ever since Barry brought that unnatural thing home with him. What on earth were you thinking, Victor?" Cynthia accused. "Surely you realised such a freakish toy would scare the life out of a toddler."

"Don't go blaming me, it was all Marigold's doing," I protested, quite happily throwing my wife under the bus for once. "I told Marigold it was perfectly ghastly and more disquieting than a stuffed clown."

Unable to saddle me with the blame, Marigold came over all flustered and defensive that her carefully chosen gift had gone down like a lead balloon.

"Dirty," Ana called out, still pointing at the rabbit.

"It's just a little dirty, darling," Marigold told Ana. "It had to come all the way back from Arcadia on the roof of our car."

"I told you it needed throwing in the washing machine for a good boil wash before giving it to Ana," I said. "Goodness only knows how many germs it picked up on the roof."

"I didn't see you attempting to shove that

enormous thing in the washing machine," Marigold snapped. "It is much too big for the drum."

I felt particularly pleased to see that Anastasia was continuing to demonstrate an interest in hygiene matters, something Cynthia complained that Ana had no doubt picked up from me and her *yiayia*. Although technically Violet Burke isn't actually Anastasia's grandma, Ana is extremely fond of my mother and insists on calling her *yiayia*. Personally, I considered that Violet Burke was a much better role model of a grandma than Anastasia's actual grandmother, the insufferable Anne Trout.

"I think I'll take Ana up to bed and try to settle her," Cynthia said. "All those tears have worn her out."

Clucking over her niece, Marigold asked, "Do you want Aunty Marigold to come up with you? I can help mummy to tuck you in and read you a story?"

Nodding vigorously through her sniffles, an innocent smile that would melt the stoniest heart broke out on Anastasia's tear-stained face.

As the two women made their way upstairs, fussing over Anastasia, Cynthia turned back to hiss at Barry, "Do get rid of that stupid stuffed rabbit. I don't care what you do with it, but I don't want it upsetting Ana again."

"What am I supposed to do with it?" he

demanded.

"Why not get Victor to palm it off on Guzim?" My sister-in-law sent a scathing look in my direction, clearly under the mistaken belief that despite my denials, I was in some way responsible for procuring the terrifying bunny. "That Albanian of his has quite the reputation for bedding down with rabbits."

"I'll drop it in on Guzim later," I volunteered, rather amusing myself as I considered the likely reception it would get from the Albanian shed dweller. Knowing Guzim as I do, I expected he would declare his undying love for the thing.

As Barry and I headed outside to the patio, the sound of Marigold singing an off-key lullaby to her niece drifted downstairs. Tossing the stuffed rabbit aside, Barry grumbled, "I'm tempted to hurl the damn thing in the pond."

"Indeed. Might as well just drown the thing," I suggested, thinking at least that way, I could avoid the risk of making myself a laughing stock later by carting it back through the village later.

"Cyn will probably complain it's not ecological or some such nonsense. She won't want it contaminating the pond."

"Well, one of its ears is already dangling below the surface of the water," I pointed out.

Barry made a grab for the rabbit. After

wringing its ear out, he left it lying on the patio by the side of the pond. "I'll leave it there. It will remind you to take it with you later."

"It will probably put us off our food," I quipped.

Partially hidden under a red callistemon shrub, otherwise known as a bottlebrush because of its floral resemblance to a bottle cleaning brush, Kouneli crouched on its haunches, its ears pinned back, stealthily eyeing up the stuffed rabbit as though it was some kind of seductive prey. Slowly creeping forward, the vile cat made its move, springing in the air and descending on the inanimate stuffed toy, stabbing randomly at the rabbit with its swollen appendage. Clearly frustrated by its failure to have its wicked way, Kouneli attacked the rabbit with its claws, ripping a hole in the fur, leaving its stuffing exposed. Moving swiftly to grapple the stuffed toy away from the cat, Barry slung Kouneli in the kitchen before reiterating Cynthia's demand that I take the now damp and bedraggled rabbit away with me when I left.

Before I'd even had chance to plonk myself down in a deckchair, I was targeted by a vicious mosquito. Grabbing my arm, Barry dragged me into his man cave, otherwise known as the garden shed, with the enticing offer of dabbing some vinegar on my bite.

V.D. BUCKET

Grabbing a couple of beers that had been chilling in a bucket of fast melting ice, Barry slung the water out of the bucket. Upending it, he offered the bucket to me as a makeshift seat. Clinking his bottle against mine, Barry exhaled in relief.

"We can catch up in here without our wives butting in on our conversation. It's just like the old days when we used to take refuge in your downstairs storage."

"Those were the days," I sighed, thinking wistfully of the time before the downstairs storage had been converted into a home for my mother. Barry and I had whiled away many a happy hour in the shuttered and cobwebbed gloom of the unrestored *apothiki*.

"How's things?" Barry asked.

Even though there was no danger of our wives overhearing us, I leaned in close, hissing, "Well, not a word of this to your sister or I'll end up in the doghouse."

Raising his eyebrows questioningly, Barry waited for me to elaborate.

"You know I left Guzim in charge of Marigold's precious cats…"

"What's the idiot gone and done now?"

"He's only gone and lost one of them."

"Crikey, I see what you mean about the doghouse. Wait, how come you're not already in strife?

BUCKET TO GREECE (VOL.14)

We'd know about it if you were."

"Amazingly, Marigold doesn't actually know anything about it. I can't believe I've been able to keep her in the dark. Considering all the fuss she made about missing the cats whilst we were in Arcadia, once we were home, she barely gave the time of day to Clawsome and Pickles."

"So, it's Catastrophe that Guzim's gone and lost. It will be a catastrophe for sure, if Marigold finds out." A wry laugh followed Barry's words, even though there would be nothing to laugh about if Marigold cottoned on.

"I've sent Guzim out to search for the thing now. With a bit of luck, he'll find it and sneak it back in the house before Marigold is any the wiser."

"You'll be for it if Guzim doesn't find it."

"If he hasn't found it by ten o'clock, I'll be joining him in the search. I'll have to make some excuse to sneak away early to meet him. Cover for me?"

Slapping me on the back, Barry confirmed, "You don't need to ask."

"How's the rental ruin coming along?" I asked. "I'm guessing you're way ahead of schedule if you can afford to take the evening off."

"Not exactly. Cynthia threatened to have my guts for garters if I didn't take the evening off to spend with the family. She's sick of me putting in so many hours and spending her evenings without me," Barry revealed. "Blat has proved to be such a good worker that me and Vangelis have taken him on full time. Blat's over at the wreck now, putting the finishing touches to the pointing. He was glad of the overtime. Once the pointing is out of the way, we can crack on with the rest of the work."

"What's up next?"

"I want to get the shutters and windows installed before we tackle the rest of it; there's so much to do, installing the bathrooms and kitchens, tiling, plastering..."

"It all sounds exhausting," I said, hoping Guzim had cracked on with the weeding whilst I'd been away. I'd be in no mood to tackle an overgrown jungle after a hard day's repping.

Not for the first time, it crossed my mind that the limited renovation needed on our own house in Meli had been a doddle compared to the amount of work required at the rental property. It was imperative that we cracked on with the renovation without delay. Expenditure on the project would be an endless drain on our finances, continuing to bleed our bank accounts until the moment it produced some rental income.

"I'm glad you took Blat on full time. He struck me as a decent sort and I must admit to being rather charmed by little Tonibler...such a character, modelling himself along the lines of a young Tony

BUCKET TO GREECE (VOL.14)

Blair."

"I think that's Blat's doing. He's obsessed with Teflon Tony and the great Great Britain." I smiled at the way Barry emulated Blat's way of describing our native land.

"I intend to offer Tonibler another English lesson. He was terribly keen and has the makings of an excellent student."

"I reckon the lad might come in handy if we've any complicated measurements to work out. Vangelis is forever stuffing up how much paint we need for a job. The van's full of tins waiting to go back for a refund, he always buys far too much. Young Tonibler's a bit of a maths whizz."

"That's handy if you have any local work on…"

"We do. We've made a start on that renovation job for John Macey," Barry groaned. "Ever since he signed the deal on that house in the village, he's been hanging around like a bad smell, supervising the work we're doing. Still, at least I've found a way to get shut of him."

"How so?" I enquired.

"Well, he never shuts up, and I do mean never. He's worse than Sherry for prattling on. I generally try and tune him out but my ears pricked up when he was banging on about having done some repping work in Crete; the way he carried on about it, he obviously thought he was the dog's bollocks at it. Seeing that Cynthia's still a rep down after that business of that Dennis bloke being drunk on the job, I introduced John Macey to Cynthia. She offered him some work on a trial period." Looking a tad guilty, Barry avoided my eyes as he added, "You might as well know, Cyn's got Macey shadowing you on Pegasus tomorrow. She wants you to show him the ropes."

"I've no problem with that. I really can't see why you've taken against him, Barry. Macey struck me as perfectly amiable, perhaps a tad full of himself, but nothing excessive. Smug Bessie was practically begging for the rep job and anyone would be an improvement on her. She's absolutely insufferable."

"We'll have to agree to differ, Victor. I'm not the only one who can't stand him…"

"I know that Marigold wasn't too keen…"

"I meant Vangelis, and you know how easy-going Vangelis is. He hates the way that Macey keeps popping up, forever changing his mind about how he wants things fixing on the house. Vangelis reckons that working for Macey could end up being even more of a hellish experience than working for Sherry."

"Just think of the money…"

The shed door creaked open and Cynthia appeared. "What on earth are you two doing skulking away in the shed?"

"I was just getting some vinegar for Victor to keep the mossies at bay..."

"You haven't even started the disposable barbecue yet," Cynthia nagged.

"I'm on it now." Downing the dregs of his beer, Barry reluctantly followed his wife back to the patio where Marigold had comfortably ensconced herself in a deckchair.

"You might have thought about lighting the barbecue instead of skulking off to the shed," Cynthia harped.

"I wanted to wait until everyone is here," Barry said.

"We're all here..."

"Not quite." Barry hesitated. I wondered who else he'd invited to join us without taking the reasonable precaution of clearing it first with his wife.

"I'd better grab another plate if you've invited Vangelis along," Cynthia said, glancing across at the outside wooden table laid for four. The smile she gave Barry indicated she didn't mind that he had roped Vangelis into joining our family gathering. Vangelis is, after all, Anastasia's godfather.

"No, it's not Vangelis. I ran into Litsa in the village earlier and invited her to join us."

"Really, Barry. I'd hoped we'd have a relaxing family evening," Cynthia chided, her face turning just a tad green as her jealousy raised its ugly head. I could never quite fathom Cynthia's annoyance at the special relationship that had developed between the sweet, elderly Greek pensioner widow and Barry. If anything, it should be Litsa that was envious of Cynthia since the English woman had snatched up Barry and taken him off the marriage market, so to speak.

"Litsa always treats me like family," Barry stated, rolling his eyes behind Cynthia's back.

"Now we'll have the mental challenge of speaking in Greek all evening and trying to work out what Litsa is talking about. I wanted to give my brain a rest this evening." Considering her competence in the Greek language, Cynthia's gripe wasn't very convincing.

"Barry and Litsa have always been able to understand each other, even before Barry had mastered a word of Greek." I couldn't resist throwing fuel on the fire.

Firing a filthy look in my direction, Cynthia flounced off to the kitchen. "I'll go and get the food for the barbecue."

"I wonder what sort of meat Barry is planning to incinerate," I hissed to Marigold.

"You needn't josh, Victor," Barry said. "Cynthia knows how anxious you are about the food not being cooked through thoroughly and the risk of us all coming down with food poisoning. She's sorted out a few jars of sausages in brine she picked up in Lidl. Since they're pre-cooked, I only have to bung them on the barbie to brown them."

I grimaced at Cynthia's lack of imagination when it came to sausages. Rather than selecting the excellent local *loukanika* infused with orange peel, Cynthia always went for the lazy option of opening a jar of ready-cooked wieners. Just the thought of her toad-in-the-hole was enough to trigger a bout of indigestion.

"I should have brought the Gaviscon," I whispered to Marigold.

Not being a fan of a briney wiener, Marigold crinkled her nose in distaste. "Perhaps we should just stick to the salad."

"There's no need for that," Cynthia said snootily, sneaking up behind us, carrying a tray laden with two jars of wieners and some suspicious looking parcels wrapped in tin-foil. "I've popped some potatoes in foil to add to the barbie."

Barbecued potatoes filled with lashings of butter ought to sound like a tempting addition, but I doubted they would be. Knowing Cynthia, the potatoes were likely still raw within their shiny wrappers and would remain stubbornly raw by the time the last of the embers were extinguished. I may sound like a terrible food snob, but it hadn't escaped my notice that my sister-in-law didn't even have the nous to rinse the brine off the wieners, simply plucking them from the jar and passing them to Barry to cook.

Settling down in an adjacent deckchair, Cynthia pulled out the work rotas and went into office manager mode, leaving Barry in charge of the barbecue. At least Cynthia always extended the hand of nepotism to me as her brother-in-law, allowing me first pick when it came to claiming which trips that I fancied leading. After telling her that Barry had already brought me up to speed on John Macey joining the team on a trial basis, Cynthia filled me in on the trips she had provisionally marked me down for.

"I've put you down for three trips over the coming week, Victor. The Lazy Day cruise with Vasos tomorrow, the Vathia tour, and your usual Gastronomic Walking tour around town."

"Excellent. What have you lined up for Macey?"

"Well, he's with you tomorrow and then I've put him down for the Moonlight Cruise on Pegasus and the evening trip to an authentic old world taverna in a mountain village…"

"The old world taverna where the microwave pings," I mocked.

"That's the one. It's very popular."

BUCKET TO GREECE (VOL.14)

"Did I hear you right, Cyn?" Barry said. "You've got Macey doing two evening shifts. I thought the whole idea was to get him out of the village during the day so he won't get under our feet when we're working on his house."

"Well, he's on day's tomorrow."

"Come on, Cyn. Juggle your rotas a bit," Barry wheedled.

Scrunching her face in concentration, Cynthia stared at the rotas.

"Look, you could swap him over to the Diros trip and roster Judith on for Moonlight Cruise," I suggested.

"Yes, that works. But I can't switch any other trips around this coming week, it just doesn't work. Sorry, Barry, that's the best I can do," Cynthia said.

"Just make sure that Macey is on all days when you sort out the next lot of rotas," Barry urged.

"Let's see how he gets on during his trial period first. He might be a bit rusty. It's a few years since he did any repping," Cynthia said.

Moving to my side, Barry leant over my shoulder, the brine from his barbecue tongs dripping onto my button down as he whispered, "Can't you fiddle the customer satisfaction surveys to give Macey a glowing rating to make sure he doesn't get sacked? Come on, you know I'd do the same for you."

"Barry. The sausages are burning, jump to it," Cynthia shouted, prompting her husband to catapult himself back to the disposable barbecue.

"I reckon the sausages are nearly done," Barry said a short while later.

"I'll go and grab the salad then," Cynthia said. Asking Marigold to help her, the two women trotted off to the kitchen. Their exit couldn't have been timelier since the second they were out of sight, Barry pointed his tongs towards the shrubbery. "What on earth is Guzim doing creeping around the edge of the ecological pond? And what's he doing with those ludicrous pompom things on his feet?"

"Since he didn't announce his arrival by ringing the doorbell like a normal person, I expect he must have manipulated a loose plank in your fence," I replied, rushing over to my gardener.

Grabbing Guzim by his arm, I demanded to know what he thought he was doing here. "*Ti nomizeis oti kaneis edo?*"

"*Prospatho na vro ti gata.*" His reply that he was trying to find the cat sent my blood pressure soaring: could he be any denser?

"*Eisai ilithios?*" Admittedly, asking him if he was stupid, was a stupid question. Of course, he was stupid: it went without saying.

Dragging Guzim by the arm, I told him that he couldn't be seen looking for Mrs Bucket's cat in front of her, warning him that my wife could return to the garden at any moment.

"*Mou eipes na psaxo pantou. Mou eipes na min afiso kamia petra,*" Guzim whined, saying I had told him to look everywhere and told him to leave no stone unturned.

"*Ochi brosta stin Kyria Bucket, kretina,*" I retorted, saying, 'Not in front of Mrs Bucket, you cretin.'

As I shooed Guzim away through the undergrowth, he deftly caught the charred wiener that Barry generously tossed his way. As my brother-in-law and I watched Guzim skulk away, Barry slapped his forehead. "You forgot to give him that blasted stuffed rabbit."

"I'll take it over to him later."

"Take what to whom?" Marigold trilled, returning to the garden carrying a bowl of salad.

"Nothing," Barry and I replied in unison.

"Was someone just in the garden with you two?" Cynthia said suspiciously, juggling a tray of rather anaemic looking cheese pies that had failed to brown in the oven.

"No."

"Strange, I could swear I saw…"

"Good grief, you've been a tad heavy handed with the olive oil, Cynthia," I interrupted, hoping to distract her from the idea that anyone had been in the garden. "The salad's practically floating around in the stuff."

Ignoring me, Cynthia started to plate up the salad and *tyropites*, the excess oil from the salad immediately turning the pallid cheese pies soggy.

"Shouldn't we wait for Litsa to arrive?" Barry said.

"Well, what time did you tell her to come?" Cynthia asked.

"I just said this evening."

"Then she probably won't turn up for hours. The Greeks consider it is still afternoon until it goes dark," Cynthia snapped. "We may as well eat now that the sausages are done."

"These spuds are still rock hard, Cyn. Ouch." Barry burnt his fingers examining the foil wrapped potatoes that Cynthia had, as I'd predicted, most definitely neglected to cook before sticking them on the barbecue. "Here, take a couple of sausages, Victor. There's no need for you to go sticking your food thermometer in them. They're burnt to a crisp."

"I like them well done," Cynthia said, daring the Buckets to make any more disparaging remarks about the food on offer.

Fortunately, Litsa's arrival spared us from having to make a pretence of enjoying the dismal food since the elderly lady came bearing tempting dishes she had lovingly prepared in her own kitchen. I rushed forward to relieve her of the pies and salad she was carrying, whilst Barry solicitously guided her to the table.

My taste buds sprang into life as I removed the clingfilm from an enormous bowl of salad, asking Litsa if it was artichoke salad. "*Einai afto salata ankinaras?*"

"*Nai*," she confirmed as I gazed hungrily at the wonderful mix of penne pasta, *zimarika penes*, fresh artichokes, *freskes ankinares*, cherry tomatoes, crumbled feta, and parsley.

To accompany the salad, Litsa had brought some home-made *spanakopites*, spinach pies, nicely browned and still warm from her oven.

Not standing on ceremony, Barry grabbed one of Litsa's pies, the cheese oozing out as he bit into it. "*Teleios*," he proclaimed, declaring the pie perfect.

"You didn't say that about my *spanakopites*," Cynthia complained jealously.

"Well, all you did was sling a tray of frozen pies from Lidl in the oven," Barry pointed out.

"At the wrong setting," I couldn't resist adding. No one could ever accuse Cynthia of being a domestic goddess.

Spooning some of the artichoke salad onto her plate, Marigold whispered to me, "It's a pity that Barry didn't find himself a Greek wife. We'd never have been fobbed off with frozen pies."

V.D. BUCKET

I suppressed a snort at the irony of Marigold's words. She wasn't above shoving a packet of frozen *tyropites* and *spanakopites* from Lidl in the oven whenever she had her friends over for a girls' night in, though naturally she tried to pass them off as home-made by tarting them up with a sprinkle of oregano.

Barry was at his most charming as he fussed over Litsa, showering the old lady with compliments that brought a blush to her cheeks. Glowering at Litsa across the table, Cynthia muttered to Marigold, "Look at the way she's trying to win Barry over with her fancy cooking. Turning up with her home-made salad and pies; I bet she only did it to make me look like an amateur cook next to her."

"Well, there's an obvious solution that's right under your nose," Marigold said. "You wouldn't need to feel inferior in the kitchen if you got Barry to take over the cooking."

"Barry and cooking don't go together," Cynthia scoffed.

"You would have said the same thing about Victor before we moved to Greece, but just look at him now. These days, I never need to rustle up a meal when we have company. I get Victor to do it and he's in his element."

"Marigold is turning into quite the lady of leisure," I told Cynthia. "She has Violet Burke in to do the cleaning and Blat's wife, Blerta, to do the ironing."

"Lady of leisure indeed," Marigold scoffed. "I do most of the run of the mill cooking and all of the washing, not to mention the shopping. Don't forget, I have three cats to look after, all the pot plants need deadheading, and there's my work in the community."

"Work in the community?" Barry asked sceptically.

"I hardly ever miss the monthly meeting to beautify the cemetery," Marigold said.

"To be fair to Marigold, she is past retirement age so it's not surprising that she wants to take things a bit easier." My wife flushed with anger at Cynthia's snide comment.

"We're just teasing you, Sis." Barry attempted to calm the waters before they erupted. Winking at me, he added, "After all, you've got your work cut out for you, being married to Victor."

The remainder of the evening passed pleasantly enough. I derived great satisfaction in surreptitiously feeding all of my and Marigold's charred wieners to Kouneli. With a bit of luck, the mutant cat would end up vomiting in the ecological pond. With the hour fast approaching ten, I realised I would need to get a move on to meet Guzim at his shed: I know from experience that the Albanian can get a strop on if he's kept waiting. Needing to make some excuse that wouldn't trip Marigold's radar to something being amiss, I announced I was stiff from spending so long in the Punto and could do with a stroll.

"I'll come with you, darling," Marigold offered.

"No, don't. Really, don't. When I said stroll, I actually meant a very brisk walk. You wouldn't be able to keep pace in those heels."

Catching my drift, Barry winked at me, before cajoling, "Stay a while, Sis, it's early yet. It's not as though you have to be up with the lark for anything."

"That's where you're wrong. I'll need to get up early enough to be out of the way before Vi turns up to clean. I'm in no mood to endure one of her running commentaries on my lax standards. My mother-in-law has no filter. I suppose she thinks she can get away with it because we're related."

"I've heard that she's just as mouthy with all her other clients," I said. "You'll see Marigold safely home later, Barry?"

"Of course. If you're determined to leave so early, take that blasted rabbit with you and drop it off with Guzim. I don't want Anastasia having nightmares."

"Guzim will end up spoilt. We already bought

him some lovely shoes in Arcadia," Marigold grumbled, her nose still put out of joint that her special gift had been rejected by our darling niece.

Chapter 15

Guzim is Beyond Confused

Walking briskly home to keep my pre-arranged ten o'clock secret rendezvous with Guzim, I was in two minds over whether or not to be thankful for such a dark, moonless night. On the one hand, the lack of moonlight meant I would be spared the taunting sniggers of any villagers who might cross paths with me carrying the ridiculous, life-size stuffed rabbit: on the other hand, if Guzim hadn't already located Catastrophe, the impenetrable darkness would hinder our search.

Since I really was in no mood for traipsing

around in the dark looking for the blasted cat, I had high hopes that the moronic Albanian would be able to report he had located the missing feline. At least I was confident that Violet Burke hadn't slung Catastrophe in a passing pickup as she'd done with Cynthia's vile, mutant moggie, Kouneli. Being on our second honeymoon when Marigold's precious cat went missing, gave my mother a cast iron alibi. I must confess to finding it quite ironic that after bleating at length about how much she missed the cats whilst we were away, Marigold had failed to even notice she was one cat down on our return.

Guzim popped up in my path out of nowhere as I crossed the garden by torchlight, the forlorn expression on his face hinting that all attempts to bag the cat had been a dismal failure. I will spare any readers the convoluted, confused translations that I am forced to endure in all my encounters with the Albanian shed dweller and instead simply summarise the gist of it without penning any guttural Greek or any of Guzim's Albanian expletives

"No sign of the cat?" I asked.

"I look everywhere..."

"No luck in the bins?"

"Much luck in the bins." Guzim broke into a wide toothless grin. I experienced a moment of sheer relief at Guzim's response. If he'd found Catastrophe in the bins, I could sneak the cat back in

V.D. BUCKET

the house and give it a quick blast of Lidl air freshener before heading to bed with a clear conscience, leaving Marigold none the wiser that her precious feline had ever been on the missing list. My moment of joy evaporated when Guzim began prancing about in the torchlight, full of himself as he announced, "See, I find this shirt in the bins. It was the big luck to find it."

Shining my torch at his torso, I saw that Guzim had decked himself out in a red and black polka dot blouse featuring puffed sleeves and a plunging V-neckline. I could swear that I'd seen the blouse before. Since Guzim lacked the bust to carry it off, the blouse hung loosely over his scrawny chest.

"I hate to disillusion you, but that isn't a shirt…"

"It is…"

"No, it isn't. It's a woman's blouse."

"It is a shirt," Guzim defiantly argued. "I like it much because it is in the colours of the Albanian flag…"

"That doesn't do anything to make the blouse manly. You'll give people the wrong idea if you go around wearing women's clothing. Anyway, the red clashes something awful with the pink pompoms on your slippers."

I racked my brain, convinced I had seen one of the expat women wearing the very same blouse recently. It definitely wasn't one of Marigold's cast-offs since the neckline was a tad risqué for her liking and I very much doubted that Doreen would have chucked it out when she had the jumble sale coming up. Catching a whiff of dog, it came to me: Guzim was wearing a spotted reject last seen on Moira Strange. The lingering scent of damp Goldendoodle could well have hindered Guzim's search for the cat. Catastrophe, having a keen sense of smell, usually ran a mile, terrified if Waffles accompanied the Stranges whenever they dropped in on the Bucket household.

Since I was on a hiding to nothing, I gave up trying to convince Guzim that he looked a right plonker. His dire fashion sense was hardly anything new, though in his defence, he had at least paired the women's blouse with shin-length denim shorts rather than skin-tight Lycra.

Having allowed the Albanian shed dweller to side-track me from the important business of searching for the missing cat, I unburdened myself of the enormous stuffed rabbit by chucking it in Guzim's direction. Taken by surprise, Guzim almost toppled over as the flying object hit him square in the chest. I couldn't wait to boast to Barry about my impressive aim; my brother-in-law always used to relentlessly mock my efforts when I attempted to play ball with Benjamin back in my son's childhood days.

"What is it?" Guzim asked as though he'd never encountered a giant stuffed rabbit before.

Since I had no patience to point out the patently obvious and end up in some nonsensical discussion, I thought fast on my feet. "It's a gift for Victor Mabel. Think of it like a teddy bear."

Surveying the life-size stuffed rabbit with a baffled expression, Guzim demanded, "How am I supposed to get it to Albania? It would need a seat on the bus. I would have to buy it a ticket."

"For goodness' sake. If they refuse to transport the rabbit in the luggage storage bins, I will pay for its blasted bus ticket," I said in exasperation, realising it was going to cost me dearly to get rid of the thing. Taken aback by Guzim's ungrateful response, I wondered what had happened to his usual over-the-top reaction to my generosity.

"You will pay the bus fare?" he wheedled.

"I've just said so, haven't I?" Guzim backed away from me as though he expected to receive a good kicking. Admittedly my tone had been a tad curt but I was yet to raise a foot to the scrawny Albanian, no matter how much I was tempted.

Realising that I had failed to take Guzim's permanent penury into account, I felt a pang of guilt. It was perhaps a tad thoughtless of me to try to palm off the grotesque stuffed toy as a gift to Guzim's latest offspring if he imagined it would end up costing him a day's wages to banish the bunny to Albania.

"Come on, let's get a wiggle on and start searching for the cat. Where have you looked so far?"

"Everywhere," Guzim replied despondently. Clearly, the enormity of losing Catastrophe was worrying him, as well it should. Marigold would make mincemeat of him if she ever found out. "Do you have a photograph of the cat?"

"Why do you want a photograph?"

"Because when I look in the bins, they were full of cats. I could not remember exactly what Mrs Bucket's cat looked like. I think she might notice if I bring the wrong one..."

"Oh, she'd notice all right." The very idea that we could pass off some flea infested feral as Marigold's pedigree pet was absurd, even though its pedigree was a tad dubious. Much as I detested the prospect, I realised that we had no choice but to make the bins our first port of call and have a good rummage. As a pampered imported domestic, Catastrophe was clueless how to hunt for food. It wasn't beyond the realm of reason that if she was attempting to survive in the unfamiliar outdoors, she might have been driven to look for scraps amongst the garbage rather than attempting to chase down a live mouse and transform it into a tasty dinner. Even the sight of a lizard in the house sent Catastrophe running for cover, the cat sharing my wife's irrational fear of lizards and geckos.

Guzim manoeuvred the stuffed rabbit into his shed before falling into step beside me. As the two of us made our way to the village bins, I had a horrible flashback to the time I had been stuck in the bins with Milton. I didn't intend to make the same mistake twice. If there was any climbing inside the rancid metal receptacles to be done, Guzim would be the only one doing it.

I couldn't help noticing that despite Guzim being the one at fault for losing the cat, he seemed to have a bit of an attitude. Dragging his feet, he curled his lip and gave a surly, one syllable response when I enquired how my namesake, Victor Mabel, was getting on. Losing patience, I demanded an explanation for his glumness, determined to get to the bottom of whatever had soured his mood.

As I shone the torch in the churchyard in the hope of uncovering Catastrophe, Guzim lowered himself onto the wall outside the church. Emitting a dramatic sigh, he admitted he was confused.

"That's nothing new," I quipped. Noticing he was about to clam up, I apologised. Encouraging him to unburden himself, I prepared to sympathise, even though it would be hard to be sympathetic if he'd gone and got Luljeta pregnant again.

BUCKET TO GREECE (VOL.14)

Guzim told me that whilst he was searching the village earlier for Catastrophe, he had run into an Albanian woman, Agnesa, who Papas Andreas had paid to clean his mother's house. When Agnesa had duly admired Guzim's new shoes, he had told her they were a gift from his generous employers, confiding he felt very grateful that we Buckets lavished him with such wonderful gifts. To Guzim's surprise, his innocent statement had unleashed a vitriolic outburst from Agnesa. She told Guzim that the Albanians that worked in Greece were far too deferential towards the Greeks, the Greeks treating the Albanians as little more than servants. She went on to fill his head with nonsense, telling Guzim he was entitled to more than a pair of poxy shoes from his foreign employers.

Poxy indeed, I thought. Two seconds ago, Guzim had claimed the meddling woman had been coveting his knock-off *tsarouchia*, which we had so generously gifted to him.

As Guzim regurgitated Agnesa's ridiculous opinions that the Albanians must make a stand and demand the Greeks shower them with extras on top of their wages, he sounded as though he had been brainwashed by a compatriot with a lingering loyalty for the now defunct Communistic regime back in their homeland.

"The Agnesa say me, if the Victor Bucket was

poor and had to leave his country to seek work in the neighbouring Albania, it would be me, the rich Guzim, giving the shoe to the Victor Bucket."

"And I'm sure that if our circumstances were reversed, I'd be very grateful for your generosity and thank you accordingly," I said.

"I not explain the well." Guzim scratched his head before continuing. "I am the poor Albanian in the foreign Greece, so you must to give me a towel on top of the shoe. I am entitled."

It seemed that a stuffed rabbit wasn't enough for the ungrateful wretch. Entitled indeed.

"A towel? Why on earth should I give you a towel? You aren't even wet?"

"The blanket then. You must to give me the blanket. It is my right."

"Your right? You sound as though Arthur Scargill has been bending your ear."

"*Ti?*"

Realising it was a mistake to reference the bolshie union leader since it was lost on Guzim, I hurriedly moved on with another argument to counter his demand. Thinking of his stinky bedding covered in rabbit hairs, I pointed out, "You've already got a shed full of mangy blankets. And didn't Doreen knock you up some nice patchwork thing on her sewing machine?"

Blinking rapidly as though attempting to make

sense of his thoughts, Guzim's face was a picture of confusion as he struggled to find the right words.

"If I was the rich man in Albania and you were the poor Greek who came to my home, I would give to you the blanket and the shoe." I amused myself with the thought of how easily Guzim had given up his demand for a towel. "The Agnesa say me, I should not to thank the Greek for the shoe, the shoe is the scrap from the rich Greek table…"

"I draw the line at putting one's shoes on the table, it's a deplorably unhygienic habit. I'll have you know that Mrs Bucket bought you those pom-pomed things currently gracing your feet from an actual shop. They aren't your usual cast-offs; they are brand new."

"The Agnesa say me, I should accept the shoe without offering the humble thanks because if you were the poor Greek, you would not thank me for the shoe."

"Hang on, there's just a few flies in your ointment," I pointed out to my brainwashed gardener. "Firstly, I am not a poor Greek, but British. Like you, I am a foreigner in Greece. If I was to travel and visit you in your homeland, I would naturally thank you for any hospitality you offered me because I am nothing if not polite. If I give you something, it is only good manners for you to thank me, but there has certainly never been any sort of expectation on my part that you should prostrate yourself on the ground and gush your thanks effusively; in fact, it's downright annoying. A simple thank you will suffice."

Guzim stared at the ground, a hangdog expression on his face as I continued to speak.

"This Agnesa person sounds as though she has a chip on her shoulder and her sense of entitlement won't win her any friends and likely lose her any employment. Papas Andreas was most perturbed to hear that Agnesa demanded that Kyria Maria must give her the blankets off her bed. Agnesa was paid for her work, and that should be the end of it. She won't be getting any more cleaning work next door, I can tell you that."

Guzim's mouth opened and closed in a fair imitation of a bewildered goldfish. I presumed he was struggling to understand me since I had found it a bit of a challenge to come out with such a lengthy spiel in Greek: indeed, some of it may well have been nothing but gibberish. After a minute of silence, Guzim slapped himself on the head before hurling his body onto the ground and making a grab for my shins. "The stupid woman must be the idiot to say me I must demand the towel. Thank you for the shoe. I will be proud to wear the shoe everywhere. No other Albanian have this shoe, I think the Agnesa speak from jealousy."

BUCKET TO GREECE (VOL.14)

"Oh, do get up, Guzim. I haven't got time for this," I ordered, offering him a hand. "We need to concentrate on finding Catastrophe before Mrs Bucket discovers she's missing."

Chapter 16

A Fruitless Search

Controlling my gag reflex proved impossible. The putrescent stench of decomposing leftovers drifting from the overflowing village bins assailed my olfactory senses, the disgusting odour suspended in the warm night air. By the look of things, the bin men were likely on strike again. The beam of my torch exposed plenty of action in the reeking rubbish receptacles. A multitude of scraggy, feral felines scrambled to escape the beam of my flashlight, hurling themselves on the ground and attempting to take cover under the narrow space between the bins' wheels, or burrowing beneath bags of rubbish.

A kindle of cowering kittens bore a suspicious resemblance to Cynthia's vile mutant moggie. Branded with the same distinctive black stripe across their faces, it led me to speculate that Kouneli may well have engaged in a recent rampage of indiscriminate rape. Moreover, the sheer number of grubby cats hanging about made me think that Edna must have been rather remiss in her usual efforts to offer the bin strays a home.

Crossing my fingers, I hoped the cats that had been busy rooting through the rubbish when we arrived had killed off any rats and other revolting vermin that might have joined them. One persistent cat remained undaunted by my flashlight. A slimy lettuce leaf adorning its head, it stared me down defiantly, more intent on licking its way through a squashed cream cake than making its escape. It struck me that Norman may perchance have made a late-evening trip to the bins, his rejected patisserie confections attracting a clowder of cats.

Although there was no immediate sign of Catastrophe, that didn't mean she hadn't taken refuge in one of the bins. Considering how lazy and obese she was, if she had indeed ventured in, she could be well and truly stuck. There was nothing else for it; Guzim would have to go in. I can't say that I exactly relished the thought of carting a refuse contaminated cat home in my arms, not to mention I would need to hose it down under Guzim's outside shower and give it a quick spritz of Lidl air freshener before allowing it back in the house. Any lingering stench of the bins would surely rouse Marigold's suspicions.

Despite his earlier sullenness, Guzim didn't need telling twice. Stripping off his new shoes, he placed them neatly next to the bins, mumbling he didn't want them to get dirty. Declining my offer of a leg up, Guzim executed a quite impressive face-first lunge into the nearest bin, a bulging black plastic sack containing the contents of a toilet bin offering a soft landing. Naturally, I assisted Guzim in spirit if not in body, directing my torch beam to illuminate his search. Digging through the mounds of stinking garbage and the odd cat that had hunkered down, Guzim cleared a path by randomly chucking bags of rubbish on the street.

"Watch it," I shouted in Greek as a bulging plastic bag with a slimy exterior only just missed my head, its icky contents spilling out perilously close to my feet.

I couldn't swear to it, but I think Guzim's fleeting look of disappointment, coupled with his muttered response of something along the lines of "My aim was off," made me consider that he was perchance engaging in a spot of payback for the way I'd almost taken him down with the tossed rabbit,

BUCKET TO GREECE (VOL.14)

earlier.

Knee deep in rubbish, Guzim declared there was no sign of Catastrophe.

"Perhaps it's a fruitless search," I admitted in Greek. "On reflection, it strikes me that the bins may not be an attractive proposition for Mrs Bucket's pampered pet. Likely Catastrophe is too well-bred to go grubbing around in the bins with the sort of alley cats that made it their regular hangout."

"You want me to find you the fruit?" Guzim's question was quite bizarre.

"What?"

"You just say me you are the fruitless."

"It's a figure of speech. As a retired public health inspector, do you really imagine I'd start chowing down on fruit from the bins?"

Extending a bruised banana towards me, Guzim said, "You can have it. It is fine. See, it has the skin on."

"I don't want it."

"Is okay."

"Really, I don't want it," I insisted.

"I have it." Claiming ownership of the banana, Guzim gave me a flash of his toothless gums before commencing to peel it. Lurching towards the bins, I grabbed the fruit from his grip and hurled it into the distance, promising I would buy him a whole bunch of bananas the next day if he promised me that he would never again resort to eating food salvaged from the bins.

"I not to understand the problem. Earlier, I find the tomatoes and cheese sandwich…"

"Have you never heard of food hygiene, you moron? You could come down with something deadly if you eat anything scavenged from the bins…there's plenty of perfectly clean tomatoes growing in the garden. You know you can help yourself…"

"But you not to grow the cheese…"

"Well, don't expect any sympathy from me if you come down with a nasty case of salmonella or botulism…"

"Victor, is that you?" Recognising Barry's voice, I called back in the affirmative. "I thought it was you. Couldn't imagine anyone else prattling on about salmonella at this time of night. I never knew that the Greek word for salmonella is *salmonella*, you learn something new every day. I've just seen Marigold home. Thought I'd try to find you and help with the search. Not a word to Cynthia though; she'd skin me alive if she knew I was helping you…"

"Why on earth?"

"Because you never joined in the search for Kouneli when he went on the missing list," Barry explained.

"Surely she wouldn't be so petty," I scoffed.

"Have you met my wife?" Barry retorted.

"Anyway, it would have been pointless joining the search for Cynthia's cat. I knew full well that my mother had slung the dratted thing in the back of a passing pickup."

"You never said a word when Cynthia was sticking up those posters of Kouneli in the village," Barry persisted.

"Well, it was for Cynthia's own good. She'd probably have come over all hysterical if she found out that Kouneli could have been driven halfway across the country...she does have form when it comes to histrionics," I said, recalling how hysterical Cynthia had been in full bridezilla mode.

"The only reason I'm prepared to help you now with the search for Catastrophe is to spare you ending up in the divorce courts if my sister finds out..."

"That's a tad dramatic, Barry. Don't forget, we've only just renewed our vows...that's sure to buy me some brownie points for the foreseeable."

"Fair point. You might get off more lightly with just a couple of weeks in the doghouse, though I expect Guzim will cop it..."

"*Ti?*" Guzim's ears pricked up at the sound of his name.

"*Megalos belas. Kaki chameni gata.*" Mangling his

Greek and omitting his grammar, Barry told Guzim, 'You big trouble. Bad lose cat.'

Guzim visibly flinched at Barry's reprimand. I braced myself for the Albanian coming out in a fit of hysteria that would rival Cynthia's most hysterical bridezilla moment.

"I think you're wasting your time going through the bins," Barry opined.

"Well, can you think of a more likely place where the cat might be?"

"I can, actually. As I headed over this way, I noticed a light on in the Hancocks' house. It got me thinking: likely Edna has taken Marigold's cat in."

"But Catastrophe isn't a half-starved stray. Surely Edna would have recognised that it's a tame domestic..."

"You'd think, but Edna's got form when it comes to catnapping." Barry broke into laughter, apparently amused by his own witty pun.

Recalling how Edna had indeed kidnapped a cat belonging to an Athenian woman, stubbornly refusing to relinquish it to its rightful owner until I had intervened and calmed the waters with a bribe of Norman's fondant fancies, I agreed Barry's idea was worth exploring.

"Give Guzim a hand out of the bins and we'll head over to the Hancocks' house now," I said, cringing at the sight of the cretinous Albanian openly licking a bit of cream cake off the sleeve of Moira Strange's blouse. Obviously, my dire warnings about the consequences of consuming food from the bins had gone clean over his head. I hoped he gave his hands a good hosing before handling any of my veg.

Striding briskly towards Milton's place, I made a point of walking downwind from Guzim since he stank even more than usual. In two shakes of a lamb's tail, the three of us arrived at Milton's. It struck me that the Hancocks' home was conveniently sited near the bins, convenient for Edna's compulsive habit of foraging for ferals that is. Perhaps it was time to suggest to Milton that he should persuade his wife to change her habits. If he could prevail upon her to forage the fields for free food in the form of *horta* instead of searching the streets of Meli for cats, any *horta* she picked wouldn't eat them out of house and home as the cats did. Insisting on keeping so many cats meant the Hancocks permanently lived beyond their meagre means.

Despite an upstairs light inside the house indicating the residents hadn't yet retired for the night, there was no response to Barry's sharp rap on the door.

"Perhaps they've already gone to bed," Barry suggested.

"Then knock again and wake them up," I told

him bluntly. If there was even the slightest chance that Edna had taken Marigold's cat in, I intended to retrieve and return it before my wife got wind of it.

Barry's second rap elicited a response.

"*Perimene. Erchomai,*" a deep male voice shouted from within, saying, 'Wait. I'm coming.'

"That doesn't sound like Milton." Barry does like to state the blatantly obvious, a trait he shares with his sister.

The electronic whir of Milton's stairlift gave some indication of why it was taking so long for the door to open. I recalled Milton's stairlift hardly represented a fast mode of transport. We were in fact left waiting for another five minutes before the door was finally thrown open by a stocky, unshaven chap clad in pyjama bottoms and a grubby grey vest. Clearly not Milton, he looked familiar but I couldn't quite place him. It was only when I spotted the crutch that was keeping him upright that it dawned on me that this was Milton's new chum, Kyriakos, a local recluse who'd had the misfortune to break both his legs whilst in the grip of a delusion that he could fly off his balcony. Since I had only met him once, briefly, in Milton's company, it was understandable that I didn't at first recognise him in his night attire.

Kyriakos' memory was clearly better than mine since he immediately addressed me by name,

BUCKET TO GREECE (VOL.14)

speaking in broken English as he joshingly reminisced about winding Milton up by teaching him inappropriate Greek words that would have made Edna blush. Despite the lateness of the hour, Kyriakos immediately invited the three of us in, explaining that Milton had invited him to stay in the house to cat sit for the Hancocks who were up at the hospital.

"I'd clean forgotten with being away that Edna was scheduled to have her cataracts done," I said.

"I think Cynthia might have mentioned something..." Barry added.

"So, is Milton staying over at the hospital with Edna?" I asked.

"It is the Greek way. The Milton tell me the English way is to send the family home. This is much the superior, I think. It give the patient some the needed peace from the relative." The way in which Kyriakos practically spat the word relative made me recall that Milton had told me that Kyriakos had the misfortune to live under the same roof as both his wife and mother: I say misfortune since the two women apparently loathe each other.

It was their constant arguing that drove Kyriakos into a state of depression, his maudlin mood in turn leading to the overdose resulting in his foolish, drug-induced fancy that he could fly off the balcony. Even when Kyriakos was incapacitated in hospital with two broken legs, he couldn't get any respite from the constant bickering between his wife and mother. The way they went at each other hammer and tongs over his hospital bed, explained Kyriakos' vocal support for the way that the British National Health Service adhered to strict visiting hours, making no bones about turfing superfluous relatives out at chucking out time.

"I was in the bed," Kyriakos said.

"Sorry for waking you," I replied, even though I felt absolutely no remorse.

"You not to wake me, I reading. The Milton to leave me the book he write. I find it very the difficult to read the English word. The book he name delicious; it confuse me. I think the delicious to translate to the *nostimo*."

"It does…"

"So why the book he the full of the sex instead the recipe? I think the English must be very the terrible at make the love."

"I thought you knew that Milton penned porn," I said.

"I think he to pull my leg."

"No, it's true." Changing the subject, I said, "So, you're staying here to cat sit whilst the Hancocks are at the hospital. You'll have your work cut out for you with the number of strays Edna has adopted from the streets of Meli."

BUCKET TO GREECE (VOL.14)

"The Edna, he is the cat mad," Kyriakos sneered, his lip curling in contempt.

"I get the impression you're not a cat lover," Barry observed.

"I love the cat," Kyriakos declared. "The one or two is the normal, is good. To have twenty the two is crazy, is mad."

"Too right," Barry agreed.

"It's a cat that has brought us to your door this evening," I said. "One of my wife's cats has gone missing and we wondered if Edna had perhaps taken it in. She has such a habit of adopting strays."

"I not to know…so many the cats here, it could be. *Ela*, come through, see if you can to see the cat of the wife," Kyriakos invited, ushering us through to the living room.

At first glance, there seemed to be fewer felines than usual cluttering up Milton's living room. Although there appeared to be about a dozen cats scattered around, littering every seat, I didn't find myself knee-deep in the creatures as I'd been on my more recent visits to the house. Perchance Kyriakos had settled some of them down for the night upstairs, or maybe they were sprawled out in the kitchen, contaminating the worksurfaces where food was prepared.

"You see the wife cat?" Kyriakos asked. "What it to look like?"

"It looks like a cat." Barry never tires of stating the patently obvious.

"Any special the mark?"

"It only has a partial tail."

Adroitly balancing on his crutches, Kyriakos immediately started manhandling the cats, rolling them over in order to get a good look at their tails. Disturbed from their slumbers, the clowder commenced hissing and meowing in outrage, creating a caterwauling cacophony of a din. "It could be I to throw the cat out. There were too the many, too the many for the normal. I throw some. It is to like staying in the cattery. You to see the smell? And the hair? You to see the hair?"

"I can see the smell of cats," Barry chuckled.

"And it's hard to miss the cat hairs," I agreed. "There's enough lying around for Edna to crochet a blanket out of the things."

"I think the Milton wife not how to say, right in the head?" Kyriakos posited.

I reflected it was all a bit of a rum going on. Having agreed to cat sit, it struck me as a bit of liberty for Kyriakos to go turfing half of Edna's cats out on the street; it was after all their home. Admittedly, I would have been sorely tempted to do the same if I'd been in his position, but there again it was most assuredly a position I would never have been stupid enough to put myself in. Putting up with Marigold's three cats was quite enough for me to cope with, without taking charge of a couple of dozen of the Hancocks' pets. I metaphorically patted myself on the back for having the good sense to turn Milton down flat when he'd asked me to cat sit.

"I throw the cat out but they to come back," Kyriakos despaired.

"Well, they've been living here since Edna snatched them from the jaws of the bins. They likely think of the house as their home," I said. Certainly, Marigold's imported domestics ruled the roost in our house. "How do they keep getting back in?"

"I must to leave the window open. The smell too bad without the fresh hair…"

"Air. Fresh air," I corrected.

The sound of electronic whirring distracted Kyriakos from his examination of tails. Leaning on his crutches, he hobbled slowly into the hallway, almost coming a cropper as he tripped over a couple of the cats he had so rudely woken.

"*Pou pas*?" he shouted at Guzim, asking him where he was going.

"*Pouthena*," meaning 'nowhere' Guzim sheepishly replied, having been caught bang to rights taking a joy ride upstairs on Milton's stairlift. I recalled that Edna had put her foot down at Milton's fancy dress party, refusing to let the Albanian shed dweller in his guise of a scarecrow, test out the new mechanical device that had so intrigued him. Watching Guzim ascend the stairs at a speed that failed to rival a crawl, an enormous grin of delight plastered across his face, it seemed to be a case of that while the cat is away, the mouse will play.

"*Mou aresi.*" Guzim proclaimed he loved it, demanding we look as he informed us the chair moved. "*Koita, i karekla kineitai.*" My moronic gardener clearly derived some childish pleasure from the novelty of gliding upwards on the torturously slow stairlift.

"*Otan ftasete stin koryfi, anazitiste ti gata tis Kyrias Bucket,*" I said, telling him that when he got to the top, he must look for Mrs Bucket's cat.

Considering the snail's pace of the stairlift, I exchanged a rueful glance with Barry, the two of us settling in for a long wait.

Chapter 17

Victor Takes Pity on a Pitiful Creature

There was not so much as a smidgen of evidence to indicate that Edna had catnapped Catastrophe and sequestered it in her cat-ridden home. Warning me that Marigold may well get suspicious if I rolled in at some unspeakable hour, Barry convinced me it was time to call off the search and call it a night. Since Guzim was having the time of his life playing on the fairground attraction of Milton's stairlift, we left him behind, the Hancocks' cat-sitting lodger apparently glad of his miserable company. As Kyriakos showed us out, he used one of his crutches to brusquely push away a tiny kitten meowing piteously on the doorstep. Striding over the kitten, Barry bade me good night, our homeward paths taking us in opposite directions.

Something about the mewling creature that Kyriakos had heartlessly refused admittance to, caught my attention. Bending down to examine it more closely, I felt a lump in my throat when I spotted the outline of its spine clearly visible beneath its bedraggled tawny fur. It was obviously starving; although possibly only a few weeks old, its emaciated appearance gave its features a wizened look. Barely having the strength to remain upright, the kitten flopped to the ground; with one eye gummed closed, the pathetic creature looked at death's door. Too sickly to make another sound, it used its one good eye to plead with me to save its life.

In light of its grungy appearance, I have no idea what possessed me to swoop up the dirty kitten and carry it home, throwing all caution to the wind concerning the possible communication of any zoonotic diseases it may be harbouring. I just had a terrible feeling that if I didn't intervene, it would be dead by morning. I couldn't in all conscience bear to have its death on my conscience.

Reaching the house, I laid the kitten down gently at the top of the outdoor staircase whilst I rushed inside to retrieve a shoebox and a couple of towels, grabbing a pot of Greek yoghurt from the fridge. Dolloping a spoonful of yoghurt down next to the kitten, I watched as it made a feeble effort to extend its tongue. Realising it was too weak to eat, I rushed back inside, rummaging through the cupboards in search of one of Anastasia's baby bottles, filling it with watered down milk.

Settling down on the doorstep, I wrapped the shivering kitten in a towel and offered the bottle, a glimmer of hope stirring in my chest that the kitten might survive as it made a valiant effort to suck. Quickly sated, the kitten slept as I settled it inside the shoebox. Since the night was mild, I felt no qualms about covering it with a towel and leaving the shoebox on the doorstep. Since the stray was potentially a carrier of germs that may be passed on to our household's indulged felines, Marigold might have kittens if she discovered it in the house the next morning. I wasn't quite sure how she would take it if she clocked that I'd gone soppy over a kitten, especially after I had gone to great lengths to rid the Bucket household of Tesco.

A scalding shower washed away the lingering stench of the bins and hopefully anything communicable I may have picked up from the kitten. Lathering up, I reflected that I had no explanation for why I was able to stride heartlessly by a dozen ferals congregating in the bins, yet allow one helpless, pathetic kitten to tug on my heartstrings.

I sighed in relief to see that Marigold was sleeping soundly, something she'd never have managed if she had any clue that Catastrophe was missing. Just before I drifted off to sleep, I hatched a plan for dealing with the sickly kitten the next morning.

Arms folded rigidly across her ample bosom, Violet Burke stood in the *apothiki* doorway in all her candlewick glory, looking every inch the bolshie, hair-rollered harridan. Without her usual thick application of slap, her wrinkles stood out prominently, reminding me she was getting on in years. Gawping at me suspiciously over the top of her rectangular spectacles, she dispensed with the usual morning pleasantries.

"Have you lost your marbles, lad, knocking on at this hour? It's barely morning yet."

"I won't beat about the bush, Mother. I need a favour," I stated in a tone that brooked no argument.

"It's not like you to bother asking…"

"I need you to take this sickly kitten in until I get home from work," I said firmly, brandishing the shoebox under her nose.

"'Appen you're confusing me with that cat soppy wife of yours?"

"I'm not sure how Marigold will react to a stray

of unknown pedigree that may have been in the bins," I admitted.

I had left Marigold to enjoy a much-needed lie-in, sneaking the shoebox away before she could discover its sickly contents. I knew my wife well enough to know that if she'd cottoned on to the kitten's presence, she would immediately make sure that none of her precious imported felines were anywhere in its vicinity until it could be checked out for fleas and other potentially contagious nasties. I was hoping to keep Catastrophe's disappearance from Marigold for a while longer, in the hopefully not futile hope that the cat would somehow manage to return home under its own steam as Kouneli had done, leaving my wife none the wiser that it had ever left home.

"My goodness, it's a scrawny little mite and no mistake," Vi said, her wrinkled features softening into a concerned crumple as she peered into the depths of the shoebox. "You reckon some heartless beggar has been mistreating it?"

"The thought has crossed my mind. Its fur is in a terrible state. It has some bald patches and I could feel all its bones when I picked it up. I'm worried about its right eye; it was glued together with gunk. I cleaned it out with some antibiotic drops applied to some damp toilet paper but it still looks infected. I'll give it another clean out when I get home from work."

No sooner had I finished my sentence than the tip of the kitten's tongue poked through its parched lips, the kitten opening its one good eye to look plaintively at my mother. The pitiful movements clearly took all the kitten's strength. Whilst the prudent course of action might be to rush it to a veterinarian, I worried that two hours stuck in a cat box in a moving vehicle might finish it off.

"If you take it in for the day, it will be a good chance for you to practice your mothering." If it would help my cause, I had no qualms about reminding Violet Burke that she had been rather remiss in the whole parenting department.

"If I take it in, do you reckon it'll be all right on its own when I bob out to do my cleaning jobs? I can pop back in between, like." Surprisingly, I detected concern in her voice.

"It's barely got the strength to eat, let alone move. It only managed a couple of grams of watered-down milk this morning from one of Anastasia's bottles."

"I'll try and get hold of Sampaguita, lad. She's got a right good way with ailing creatures. 'Appen she'll know the best way to keep the little runt alive."

"An excellent idea," I agreed, amazed that my mother had given in so readily. It appeared that we had something else in common beyond our mutual obsession with hygiene. Whilst neither of us claimed to be cat friendly in general, it seemed we were both a sucker when it came to a neglected and maltreated underdog.

Chapter 18

The Ship's Cat

Clocking my watch for the third time in two minutes, I sighed in frustration at John Macey's seemingly lackadaisical approach to timekeeping. It really wasn't good enough of him to leave me standing around like a spare part, twiddling my thumbs outside the tourist office. Since he would be shadowing me for the day, I would have expected him to act in an accordingly deferential manner, since technically, I was his superior. I considered his unpunctuality not only the opposite of deferential, but bordering on impertinence.

"About time," I muttered under my breath,

spotting Macey dodging his way between a moped and a car that appeared at first glance to be steered by a canine. On second glance, I was relieved to notice that although the dog's paws were draped over the steering wheel, its body was firmly planted in the passenger seat. I considered it quite negligent of its owner to fail to strap the canine in with a seat belt. The fine for humans failing to belt up was in the region of three hundred euros, yet pets could apparently get off scot-free.

After dicing with death, dashing across the busy road, Macey strode swiftly towards me, kitted out in his pristine new repping uniform. With his grey hair tucked away inside the compulsory cap flaunting the company logo and with oversized dark sunglasses conveniently concealing his slug-like eyebrows, I must admit he had made every effort to look the part of a tour rep. The unsightly damp patches under his armpits were an unfortunate consequence of being forced to wear unsuitable polyester in the heat. I made a mental note to slip another reminder about the benefits of cotton uniforms into the staff suggestion box.

"Good morning, Vic."

"It's Victor and you're late," I informed him a tad churlishly. I do loathe tardiness and Macey finally deigning to show up a full seven minutes after the allotted meeting time was hardly an impressive start for his first day on the job.

"Sorry about that." Macey sounded genuinely contrite. "I got stuck behind a concrete mixer on the mountain road...it was impossible to overtake the thing."

"You must factor in the likelihood of hold ups when you calculate your journey time," I chided, determined to rub his nose in his lateness to ensure it never happened again. "It really wouldn't do if you turned up late to Pegasus. One can hardly expect *Kapetanios* Vasos to handle the meet and greet on his lonesome when he doesn't speak a word of lucid English."

Perchance if we had driven up to the tour office together, I might have taken the time to spill the beans to Macey about some of Vasos' unique peculiarities, rather than leaving him to form his own impression. However, in light of Macey's inexcusable insouciance, I simply apprised him that he would need to communicate in Greek with the non-English speaking *Kapetanios* and his crew of one. Since Macey hadn't made every effort to be the consummate professional and turn up on time, I didn't bother to warn him that Vasos was prone to coming out with random English words without any context, nor that his sidekick, Sami, was mute.

"You must always make a point of being early for any trips on Pegasus," I schooled him as we walked briskly towards the harbour. "Even though it isn't technically in your job description, half the time, you will need to wake the captain and drag him out of his pit if you wish to avoid a passenger mutiny."

"He sleeps on the boat?"

"It has been known. It rather depends how much *ouzo* he downed the night before; too much leaves him incapable of staggering home. In addition to ensuring that Vasos is upright and capable of steering the vessel, you will need to check that Pegasus is in shipshape and Bristol fashion..."

"I don't think you can say that anymore. The papers were full of it being politically incorrect last month," Macey interrupted me.

"What? Shipshape?"

"No, Bristol fashion."

"Have you lost the plot? It's a nautical term and I haven't heard that Bristol has been forcibly name changed..."

"It's becoming a minefield these days..."

"What? Bristol?"

"No, what one can say..."

"I don't think the Greeks worry unnecessarily about such things," I said, thinking Macey was in for a shock when he heard some of the meaningless guff that Vasos comes out with. I'm pretty sure that someone somewhere would take offence at the way

V.D. BUCKET

Vasos referred to women as beautiful towels, but it would be a sad day in my mind if such innocent compliments were banned. "Now, *Kapetanios* Vasos can be a tad lax when it comes to standards. It will be your responsibility to make sure that Sami gives the toilet a good mopping out before the tourists turn up and you must check that all the inflatables are full of air."

Admittedly, I fibbed about the inflatables. Since Marigold was of the opinion that Macey is full of hot air, it would amuse her to think of him having an outlet for his excess with a spot of mouth to mouth.

"So, I need to give the boat the once-over before greeting the passengers," Macey confirmed.

"Certainly. If Vasos has been indiscriminately scattering pie crumbs around, they must be swept up. We can't enforce the No Eating onboard rule if the passengers end up knee-deep in bits of old pie. You can never be sure what state Vasos may have left the boat in if he was out carousing the night before."

"Carousing?" Macey drew out the word as though it was an alien concept.

"Drinking and attempting to pick up women. Usually unsuccessfully," I admitted. "Vasos is a great one for making *kamaki*."

Fortunately, I had yet to walk into the

wheelhouse and catch Vasos slumped out in a compromising position with a member of the fairer sex, thought it wasn't for lack of effort on his part. Admittedly, I had once caught him passed out next to an equally comatose Russian sailor, who may or may not have been trying to claim political asylum on Pegasus. Vasos had been far too hungover to make a coherent case on behalf of the swarthy sailor and it certainly didn't help that Vasos' Russian comprehension was on a par with his English. Since the still soused sailor couldn't produce a valid ticket issued by the tour office, it had fallen on me to chuck him off the boat despite Vasos' protestations that he was happy to harbour the Russian as a stowaway, no doubt thinking he would make an ideal drinking buddy.

"So, I take it that you have a list of the names of the passengers to check off as they arrive?" Macey asked.

"I collected it from the office before you turned up. We have a good turn out today; forty-two souls. When we greet them, we will need to make a note of their individual lunch preferences. They have a choice today between *gemistes piperies*…"

"Stuffed peppers," Macey interjected.

"And *souvlaki kotopoulo*…"

"Chicken *souvlaki*," Macey translated, determined to show off his knowledge of Greek with a smug complacency that reminded me of Smug Bessie. It struck me that Macey might not sound quite so full of himself when confronted with Vasos' interesting take on the English language. Coping with the captain's linguistic bloopers takes a special skill that can't be mastered in an instant.

"It goes without saying that the passenger count at every stop is crucial. The company really does frown on us losing any tourists…"

"I'm sure this whistle will come in very handy if the count is off," Macey suggested, clearly itching to blow his whistle as a show of authority. I suppressed a snort at the thought that he could well be too out of puff to summon a hearty warble on his whistle after blowing up any leaky inflatables. I must confess to a fleeting and wicked urge to tamper with the onboard flotation devices, before repressing the temptation. Sabotage has a nasty habit of coming back to bite the miscreant and it really wouldn't do to lose any tourists in the Mediterranean.

We had almost reached the harbour when my mobile phone trilled. Spotting Marigold' name displayed as the caller, I halted, telling Macey I needed to take the call. I was surprised when he came to an abrupt standstill beside me; rather than putting some distance between us to afford me some privacy, he shuffled impatiently beside me, blatantly earwigging my conversation.

"Victor." Marigold's strident tone sent alarm bells ringing, the way she verbalised my name alerting me that I was about to get it in the neck. It is amazing how a single word can carry such portentous weight, indicating trouble ahead. I hazarded a guess that my wife had finally noticed her precious feline was missing. The previous evening's search had been a resounding flop, Catastrophe still failing to put in an appearance when I'd slopped the cat food into her bowl before leaving the house that morning. "Victor. Did you shut Catastrophe in the wardrobe in the guest bedroom this morning?"

"What?" Deliberately non-committal, I managed to insert suitable outrage in my tone at the very suggestion. My faux indignation concealed my relief that the cat had apparently turned up in the wardrobe and I wouldn't be forced to spend another night traipsing through the dark streets and fields of Meli.

"Catastrophe just gave your mother a funny turn. Vi went to get some clean bedding and the cat sprang out at her like a thing possessed, scratching your mother in her desperate rush to get to her water bowl. She lapped up the water as though her life depended on it."

"Make sure my mother puts some antiseptic on the scratch. You never know where the cat has been." By now I actually had a pretty good idea where the cat had been. Catastrophe had most probably spent two full nights locked in the guest room wardrobe; so much for Guzim insisting he had conducted a thorough search of the house. The cretinous Albanian must have been the one to slam the door on the cat two days ago.

"She's been in the wardrobe, Victor, I already told you that. Did you somehow accidentally lock her in there this morning? I can't think how else the cat ended up in there."

Weighing up my options, I decided to shoulder the blame. Owning up to accidentally shutting the cat in the wardrobe for a couple of hours was a small price to pay when the alternative was the truth coming out that the cat had in reality been stuck in there for two full days. "Guilty as charged, darling."

"Really, Victor. You need to be more careful. Catastrophe is a very sensitive feline. Oh, for goodness' sake. Vi's just said the cat has piddled all over the clean bedding in the wardrobe. I'll have to put an extra wash on now." As Marigold hung up on me, I reckoned I'd managed to get off quite lightly, though I would most definitely be having words with Guzim later.

Directing my attention back on Macey, I noticed he was engrossed in reading something.

BUCKET TO GREECE (VOL.14)

"What have you got there?" I asked him.

"Just some notes that Cynthia compiled about repping on the Lazy Day Cruise. To be honest, Cynthia's style leaves a lot to be desired. She certainly believes in overdoing the bangorrhea. I say in all modesty, that excessive bangorrhea is a habit I find quite intolerable."

I must admit that I had no idea what Macey was wittering on about. Although reluctant to admit that the meaning of bangorrhea eluded me, I had to ask.

"Bangorrhea?"

"Yes, indeed. I find it the most tedious habit when an excessive use of exclamation marks blot's one's writing. There is certainly nothing to exclaim over in Cynthia's notes."

"A quite unnecessary habit," I agreed, attempting to hide my inner elation. Naturally, I would consult a dictionary to make sure such a word existed before teasing my wife about her own bangorrhea. I couldn't believe there was actually a word for Marigold's addiction to plings. I was going to have such fun teasing her about it later.

"I hope that we aren't going to be late to the boat, what with you stopping to take a personal call," John Macey said, his slug like eyebrows gliding over the rims of his sunglasses in disapproval. As the two of us resumed our quick pace to the boat,

V.D. BUCKET

I fumed silently, Macey having the cheek to lecture me by slinging my earlier words back in my face. "You must factor in the likelihood of receiving personal telephone calls that could hold you up when you calculate your journey time."

Rounding the corner, Pegasus came into view. "Is that the boat?" Macey asked.

"Yes, that's Pegasus." Spotting a short squat figure on the gangplank, waving vigorously, I sighed in relief. At least for today, I would be spared the unpleasant task of rousing Vasos from a drunken slumber. "*Kapetanios* Vasos is up and about already. With a bit of luck, he might even have downed a coffee and be halfway sober."

"*Kalimera, Victor, Mucky mou,*" Vasos bellowed as we approached.

"Mucky? You look perfectly clean to me," Macey opined in confusion.

"Oh, he means nothing by it. It's just a turn of phrase," I assured Macey before calling out a greeting to Vasos, introducing John and explaining it was his first day on the job. "*Kalimera, Kapetanios. Eisai kala? Aftos einai o John. Einai i proti tou mera sti douleia.*"

"*Yasou, Gianni,*" Vasos shouted, immediately greeting John with the Greek version of his name before dropping a meaningless "Beautiful Fray" into the mix. Violet Burke's influence was certainly

BUCKET TO GREECE (VOL.14)

rubbing off on Vasos. Since the pair of them had forged an unlikely friendship, the Greek Captain's nonsensical English vocabulary had expanded in leaps and bounds. Before we reached him on the gangplank, he managed to throw out a few new favourites he had picked up from my mother, yelling out a string of unrelated, "Peas, Fat, Mushy, Warrington, Bottoming and Bentos," leaving John Macey beyond befuddled.

"Is he quite the full shilling?" Macey hissed.

"That's debatable," I replied as Vasos bounded across to the harbour and smothered me in a hearty embrace.

"I love you, Victor," Vasos declared, prompting Macey to nudge me and enquire if the captain was gay.

"Only in the sense that he's full of the joys of spring. He has quite an eye for the women, as you will no doubt soon discover," I said.

"Well, I say in all modesty that I'm not one to judge," Macey declared in a decidedly judgemental tone.

Releasing me, Vasos treated John Macey to a bone-crushing handshake before shouting it was a radiant day and he was in the mood for ogling all the ravishing women that would soon drape themselves over the deck. Giving his binoculars a quick polish on his grubby tee-shirt, Vasos winked at

Macey, informing him that on a good day, some of the women sunbathe topless. *"Se mia kala mera, merikes apo tis gynaikes kanoun iliotherapeia toples."*

"Did he just say…?" Macey's sentence was left unfinished as he second guessed his competence at translating.

"I'm afraid he did," I admitted. "Fortunately, it's rare for the female passengers to sunbathe topless…I never know where to look. I find it most unseemly."

"I'm with you there," Macey agreed, even though I had spotted him sporting indecent budgie smugglers on the beach during our vow renewal service. I supposed he could just be a fashion victim rather than an unaware exhibitionist.

"Pao yia kafe, theleis?" Vasos announced he was going for coffee, asking if we wanted any.

Declining the offer, I told Macey that we needed to check that conditions on Pegasus were up to scratch before the tourists began to arrive. Noticing that Macy appeared a tad wobbly as he traversed the gangplank, I fervently hoped that it wasn't an indication he had wobbly sea legs. It wouldn't do for the latest recruit to come down with a case of virulent seasickness. He would be as much use as a chocolate teapot if he spent the day turning green and hurling over the railings. Although Sami wasn't able to vocalise his displeasure when forced to mop up vomit, he certainly made his feelings known by the petulant way he brandished the mop.

No sooner had a vision of Sami slopping the mop invaded my mind than Vasos' mute sidekick appeared in person, dragging the mop and bucket out of the onboard toilet, the proverbial cigarette clamped between his lips, another one inevitably tucked behind his ears ready to be lit from the current dog end. Raising his eyes, Sami caught sight of me. His weatherworn features instantly transformed as he broke out in a cheery grin stretching from ear to ear, the cigarette falling to the deck as his lips parted. I was beyond taken by surprise. I had never once observed Sami expressing any emotion beyond a bored scowl whilst carrying out his duties. In his defence, his life of drudgery was hardly anything to smile about.

Macey echoed the greeting of *kalimera* that I directed at Sami, the new rep immediately tutting with disapproval when his greeting remained unreciprocated. "How rude."

"Sami doesn't have much to say for himself," I explained.

"Surely a simple good morning isn't beyond him..."

"It is actually. He's mute..."

"As in mute, mute? You can't go around saying

that these days?"

"What are you, the language police? Sami isn't able to verbalise…"

"So, he's non-verbal?"

"Exactly, mute means an inability to verbalise," I pointed out in exasperation. If Macey insisted on keeping up this pedantic streak, I could well be tempted to help him on his way to becoming 'man overboard.' I was beginning to sense why Barry and Marigold found him so annoying.

Discarding his mop and bucket, Sami tugged on my arm before gesturing with a gnarled finger that I should follow him. Instead of shuffling along the deck with his head slumped in typical hangdog style, there was a veritable spring in Sami's step. Macey fell into step beside me as I trailed after Sami, wondering at the sudden cheery change to his usual surly disposition. Since Sami doesn't speak, or should I more accurately say, doesn't understand English, I filled Macey in on what little I knew about the deckhand. Of course, I couldn't speak with any accuracy since everything I knew about Sami had come second-hand from Captain Vasos, hardly the most reliable source considering he is half-cut most of the time.

"Years ago, when Sami was a lad, he was fished out of the sea close to the Island of Samothrace, clutching a soggy cat. Because he was unable to verbalise his name, the crew that rescued him christened him Sami after the island and adopted him as the ship's mascot, making his feline friend the honorary ship's cat."

"And they kept him onboard?"

"Apparently, rumour has it that when the ship turned course with the intention that Sami would be dropped off at the nearest spot of dry land, he chained himself to the mast, shaking his head like a madman and screaming silently. Presuming he had escaped some hellish existence that he clearly didn't want to return to, they let him join the crew. In gratitude, Sami took to swabbing the decks and general skivvying with an enthusiasm that drew the respect of the hardened crew. According to Vasos, Sami's feet didn't touch dry land for years."

"What a fascinating story," Macey commented. "And you've no idea when his rescue took place?"

"None at all," I confirmed. "But rumours persist that the rescue may have been enacted during wartime. The only thing that I know for sure is that Sami's enthusiasm for mopping has most definitely waned over the years. He approaches it with a very sluggish attitude these days. I often think that if he was able to speak, I would be subjected to a litany of grumbles every time I tell him the lavatory is in need of a good swabbing out."

Sami's steps led us down to the cabin below

deck where Vasos stored his ample supply of ship's *ouzo*. Reaching into a cardboard box, Sami retrieved an enormous cat, immediately cuddling it close to his chest.

"Goodness, that's a big one. Is it the one he was rescued with from the sea?" Macey asked.

"Hardly, Sami was only a lad at the time though it's anyone's guess how many years he's clocked up by now. It's the first time I've ever seen sight of a cat on Pegasus," I replied, pondering if Sami had found himself a new pet and wondering if Vasos knew about the feline or if it was a stowaway.

The cat was certainly a strange looking creature. About twice the size of the average cat hanging around in Meli, it was so obese that it wouldn't surprise me to hear that he had swallowed one of his smaller brethren whole. The feline was black with a dark grey underbelly and malevolent green eyes. Its ugly grey fur resembled in colour the sort of muck that Violet Burke regularly emptied out of the vacuum bag, as though it had been slopped on by an inebriated painter, covering three of the feline's four legs and finishing in a sharp line just below its mouth. It crossed my mind that if I was to sneak the creature away from Sami and smuggle it back to the village, it might well be the first feline adversary to have the nous to put Kouneli in its place.

"*Einai i gata sou?*" I said, asking Sami if it was his cat.

Sami shook his head vigorously. His action left me none the wiser because I wasn't sure if he was confirming my words by using the Greek habit of shaking his head to indicate yes. He wasn't one for nodding or shaking in general.

"*Zei sti varka?*" I persisted, asking if it lived on the boat. This time, Sami's vigorous head shakes were accompanied by him pointing his gnarled finger at the cardboard box, leading me to surmise that the cat did indeed live in the box on the boat.

"*I gata tou ploiou,*" I ventured. Sami's broad smile indicated my guess was spot on and the fat puss had indeed been adopted as the ship's cat. Sami bestowed a smacker of a kiss on the cat's lips before dropping it back in its box and miming it was time to return to his mopping.

Cringing in horror at Sami's blasé indifference to the risk of contracting a debilitating gum disease from the bacteria harboured within the feline's mouth, I warned him that he shouldn't kiss the cat on the mouth as it wasn't good for his gums. Much as I would have liked to go into more depth about the potential dangers of slobbering over the cat so closely, I lacked the necessary Greek vocabulary, so kept it simple. "*Den prepei na filas ti gata sto stoma, den kanei kalo sto oula sou."*

Sami reacted to my warning by raising a finger close to his temple and gesticulating that I had lost the plot.

"*Giati?*" I pointlessly questioned since Sami was incapable of explaining.

However, John Macey wasn't above putting in his two penn'orth worth, rather gleefully highlighting my linguistic blooper in a mocking tone. "You just told him not to kiss the cat because it's not good for his tail."

Blushing furiously at being caught out making such a basic mistranslation by confusing *oula*, the Greek word for tail, with *oura*, the Greek word for gums, I flounced off back to the deck.

It seemed that adopting the cat had injected a spark of happiness into Sami's life, a theory that was confirmed when the next time I encountered him mopping, it was with an enthusiasm that I had never witnessed before. He even managed to squirt some bleach down the onboard lav.

Giving John Macey the full tour of the boat, I showed him the untidy wheelhouse, pointing out the bench where he would generally find Vasos passed out when he failed to make it back to his bed on dry land. "I find it pays to have a good sniff of the water bottles in case the captain has filled them with *ouzo*," I advised.

BUCKET TO GREECE (VOL.14)

"It sounds as though my role will involve keeping the *Kapetanios* sober," Macey observed.

"Definitely wise to keep an eye on his alcohol intake over lunch," I recommended.

"I say in all modesty, I would never dream of drinking on the job," Macey commented.

"I'm glad to hear that. You are after all replacing Dennis who was sacked for being inebriated on the job. Cynthia said he was so sloshed that he was incapable of standing upright on the coach and fell into the lap of one of the female tourists. She made some very cutting remarks on the customer satisfaction survey."

"Well, it all appears to be shipshape," Macey declared, practically biting at the bit to begin interacting with the tourists due to arrive at any moment.

Much as I was tempted to send him off to use mouth to mouth to resuscitate any drooping inflatables, I invited him to join me on the gangplank to conduct the meet and greet. I could hardly exclude him from the most important duty he required training in. Captain Vasos, having already made it back to the boat, rushed into the wheelhouse to retrieve the canister of Old Spice aftershave gifted to him by Violet Burke. After giving his nether regions and armpits a good blitzing, he was ready to join us in welcoming the passengers.

V.D. BUCKET

"Good, hello, Gianni, mushy, yes," Vasos said to Macey, the latter visibly preening that the captain had addressed him with the grecophiled version of his name.

"You must find it a bit of a downer that your name doesn't translate," Macey said, smugness creeping back into his tone.

"It does actually," I countered. "The Greek word for Victor is *nikitis*…"

"Yes, but that means the victor. It's not an actual translation of your name as such," Macey argued.

"It could be. I just think it would sound as though I was walking around with some sort of inflated superiority complex if I introduced myself as such," I said, wondering if Macey would pick up on the irony of my remark. I was certainly beginning to pick up on his sense of superiority and answering to a Greek name would no doubt exacerbate his condition. "No one likes a know-it-all."

Being saddled with the name Victor was down to Violet Burke. For the umpteenth time, I wished that my mother had chosen my name with more care before she dumped me in that galvanised bucket and absconded, leaving me named after the limping soap salesman, Vic, and Donnie, the philandering, nice Jewish boffin GI from Brooklyn. If only Violet Burke had opted for the good Greek name, Ulysses, after the black trumpet player from Mississippi, I could have one-upped Macey having John translated into Giannis, since Ulysses wouldn't have needed any translation at all.

Chapter 19

Stalked at Sea

An attractive middle-aged woman caught the captain's eye by stripping down to her bikini and sarong before even boarding the boat. Practically knocking a geriatric day tripper off the gangplank in his eagerness to assist the woman across, Vasos boomed, "*Ela, koukla mou.*"

"Did Vasos really just call her *my doll*?" Macey hissed in my ear. "With sexist remarks like that, he's like a dinosaur out of the stone age."

"You have your historical eras mixed up; surely you know that dinosaurs died out long before the stone age?" I couldn't help but gloat at my superior historical knowledge. "And the woman appears to be happily lapping up Vasos' attention."

I watched as the woman visibly blossomed and preened as the good captain emulated a chivalrous gentleman of old by planting a kiss on her hand. Admittedly, I wouldn't welcome Vasos dribbling all over my hand since actual drool appeared to be involved, but there's no denying that some women appreciate such flattering attentions, considering them the height of gallantry. My own wife has certainly been known to bask in such sycophantic blarney, providing the flattering admirer has youth and good looks on his side. Saying that, even Marigold would see the funny side of Vasos' well-meaning efforts without branding him a sexist. Perchance Macey had higher standards than my wife.

Passing my clipboard to Macey, I delegated the task of ticking off the lunch preferences to my minion. I was pleased to note that he showed some initiative, managing to hold his ground and refuse to give in when a couple who'd brought their own sandwiches along, tried to talk him into a partial refund. I did step in to advise them that since the boat lacked a fridge, their packed lunch would likely have turned in the heat by the time we dropped anchor to eat. I suggested it might be wise to tick one of the pre-paid lunch options rather than risk a case of food poisoning.

V.D. BUCKET

It never ceased to amaze me how often this situation cropped up. I would guesstimate that it was at least a fortnightly occurrence for a couple of tourists to turn up with a packed lunch, even though lunch was included in the ticket price. I could sympathise with the ones that were reluctant to risk eating a meal from an unknown kitchen that might not adhere to strict hygiene standards. However, I ran out of patience with the packed lunch brigade that only packed their own because they were too unadventurous to sample foreign food, or the ones that brought their own to save a few bob. Invariably, such tightwads failed to offer a tip at the end of the trip.

Macey managed the meet and greet with a confident air that boded well for leaving him to his own devices on future trips. Not everyone can master a stream of simple good morning greetings without sounding bored, but his previous experience of repping appeared to stand him in good stead. As the last of the stragglers approached the pleasure vessel, I did a double take, recognising the American couple that had been stalking us in Arcadia, making small talk with my wife after they'd fed the cats in the bins at Lagadia. They certainly had some nerve following me to my workplace.

"You finish off here," I told Macey before hotfooting it to the on-board toilet before the American pair could spot me.

With the last of the day trippers safely across the gangplank, Captain Vasos took to the wheelhouse and I took over from Macey, delivering the day's itinerary to the tourists whilst ignoring the frantic attempts the Americans made to attract my attention, waving desperately in my direction. As usual, a handful of holidaymakers were disinterested in hearing me out, preferring to throw themselves directly into the important business of tanning their bodies on the upper deck until their flesh resembled Easter *kokoretsi* on the spit. It was becoming all too predictable: by lunch time, the sun worshippers would invariably be after a remedy to take the heat out of their sun reddened, painfully peeling skin.

Most of the day trippers were content to take their seats and bask in the stunning views and fresh sea air as Vasos steered the vessel towards our first destination where we would anchor up for a swim. I suggested to Macey that we split the rounds, making chit-chat with the passengers and answering any questions about the area. Making the unilateral decision to send him to the upper sundeck, I spared myself the embarrassment of having to avert my eyes from any topless sunbathers.

Unfortunately, as soon as I started my rounds, the American couple pounced on me, greeting me effusively as though I was a long-lost friend.

"I told you it was plum-out him, Ralph," the woman said. "Do you remember us? Karen and Ralph."

I adopted a suitably blank look, hoping to convey the impression I had never seen them before. Clad in my dreadful repping uniform complete with cap and whistle, I surely bore little resemblance to the suave and debonair chap they had encountered in Arcadia.

"We were in Arcadia at the same time as y'all," Karen persisted.

"I think you're barking up the wrong tree, Karen. Dad gum it, I don't plum out reckon it's the same man," Ralph argued. "How's someone on his vacation gonna to land a job on a Greek boat so darn out fast. Sure, he'd have to be top at Greek."

Tempted though I was to come out with *den katalavaino*, the Greek for I don't understand, I realised it wouldn't wash. Deciding denial was the best form of defence, I responded, "I think you must be mistaking me for someone else."

"I really could swear I'd seen you before…" Karen continued.

Hoping to convince them I was a complete stranger, I emulated Violet Burke's accent. "'Appen I have one of them faces."

"Oh, sorry. You really look like a man we saw

BUCKET TO GREECE (VOL.14)

in Arcadia. The likeness is uncanny, isn't it, Ralph?"

"'Appen you could do with a trip to Specsavers," I suggested, leaving them baffled by my reference to the English chain of opticians.

Striding away, I wondered what their game was. It had struck me as a tad too coincidental when this Karen and Ralph pair had materialised during our walk to the upper part of Lagadia after turning up in both the same café and taverna that we'd dined in, in Stemnitsa. Now here they were, presumably intent on pursuing me, kilometres away in a different prefecture. I couldn't for the life of me imagine why they were so intent on stalking me.

Before I could dwell any more on the matter, I was distracted by the actions of Mr and Mrs Heap, the couple that had brought their own sandwiches along. They were blatantly flouting the No Eating onboard rule by tucking into their sarnies even though it was nowhere near time for elevenses. About to issue a sharp reprimand, I noticed Mrs Heap suddenly freeze, the sandwich halfway to her mouth, totally unnerved when the ship's cat appeared at her feet, meowing for food. It really was a monstrously sized moggie. Not wishing to put myself in a vulnerable position between the enormous cat and the sandwich, I admit to a dereliction of duty by ignoring the situation and skipping up to the wheelhouse for a chat with Vasos.

V.D. BUCKET

"*Pos legate i gata tis Sami?*" I said, asking what Sami's cat was called.

"*Gata.*" Replying with a shrug, Vasos said the cat was called Cat. Shouting in clear, understandable Greek, Vasos told me in simple terms that the cat belonged to Sami's Moldovan girlfriend, Nastya. When Nastya's landlord discovered she was flouting the No Pets rule by harbouring a feline in her rented apartment, he told her that the cat must go. Sami swept in and saved the day by giving Gata a home on the boat, winning himself some extra brownie points from a grateful Nastya.

"*Fera i Gata edo, tha tis doso ena bol ouzo.*" I couldn't tell if Vasos was serious or pulling my leg when he told me to bring the cat and he'd give it a saucer of *ouzo*. After catching up with the captain for a while, I made my escape by telling him that I needed to check up on the new rep, telling him that Cynthia was counting on me to deliver a full report.

I freely admit to using Macey as a convenient excuse to escape the wheelhouse; the pong from Vasos' sweaty body driving me back to the deck in search of fresh air. Hopefully, at some point during the day, he would take a dip and wash away some of the sweat. As the thought crossed my mind, I remembered to give him the soap on a rope that Marigold had bought for him in Arcadia. It would of course mean that if the good captain could master the hang of lathering up, our little swimming spot in the Mediterranean would be awash with soapsuds.

Back on deck, I adopted a casual demeanour. Leaning against the railings and gazing out to sea offered a prime position to discreetly observe the new recruit without him realising what I was up to.

Macey was engaged in conversation with Mr and Mrs Clark, a married couple from Birmingham. Overhearing snippets of their exchange, it seemed that Macey was monopolising the discourse, prefacing almost every sentence with "Having lived in Greece for sixteen years," or "I can say in all modesty that I speak with authority where Greece is concerned." His spiel may have gone down well if we were taking a Lazy Day Cruise off the Cretan coast but his knowledge of the Mani was sadly lacking. I would have to lend him a thick tome or two from my collection of books about the area, to bring him up to speed. It wouldn't do for the tour company to get a bad reputation because the rep couldn't answer pertinent questions accurately.

Mr Clark, admiring the mountain range of Taygetos in the distance, asked Macey what was the highest point. "I do believe the highest point is in Sparti," Macey replied with false confidence.

Unable to tolerate such a bloop of an answer, I moved to join them, telling Mr Clark, "Actually, the summit of Mount Taygetos is *Profitis Ilias*."

"Actually, Vic, I think you'll find that *Profitis Ilias* is the name of a Cretan monastery," Macey argued.

"It's Victor," I corrected him. "It may well be that *Profitis Ilias* is the name of a Cretan monastery but it is certainly the name of the highest point on our local mountain range."

The way in which Mr Clark's head swivelled left and right as Macey and I continued to argue the point, put me in mind of a spectator at a tennis match. Admittedly it wasn't very professional of us to conduct a heated discussion in front of the day trippers.

"Remind me again, Vic, how long have you lived in Greece?" Macey's tone was condescending to say the least.

"Just coming up for three years…"

"Ah, well, in that case, I think you must defer to me. After living over here for sixteen years, I have more experience."

"Remind me again, John, how long have you lived in the Mani? It's less than a month or two, isn't it?"

With Pegasus nearing our first swimming stop, I pulled rank, sending Macey down below to collect the inflatables, instructing him to scrutinise them for holes in case Gata's claws had left any marks.

BUCKET TO GREECE (VOL.14)

When Vasos dropped anchor, I told Macey he would need to keep an eye on the swimmers in case any of them got into difficulties.

"Never fear. I say in all modesty, I got my bronze swimming certificate at school."

Much as I would have liked to best Macey by declaring I had my silver, I couldn't. I couldn't even match him with a bronze. The day before our class at school was due to jump into the water in our pyjamas at our local baths to try out for the bronze swimming certificate, Derek Little threatened to duck me under the water. Desperate to avoid the bully, I pulled a sickie from school with my mum's blessing. I doubt that Violet Burke would have been so sympathetic to my nervous plight: if she'd dragged me up instead of abandoning me in a bucket, I'm sure she would have called me a right little wuss and sent me off to school with a flea in my ear, refusing to let me chicken out of attempting my bronze.

I positioned myself well away from Macey, leaving him to assist the tourists up and down the ladder. I couldn't help but notice that he had a way of schmoozing the holidaymakers, deftly deflecting their questions about the Mani and turning the conversation around to himself.

I realised that Marigold was right when she said he never stopped boasting about having lived in Greece for sixteen years. Since the Mani enjoys many repeat visitors that return year after year, many with the dream of perchance retiring here one day, some of our trippers were more up on the area than the latest rep. Still, I presumed he would grow tired of talking about himself once he'd got a few tourist tours under his belt. At any rate, he was still an improvement on the possible alternative of Smug Bessie. Even though it might amuse me to see Vasos put her in her place, I would rather resign than show the insufferable woman the ropes.

Chapter 20

Sticking with Fanta Lemoni

With all the tourists safely herded across the gangplank to dry land, I conferred with the owner of the taverna to confirm the numbers for lunch. Animated chatter drifted over as the trippers settled at two long tables in anticipation of excellent Greek food. It's amazing how much of an appetite they had worked up, sunbathing on Pegasus' deck and taking a refreshing dip.

With my charges settled, I joined Vasos and Sami at our allocated crew table where a basket of bread and an open bottle of olive oil already graced the blue and white checked paper tablecloth.

"*Pou einai o Giannis*?" Vasos asked me where John was before turning his chair around, affording him a better view of a bikini clad woman sunning herself on the pebble beach.

Glancing around, I spotted Macey deep in conversation with my American stalkers. Assuming they were interrogating my colleague to get some dirt on me, I could only hope that Macey didn't have a loose tongue. As I debated whether or not to go across and drag Macey away by the ear, the waiter delivered the food to the Americans. Leaving them to enjoy their meal in peace, Macey sauntered over and sank into the seat next to mine.

"Were those Americans asking about me?" I grilled him.

"No, why on earth would they? They were quizzing me on local food, as it happens."

"I hope you didn't tell them about the Gastronomic Walking Tour…"

"Why? Would I do you out of a commission if I signed them up?"

"This week's Gastronomic Tour is booked solid," I improvised. In truth, I had no clue how many tickets had been sold but it would be difficult to evade the Americans if they were intent on stalking me in such a small group.

"And, of course, they wanted to know where

the best local tavernas are, the places with plenty of Greek character."

"The tour company frowns on us recommending one establishment over another," I pointed out.

"Cynthia never mentioned that but I will bear it in mind for the future. I'm afraid that I told them about the taverna in the coastal village I'm staying in. I believe you know the owner, Vasilis, and his wife, Angeliki."

"Indeed. It will be changing hands soon. Takis, a professionally trained chef, is in the process of buying the place." Making a mental note to give Takis a call to find out when his opening night would be, I exhaled in relief that Macey hadn't recommended my local taverna in Meli. Perchance he had yet to discover it.

My mobile phone trilled. *Saved by the bell*.

"I need to take this. It's my wife."

"I'm not one to judge," Macey said in a judgemental tone, doing that slug-like thing with his eyebrows again. "But that wife of yours certainly likes to keep tabs on you during your working day."

Directing one of Marigold's withering looks at Macey, I stepped away from the table and down onto the narrow pebble beach skirting the water's edge. Putting enough distance between us, I hoped to prevent Macey from eavesdropping as I answered the call.

Dispensing with the usual pleasantries, Marigold demanded, "Victor, would you like to explain why Guzim has just told me he was happy to see I'd found the cat?"

My heart sank at the realisation that the cretinous Albanian had gone and landed me in it. I might have known my half-witted gardener was incapable of keeping the cat in the bag.

"I'm sure it was just a linguistic misunderstanding, darling. You know you can never make head nor tail of Guzim's nonsense."

"It sounds as though you are trying to deflect, Victor. I understood Guzim perfectly well. It seems a bit too coincidental that Guzim seemed to think Catastrophe had been missing on the very same day that your mother discovered her locked in a wardrobe. Are you and Guzim in cahoots about something?"

"In cahoots with Guzim? Perish the thought. I expect the idiot got the wrong end of the stick." Thinking on my feet, I fibbed. "I saw Guzim in the garden this morning and mentioned Catastrophe hadn't put in her usual appearance for her breakfast slop. I asked him if he'd been overfeeding the cats whilst we were away, thinking that may account for Catastrophe not showing up for breakfast."

"Oh, I suppose that would explain it, though, if anything, Catastrophe seems to have shed some

BUCKET TO GREECE (VOL.14)

weight while we were away." Being locked in a wardrobe for two nights would likely explain the weight loss, but I had no intention of volunteering the information. Marigold's tone softened; the subject of Catastrophe instantly dropped. "Are you having a nice day out, dear?"

"I'm working," I reminded my wife.

"Floating around on the Mediterranean. It's all right for some. I have a humongous pile of ironing to do from our holiday. Those traveller's creases in your slacks don't just magically materialise, you know. I'll be sweating over a hot iron and a bottle of spray starch all afternoon."

"Why not leave it? I'll stroll over to Blat's place when I get back to Meli and see if Blerta fancies tackling the ironing in exchange for my giving Tonibler another English lesson."

"Oh, would you darling? That's so thoughtful. It means I can use my time more productively."

"You have something productive to do?" I asked sceptically.

"I simply must get together with Doreen and have a confab about the jumble sale."

So much for the established notion that women are excellent at multi-tasking: my wife was seemingly incapable of ironing whilst gossiping with Doreen.

Resuming my seat next to Macey, I was taken

aback when he said, "I suppose she's one of those jealous types."

"What?"

"Your wife. That's twice she's called to check up on you."

"You suppose wrong," I assured him. "Marigold just wanted to keep me updated about an important issue on the domestic front."

Even as I spoke, I wondered how Guzim had known the cat had returned. Since it wasn't as though Catastrophe ever ventured outdoors, it struck me that Guzim might have been inside our house again for a last desperate search. Recalling that I had made Guzim turn his key over the day before, I dismissed the thought.

"I hear that you've been making regular drives up to Meli. How are you finding the village?" I asked Macey.

His two eyebrows creased together over the top of his sunglasses, creating a hideous image of a monobrowed slug. "I didn't realise my every move was being clocked."

"The builders happened to mention you like to be on site as often as possible."

"I suppose there are blabbermouths everywhere," Macey grumbled. "I do believe that Meli is an excellent choice, though only time will tell. The village is just far enough away from the busy tourist spots without being totally isolated. The only downside is the lack of local accommodation until the house is ready to move into. I'm finding it a bit of a nuisance having to do the round-trip drive of ninety minutes every day to check up on the builders. Not to mention the cost of the hotel is adding up."

"Yes, but if you found somewhere to stay in Meli, you'd have the downside of having to drive to the tourist office. At least you're mid-way on the coast."

"But I will only need to drive to the tourist office four times a week. I do need to be in Meli every day to see what progress is being made on the house." It seemed he wasn't exaggerating when he said he liked to keep an eye on the builders.

I considered it a pity that work wasn't farther along on the ruin we had purchased. We might have been able to rent it out to Macey until his new home was ready to move into. Another thought occurred to me, which I voiced.

"Perhaps you could enquire if any of the villagers in Meli would be up for a short-term lodger." As I made the suggestion, I recalled that Manolis had hoped to turn the house he reluctantly shared with his brother, Christos, into a guest house. His plan had been scuppered because Christos was such a sex pest, but Macey ought to be safe enough from

Christos' ardent attentions, the slimy Greek only having eyes for the ladies, particularly my wife.

If Macey could cope with living in a house chock full of cats, he could approach Milton and Edna about taking in a lodger. The permanently penurious Hancocks could certainly do with the cash. Alternatively, Doreen and Norman might be up for taking in a lodger. A third person may help to reduce the hostile tension between the estranged couple. I could see a personal advantage in this scenario; if Norman became pally with Macey, it might spare me from being the primary object of Norman's friendly overtures.

"Tell me, John. Do you enjoy fondant fancies and other sweet confections?"

"What?" Macey's eyebrows did that slug-like thing again. Ignoring my question, he said, "Your idea of asking about lodgings in Meli isn't half-bad, Victor. Perhaps I could put a card up in the local shop window."

"Or ask around amongst the villagers. Have you met many of them yet? I expect by now the expats will have made themselves known to you."

"Not really, less than a handful. It seems that the English in Meli are a different breed to the ones in Crete. They were too in one's face, if you get my drift," Macey said. "A very affable chap called Norman stopped by to introduce himself when I was up in Meli yesterday, checking up on the builders. Told me all about his fascinating habit of collecting traffic cones..."

"Fascinating," I parroted in wonder. Surely Macey couldn't find Norman's hobby riveting.

"And later, I ran into an English woman in the shop...I think she said her name was Shelly...or was it Shirley?"

"Sherry."

"Well, I'm not one to judge if you want to knock back the sherry at lunchtime, but I'll just stick to my Fanta *lemoni*. It wouldn't do to be drunk on the job."

"Sherry is the name of a local expat..."

"Ah, with you. When I told her I'd bought a house in the village, she invited me along to something called the expat dining club...I'm not sure I want to get involved with any expat groups but she was most insistent I come along tomorrow evening. Wouldn't take no for an answer."

"Tomorrow evening." My heart sank. Marigold hadn't warned me that she'd be dragging me along to yet another tiresome monthly gathering of the expat dining club. I was under no illusion that Sherry was capable of knocking up a decent meal of foreign provenance. She had squandered her opportunity to improve her cooking skills at my cookery classes, more intent on making eyes at Dimitris than mastering Greek dishes. If I was forced to name the class dunce, Sherry would be awarded the pointed cap.

The waiter arrived bearing our food. Vasos, Sami and I had all opted for the vegetarian option of *gemistes piperies*. One could always rely on the stuffed peppers at this particular taverna, the cook adding some freshly chopped mint to the vegetable and rice stuffing. Macey looked rather downhearted when he saw his own plate of *souvlaki kotopoulo*, skewered chicken served with anaemic looking chips.

Casting a covetous glance at my peppers, Macey observed, "Your food looks better than mine."

"*Ti eipe*?" Vasos wanted to know what Macey had said.

"*To fagito mou fainetai kalytero apo to diko tou*," I translated for Vasos' benefit, telling him Macey had said my food looked better than his.

Vasos switched his plate with Macey's, swapping his own stuffed peppers for Macey's chicken souvlaki, confusing my colleague by winking as he said "Fray Bentos." To his credit, Macey's thanks was more effusive than I would have managed in the circumstances, Vasos already having made inroads into his peppers. Clearly, Macey was unfamiliar with the concept of contracting a whole range of nasty germs from sharing food that had already

BUCKET TO GREECE (VOL.14)

been poked around by Vasos' spittle laden tines.

Gesticulating to the waiter, Macey asked him, *"Boro na echo merika agoria se fetes?"*

Vasos and the waiter snorted in unison, my own snort following in short order once I'd mentally translated Macey's request for some sliced boys.

"Nomizo oti ennoei angouri se fetes," I intervened, saying 'I think he means sliced cucumber."

Macey reddened, muttering, "That's what I said."

"You definitely asked for sliced boys but it is an easy mistake to make," I assured him. "It reminds me of the tourists asking for grilled children rather than lamb chops from the grill. So, how's the renovation work on your little house coming along?"

"The builders you recommended have made a good start though they estimate it will be at least another month or two before I'll be able to move in. It's a terrible drag having to keep my eye on them but I can't risk them cutting corners once my back is turned," Macey pronounced rather pompously. "I get the impression that the English builder, Barry, rather resents my turning up to check on their progress. At least I always wear a safety helmet when I'm on site, which is more than can be said for the builders who seem to have zero comprehension of the importance of safety standards."

V.D. BUCKET

Bristling at Macey's casual criticism of Barry, I recalled that I'd never actually mentioned to Macey that Barry was my brother-in-law. I must admit to sharing Macey's concerns about Barry and Vangelis' lax approach to safety, scaling dodgy scaffolding without any safety harnesses and ignoring the requirement to hard hat it up. Nevertheless, I decided against spilling the beans and telling Macey about my family ties with Barry, thinking Macey may well clam up if he knew of our special relationship. My brother-in-law would surely appreciate my playing the part of a double agent, reporting back to Barry if Macey said anything untoward.

Macey turned his attention to Vasos, practising his excruciating Greek on the good captain. In no mood to attempt to put Vasos' oddball English words into some non-existent context, I polished off my peppers and excused myself to stretch my legs and enjoy a gentle stroll along the water's edge. Pausing to exchange pleasantries with a middle-aged Greek fisherman hosing down his deck, his rotund stomach straining above the belt of his saggy jeans, my attention was distracted by the sound of a fracas of sorts, further down the jetty.

"*Ti symvainei?*" I asked the fisherman if he knew what was going on. From his elevated position on his boat, he had a clearer view.

"*O Papas einai thymomenos.*" The fisherman

replied that the priest was angry, a hearty chuckle following his words.

Straining my neck to see what had apparently riled the man of God, I saw a Papas waving his arms and shouting at the two American tourists, demanding they put their camera away. Naturally, the tourists couldn't understand a word the Papas was shouting, oblivious to what they had done to enrage him. Realising it was down to me to smooth the waters, I hurried over, listening as the priest volleyed a tirade of abuse at the Americans for having the temerity to take his photograph without asking his permission first.

Addressing the Papas, I apologised on their behalf, explaining they didn't know any better, adding the caveat that they were Americans.

"*Amerikanoi.*" The way the priest stressed the word reminded me of the way I often excused Guzim's antics by explaining he was Albanian.

As the priest began to calm down, I told the American pair, "You can't just go snapping photos of the Greek clergy without asking their permission first. The Papas is particularly angry that you didn't even wait until he had extinguished his cigarette. It isn't a good look for him to be captured on celluloid whilst smoking in public. He has his exalted image to consider."

"He must be like those Amish," Karen pondered

aloud.

My mind boggled at her ridiculous comment. Although I had never ventured across the pond into Pennsylvanian Amish territory, I knew full well that the Amish style of dress bore no resemblance to Greek clerical vestments. Perhaps the Papas' long beard had confused them.

"The Amish aren't keen on having their photos taken," Ralph elaborated. "Tell him we didn't mean anything by it. I'm thinking he must be all hat and no cattle."

Thinking Ralph's southern sayings made as much sense as the English words that spewed out of Vasos' mouth, I told him, "I will if you put your camera away." I couldn't help worrying that I may become his next target. Perchance, photographing the priest had just been a ruse and I was the intended target of Ralph's camera lens.

Somewhat appeased, the Papas hurried away, casting the odd look over his shoulder to ensure he wasn't being photographed from behind. Stopping alongside the boat I had dallied by moments earlier, the Papas accepted a fish from the fisherman before continuing on his way.

Guiding the two Americans back to the boat before they could make another bloop that would put a strain on Greek-American relations, I tried to blot out Ralph wittering on about hogs in slops and other nonsensical utterings. If Vasos hadn't already scuttled off for forty winks in the wheelhouse before anchors away, I would have introduced him to the pair. He could have expanded his nonsensical vocabulary with some choice 'dandies' and 'wannas' and other assorted Americanisms.

My mood lifted as the fisherman called out to me, his outstretched hands holding a fish. Eyeing the attractive fish with pinkish hues, I asked him if it was a *barmpouni*, otherwise known as red mullet. Delighted that I had so readily recognised the fish, the fisherman slung it into a plastic bag and insisted on gifting it to me, declaring he'd had a marvellous catch that day. Accepting the generous gift, I wondered if Marigold would be in the mood for a spot of scaling and gutting later, providing the taverna could supply me with enough ice to preserve the fish during our voyage home.

Chapter 21

Ramblings of a Confused Housewife

Skipping up the outside stone staircase clutching the ice box which the taverna owner had generously furnished me with to keep my gift of free fish fresh, I couldn't wait to playfully tease Marigold. Discovering that her excessive use of plings had an actual name that sounded like a certifiable condition, had made my day, despite the information being imparted by the know-it-all John Macey. Bursting into the grand salon, I could barely contain myself, bursting out, "Honey, I'm home. Do you know that you have a terrible case of bangorrhea?"

BUCKET TO GREECE (VOL.14)

"What? Don't be so silly, darling. I've never heard anything so preposterous." As Marigold protested, I belatedly realised my wife was not alone on the balcony; she had company, Doreen staring at me as though I had just announced I was a serial killer. Really, Marigold might have given me due warning that she had her sidekick over. I didn't want my wife letting the cat out of the bag about my refusal to litter the pages of my book with excessive exclamation marks, only immediate members of the family knowing anything about my literary endeavours.

Doreen's lip curled in disgust. "I didn't have you down as the unfaithful type, Victor."

"What? I've never looked at another woman." Sometimes Doreen's utterings sounded like the verbal diarrhoea of someone unhinged.

"You mean it's the sort of nasty venereal disease that Marigold could have picked up from a random toilet seat?" I couldn't help but notice the frisson of excitement in Doreen's eyes. She never could resist a bit of juicy gossip.

"Have you finally lost the plot, Doreen?"

"You're the one accusing Marigold of having a terrible case…"

"You need to remove your head from the sewer, Doreen. The bangorrhea that I referred to is the word for using an excess amount of exclamation marks. Have you ever seen one of my wife's shopping lists? Don't you think it's a tad over the top to add a row of plings to grocery items such as *baclava* and *bougatsa*."

"Marigold does have a very sweet tooth," Doreen said defensively. In truth, I was quite gobsmacked that Doreen recognised the names of sweet Greek pastries. Perchance Manolis shared Marigold's addiction to sweet treats.

"Bangorrhea. It's an odd sounding word," Marigold mused. "I can see why Doreen jumped to the wrong conclusion; it would be easy to mistake it for a nasty dose of gonorrhoea."

"I believe the word derives from..." I began.

Marigold interrupted me, warning her friend, "Victor is about to dazzle us with one of his unproduceable Greek words that he's swotted up on."

"No, I'm not. I was about to say it is derived from bang, as if finishing your sentence with a bang would make it sound more exciting."

"Perhaps I'll try it out on Manolis." Blushing as she mentioned the name of her fancy man, Doreen fluffed her newly bottle blonde locks. "He does adore it when I try to get my tongue around new Greek words..."

"It isn't Greek, Doreen." Actually, it might well be Greek for all I knew. I mentally cursed Macey for failing to mention if bangorrhea was the same in translation. I happened to know that the Greek for gonorrhoea was *vlennorroia*, only because I'd looked it up as a point of interest when hosting the sexually infected Ashley, Geraldine's nylon haired suitor.

"Well, perhaps they use it in Texas," Doreen said hopefully.

"Speaking of Texas," I said before Doreen could regale us with some romantic drivel about her new Greek-Texan boyfriend; the woman never knew when to put a sock in it. "You'll never guess, Marigold. That pair of Americans that were stalking me in Arcadia, only went and turned up on the Pegasus trip today."

"You never told me that Victor had a stalker." Doreen's tone indicated she was thirsty for some juicy gossip. It must have been such a let-down to discover Marigold wasn't suffering from a nasty sexually transmitted infection after all.

"I didn't mention the stalkers because it's all in Victor's head. Haven't you noticed that my husband has a tendency to a fevered imagination and an inflated sense of his own self-importance?" Since plings aren't immediately visible in speech, Marigold punctuated her words with a dramatic eye-roll. "Just because a couple of tourists happened to crop up once or twice in the same places as us during our second honeymoon, Victor got it into his head they were following him."

"You don't think it's more than a tad coincidental that they turned up today?" I asked. "Pegasus wasn't exactly moored up around the corner from Arcadia."

"The only stalker around these parts is that creepy Christos," Marigold declared, shaking her head as though to clear it of the image of the oily Greek.

Whilst my immediate concern ought to be focused on the idea that Christos might be bothering my wife again, such an approach wouldn't win the petty spat. Instead of expressing my concern, I resorted to a caustic comment.

"Now who sounds full of self-importance, thinking Christos is attracted to you," I spat.

"Marigold isn't imagining it, Victor. Christos is quite besotted...he definitely still has a thing for Marigold," Doreen volunteered. Safely wrapped up in her own bubble of love, Doreen was no longer jealous about the unwanted attentions Christos directed towards my wife.

"As I recall, his fixation on Marigold used to inflame your jealousy until you took up with that brother of his with the pornstache..."

"Really, Victor. You know perfectly well that I'm not delusional. Christos has been making a nuisance of himself again," Marigold said in exasperation.

BUCKET TO GREECE (VOL.14)

"He was hanging around like a bad smell outside Athena's kitchen window when I was having my hair done earlier."

"Your hair looks lovely, darling," I belatedly complimented my wife.

Immediately contrite at the thought of the oily Christos harassing my wife, I let the argument drop, promising to have stern words with her ardent suitor. I had rather thought that Christos' fancy for Marigold might have faded a tad now that the tourist season was in full swing. It was common knowledge that the slimy Greek often motored down to the coast to make *kamaki* to the influx of tourist women scattered over the beaches. Perchance this year's crop was a tad light on redheads.

"Did you have a nice day out, dear?" Marigold asked.

"I was working," I reminded her. "I brought a freshly caught *barmpouni* home for dinner."

"I haven't got time to be gutting fish, Victor. Doreen and I are knee deep in plans for the jumble tomorrow. Anyway, I've picked all the ingredients from the garden for a nice Greek salad for dinner."

"I thought I could smell the aroma of a delicious home-cooked meal," I said, making no attempt to hide my sarcasm. Was it too much to expect a home-cooked meal after toiling all day? Marigold cobbling a salad together hardly made the cut.

Nevertheless, I couldn't help but smile. Marigold saying she had picked the ingredients for our meal reminded me of Guzim's complaint that cheese didn't grow in the garden, when I'd reprimanded him for his filthy habit of rummaging for food in the village bins.

"I avoid the gutting part by buying frozen salmon fillets in Lidl," Doreen volunteered.

"I don't blame you, it's a thoroughly disgusting task. It's quite amazing how adept the Greek women in the village are at gutting fish," Marigold said wistfully. "I think they must be born with a good fish filleting knife in their hands. And have you seen the way they can peel a prickly artichoke in five seconds flat? It takes Victor forever and he has to don two pairs of Marigolds in case he stabs himself."

"But we Brits have the edge when it comes to organizing a good jumble sale," Doreen boasted. "Can you imagine, none of the Greeks had a clue about jumble?"

"Not even Manolis?" I asked.

"He said they're big on yard sales in Texas. Of course, with Greece being metric, I suppose the equivalent over here would be selling everything in metres." After close to three years of enduring Doreen's company, her stupidity could still astound me. I often felt I was listening to the inane ramblings of a confused housewife.

"Speaking of jumble, I brought over some books that I'm donating to the sale," Doreen said. "I thought Marigold would like first dibs but she found them too dirty for her taste."

"Well, I am married to a retired public health inspector," Marigold quipped.

"How many copies of Milton's porn did you manage to cobble together for the jumble?" I couldn't imagine Doreen having dirty books in her house unless they'd originated from the local purveyor of porn.

"Really, Victor, everyone in the village has already thumbed through 'Delicious Desire.' They won't want to hand over good money for that filthy trash. When I said dirty, I was referring to cookery books. Lots of the pages are stuck together from where Norman spilt and smeared his ingredients."

"I put one of the books aside for you, darling," Marigold said. Intercepting my look, she assured me, "Don't worry, it's perfectly clean. It's been nowhere near Norman's kitchen. It's a manual on teaching yourself to touch type."

"I've had it for years but never got the hang of it," Doreen said.

"It could be just the thing for you, Victor," Marigold continued. "I know how it takes you forever to get anything down, stabbing at the keyboard with two fingers. The typing manual is jammed full of useful practical exercises to get you started."

"Surely Victor doesn't have anything he needs to type," Doreen jumped in as though I wasn't there.

Worrying that Marigold was about to let the cat out of the bag about my writing a book about moving to Greece, I sent her a warning look to keep her mouth shut. Neatly sidestepping the issue, Marigold told Doreen that I was forever typing up reams of notes so that I would always have plenty of pre-prepared speeches to lecture my captive audience with on my tourist trips.

"I think you should try it, dear," Marigold urged. "Think how much easier it would be to type up reports in the tourist office if you didn't need to fathom out where all the keys are."

"Perhaps Doreen ought to donate the book to the police station or the local KEP," I suggested. "I have yet to witness a single Greek civil servant that has mastered more than one-fingered typing. It takes an absolute age for anyone connected to Greek officialdom to fill in a simple form."

"Well, to be fair, there's no stipulation that they have to master the keyboard with any proficiency in order to qualify as computer literate. Did you know, Doreen, civil servants get an extra six days annual holiday just for using a computer?" Marigold asked.

Leafing through the book, I decided I would keep hold of it. If I could master touch typing it would be an excellent skill to utilise since I needed to retype the whole of my manuscript of Bucket to Greece, incorporating the numerous edits that old Scraper had sprawled in the margins of the printed out copy I'd sent him.

From the corner of my eye, I spotted Catastrophe strolling towards the balcony, pausing to arch her back and stretch her curtailed tail. Having never been so grateful to see one of Marigold's pampered imported domestics, I couldn't resist the urge to scoop Catastrophe up, relieved to see for myself that no harm had come to the cat during the time she'd been locked in the wardrobe. As the cat nestled in close to my chest, I remembered I would need to give my useless gardener a stern talking to. Since he had been left in sole charge of the cats, he must surely have been the one responsible for shutting Catastrophe in the wardrobe for two traumatic nights. Just what sort of business he had in our spare bedroom was another matter that I intended to get to the bottom of.

"Are you feeling quite well, darling?" Marigold's words might sound solicitous but I detected evidence of sarcasm in her tone. "It's not like you to make a fuss over the cats. I can't think what's got into you. Your mother showed me that filthy looking feral you foisted on her this morning."

"I might have known Violet Burke was incapable of keeping her big mouth shut," I spluttered in annoyance.

"She kept your little secret. I popped downstairs to return the Marigolds she'd left up here after cleaning and saw the scrawny kitten for myself. I recognised my towels in that shoebox. It's a dirty feral and no mistake. What on earth has got into you, Victor? Plucking random cats of unknown provenance off the street and palming them off on your mother?"

"One tiny kitten, Marigold, not random cats in plural," I objected. "I happened across the poor little mite during my stroll yesterday evening. It looked at death's door so I took pity on it. I couldn't bear the thought of having its death on my conscience."

"You could have just dropped it in at the Hancocks' place and left Edna to deal with it."

"Edna and Milton are up at the hospital having Edna's cataracts done..."

"Oh, yes. Cynthia mentioned it last night."

About to say that I didn't think the Hancocks' Greek cat-sitting lodger would have given the kitten an empathetic welcome, I stopped myself in time. It wouldn't do to be forced to explain that

BUCKET TO GREECE (VOL.14)

Barry and I had been inside the Hancock residence, searching for the cat that my cat mad wife had failed to even notice was missing.

"I deliberately didn't bring the kitten into our house in case it had anything contagious it might spread to those cats of yours," I said. "It really was in a sorry looking state, barely clinging to life."

"Thank goodness you didn't bring it in here. It has a nasty case of conjunctivitis that could easily spread to our cats."

"I'll pop down with the eye drops shortly and give it another wipe," I said. Before I had the chance to gauge how Marigold would react, I adopted a determined tone that brooked no argument. "If it survives, I want to keep it."

"It's a she, not an it," Doreen corrected me, her words letting me know that my apparent moment of weakness over the kitten would soon be general knowledge in the village.

"You want to keep it?" Marigold repeated as though I'd lost my mind.

"Yes, indeed. I have decided to keep it. And what's more, I won't be talked out of it." I rarely put my foot down so emphatically but I meant every word.

"It's so out of character for you, Victor," Marigold pronounced. "You couldn't wait to palm Tesco off on Spiros' old uncle Leo."

"Do I need to remind you that Tesco was the spawn of Cynthia's vile cat? Anyway, we kept hold of Pickles."

"I can see that you're set on keeping the kitten, Victor, so I won't stand in your way," Marigold graciously conceded. "If you manage to nurse it back to health, you'll have to get the vet to give it all the clear before you introduce her to the same living quarters as our other three."

"It's very early days. When I left her this morning, she looked at death's door. I'm hoping a bit of TLC will do the trick."

"They don't stock that at the local pharmacy." I struggled to make sense as Doreen went off on another warped tangent.

"Doreen, I think that you must be confusing your TLC with TCP," Marigold said. Sometimes I find it quite unnerving how my wife can make any sense out of Doreen's confused ramblings. "Remember that antiseptic we used to get in England, Victor? It's impossible to get hold of the stuff over here."

"That's what I said. They had no clue what it was in the pharmacy," Doreen said.

"Victor, your mother had Sampaguita round to take a look at that kitten. If anyone has the special touch, it's Sampaguita. She's so good with animals." Sidling over to my side, Marigold embraced me, whispering, "You do know that your attitude of indifference to the cats never fooled me for a moment. I knew all along that you liked them, even though you like to pretend they are a blithering nuisance."

"Perish the thought."

"If the helpless little thing struggles through, it will be quite nice to have a new kitten about the place. Once she's been cleaned up, that is," Marigold said. "You'll have to come up with a name for her."

"Let's not tempt fate quite yet. It may be wise to see if she can cling onto life before saddling her with a name," I said.

"Well, to be honest, it will be a miracle if she survives. There was only muck and mud holding her fur together over her bones," Marigold said. "Oh, I forgot to tell you. Your mother said you must pop into the taverna to see her. I've no idea what she wants with you but she said it was urgent and she was in a dreadful mood."

"I'll tootle along there now and then call in at Blat's to see if Blerta fancies doing your ironing." With a bit of luck, by the time I'd had a good catch up with Dina and Nikos, and touched base with Tonibler, Doreen might have remembered she had a home of her own to go to. I supposed I ought to be grateful that Marigold hadn't opened the Mastic

Tears or Doreen might still be hanging around by bedtime.

"You might as well take that fish with you, Victor."

"You could always freeze it or give it to the cats."

"Well, yes, if you've got time to gut it before you go…"

"I'll take it with me."

"I'll see you tomorrow night at Sherry's little gathering," Doreen called after me as I left. I could always rely on Doreen to go and put a damper on my evening.

Chapter 22

A Traitor to the Homeland

Still clutching the ice box containing the fish, I left the house, pondering the urgency of Violet Burke's demand that I call in on her at her place of work. She could think again if she expected me to help with peeling the spuds for that evening's chips. I wouldn't put it past her to demand a favour in return for taking in the sickly kitten that morning. I had no intention of allowing my mother to guilt me into skivvying in the taverna kitchen, providing free entertainment for Nikos to mock me for doing the woman's work, the butt of his jokes that I was born in a pinny.

V.D. BUCKET

Descending the outside stairs, my ears were assaulted by the sound of a full-blown barney emanating from my garden. Wondering what all the kerfuffle was about, I foolishly went to investigate: if I'd had any sense, I would have turned a deaf ear and carried merrily on my way. Alas, curiosity got the better of me.

Traipsing across the garden, I discovered Kyria Maria and Guzim going at it hammer and tongs over the garden wall, both parties chomping at the bit with self-righteous vitriol. The Albanian shed dweller was firing on all cylinders, repeatedly raising his arms and pumping his fists in Maria's direction. I hoped that his flailing fists wouldn't land on me if I was forced to intervene and physically restrain my gardener were he to take complete leave of his senses and attack Maria. By the looks of things, Maria was just as likely to start slapping Guzim around, but I had no intention of attempting to scale the garden wall to stop her.

Despite the colourful language polluting my garden, I couldn't resist a chuckle at the bizarre similarity between the two scrawny, black-clad figures, facing up as though they could come to blows at any moment. As usual, Kyria Maria's shrivelled form was attired in black widow's weeds, her sombre outfit for once matched by Guzim's unlikely choice of apparel. Instead of sporting lime-green

BUCKET TO GREECE (VOL.14)

Lycra or some oversized clashing cast-offs, Guzim looked almost normal in a plain black, though admittedly grubby tee-shirt, paired with black jogging trousers. Only the flimsy imitation *tsarouchia*, with their by now bedraggled pink pompoms, demonstrated he hadn't quite turned his back on his usual clueless fashion sense.

Drawing closer, I noticed that Guzim was forced to repeatedly rein in his arms to prevent his jogging bottoms from slipping down to expose his moth-eaten underwear. The way he continually yanked up his bottoms made me assume that Guzim had paid another productive visit to the village bins, happily scavenging a pair of joggers that had been tossed in the trash because the elastic had gone in the waistband.

Since Maria and Guzim were shouting over the top of one another, it took me a moment or two to understand the gist of their argument. It appeared that their feud was fuelled by the Albanian char that Papas Andreas had paid to clean Maria's house, the woman that had filled Guzim's head with the ridiculous notion that he was entitled to demand his employers lavish him with free towels and blankets. Although I was yet to come across Agnesa, I was yet to hear anything good about her. In light of the way that Agnesa had managed to ruffle the feathers of Papas Andreas, a remarkably tolerant man, it was a pretty safe assumption that she must be an unpleasant character.

It must have crossed the reader's mind that the sensible course of action at this point would have been for me to leg it as fast as my feet could carry me; after all, technically it was none of my business. It would be perfectly natural to jump to the conclusion that I was losing my marbles by inserting myself into the war of words erupting over the garden wall, yet insert myself I did.

I will spare my readers all the convoluted branches the argument took and paraphrase the dialogue in English, excluding the cutting insults, but including some ludicrous bloops that most stood out when Guzim struggled to find the correct word in Greek. It is all too easy to forget that Greek is Guzim's second language. Although his Greek linguistic skills far outshine mine, on occasion he struggles to find the correct Greek translation of whatever random nonsense has just popped into his tiny Albanian brain. Even amidst the volley of acerbic words exchanged between my gardener and my elderly neighbour, I must confess to finding it perfectly delicious when Guzim confused his heart for his bosom, compounding the delight when he then confused his heart for his breasts.

"It's your duty to tell the horrible woman to keep away from my house. Tell her I will flatten her

BUCKET TO GREECE (VOL.14)

with this frying pan," Kyria Maria instructed Guzim, illustrating her point by waving a cast iron pan around like a weapon. I reflected that if she had the strength to hurl it over the wall, it may well leave a nasty indentation in the Albanian shed dweller's head.

"How many times must I tell you? She is nothing to do with me," Guzim protested.

"She is. She's one of your lot. Albanian." Maria spat the word with contempt. In Maria's defence, she had a lot to put up with living next door to Guzim's shed, no doubt his antics colouring her mind against his countrymen. Maria was forced to endure Guzim's constant flashing as he hosed himself down in his underpants in full view of her bedroom window, with no regard to the prudish delicacies one would expect from someone of her advanced years. He had, on more than one occasion, disturbed her sleep by carousing and carrying on in his shed at all hours of the night with his drunken compatriots, though in Guzim's defence he had knocked such shenanigans on the head, along with the Amstel, since Luljeta produced Fatos, his first son and heir.

It struck me that Maria was holding Guzim personally accountable for the behaviour of his compatriot, a position I considered grossly unfair. I would certainly refuse to hold myself in any way responsible for whatever indiscretions any of my fellow Brits committed. Imagine the injustice of being tarnished by the same brush as Milton's porn or the locals assuming that, like Norman, I had a secret fetish for collecting traffic cones. Harold and Joan may have given the British in Meli a bad name, but the Bucket household and our extended family had redeemed the reputation of transplanted Brits by integrating seamlessly, well, almost seamlessly, into village life.

"The Agnesa is not my business. I hate her," Guzim shouted. As if to reiterate the point, he stamped his feet, his temper tantrum falling flat since there really wasn't much stomping power in his absurd pompomed slippers.

"She was round here earlier, demanding blankets again," Kyria Maria shouted.

Ignoring my neighbour, I interjected myself, questioning Guzim's comment. "You hate her. Only yesterday, she practically had you signed up as a card paying member of the Albanian communist party."

"I am not the communist. Yesterday, the Agnesa confuse me, telling me I should expect my rich employers to give me free things…"

"Yes, well best if we don't rehash all that again," I advised. It had been confusing enough to make any sense of his whingeing the first time around.

"I see the Agnesa today. She come looking for me in the village and give me the nasty tongue." Guzim emphasised the disgust in his tone by shooting a gob of spit in my garden.

"I thought she was friendly towards you...yesterday you made it sound as though she had taken you under her wing and was giving you advice, albeit misguided."

"She turn the nasty on me when she to hear that I own my own house in the Greece..."

"Where on earth did she hear such a thing?" I said with a side-splitting chuckle. "Fancy her thinking you own your own house in Greece."

"My house at the bottom of your garden." Throwing his arms in the air in exasperation, Guzim came very close to flashing my elderly neighbour as his joggers worked their way down again.

"Ah, quite." It was easy to forget how much pride Guzim took in owning his own home on his postage stamp piece of land. Still, it was a bit of a stretch to hear him describe the pink palace of love as an actual house when, in reality, it was nothing more than a rundown stone shed.

Hitching his pants up, Guzim said, "The Agnesa insult me, she say me that I am the traitor to Albania... to my the Albanian homeland."

"How so? What stuff and nonsense. You've certainly gone above and beyond in your patriotic duty of creating plenty of Albanian sprogs to keep the next generation going."

"The Agnesa say me that the Greek people and the rich foreign that live here are the nasty race. She hate them all. She say me they mistreat the Albanian because we are like the poor relation."

"For goodness' sake, Guzim, get a grip. No one mistreats you. You make it sound as though you are starved and beaten by the locals. I, for one, go out of my way to feed your curry addiction."

"Your curry is the best food I ever eat." I was happy to hear that almost choking to death on the plaster that Tonibler had lost in the prickly pear curry, had in no way curbed Guzim's greedy enthusiasm for my exotic cooking.

"Nikos gave you work over the winter with his olive harvest so you'd have money to send to Luljeta…"

"The Nikos is the slave driver…"

"No one's denying that. Don't forget I cheffed in his kitchen," I reminded Guzim. "But an honest day's work is an honest day's work and not to be sneezed at. The work Nikos gave you spared you from joining the motley early morning gathering of your compatriots, waiting for someone to come along and pick you as day labourer."

BUCKET TO GREECE (VOL.14)

"I not understand why they always pick to me last," Guzim muttered.

"And surely you haven't forgotten how the Greeks rushed to protect Luljeta and get her safely back over the border to Albania when Besnik involved her in that dreadful rabbit smuggling business. And just think of the way that Mrs Bucket and her friend Doreen went out of their way to make your home more comfortable. If you play your cards right, Doreen might be persuaded to put some elastic in the waistband of those joggers."

"I never say you or the Greek mistreat me. I say the Agnesa say it," Guzim cried. "And I to thank the Mrs Bucket from the bottom of my bosom for to make the decorate my home."

Guzim's joggers inched their way down again as he slapped his scrawny chest to give me some idea where his non-existent bosom was. "And I never to forget you give me the bus-fare to go home when Luljeta birth the Victor Mabel. I to thank you from the bottom of my breasts."

The joggers slid another inch or two down Guzim's scrawny thighs as he pounded his chest to show off his non-existent breasts.

"And don't go forgetting about that lovely stuffed rabbit I gave you for Victor Mabel." Admittedly, bringing up the stuffed bunny might be going just a tad too far in the emotional blackmail stakes since I couldn't wait to be shot of the grotesquery. Since Guzim failed to thank me profusely from the bottom of any more random body parts, I surmised he wasn't particularly grateful for my dumping the human-size rabbit in his lap.

"I don't dislike you because you are Albanian," Maria shouted over the garden wall. "I dislike you because you shower in your underpants."

"You want me to take them off?" Guzim's face flushed as though Maria had just propositioned him.

Waving the frying pan threateningly, Maria shot a look of contempt at Guzim. "And you can't control that rabbit of yours."

"You keep away from my rabbit. I know you want to cook Doruntina in your pot," Guzim shouted.

"This Agnesa make much the trouble, I don't trust her," Maria screeched over the wall. "She demand the Tina give her the job cleaning the shop and sack the Violet. I already to tell the Tina about the Agnesa demanding the blankets, so the Despina throw her from the shop," Maria said. I imagined Despina would be more than a match for anyone making demands. Whilst most of the villagers were cowed by Despina's evil tongue, I was proud of the way my mother was able to stand up to her, refusing to stand for any of Despina's nonsense.

BUCKET TO GREECE (VOL.14)

"This Agnesa certainly sounds like a trouble-maker," I said. "We should be grateful that she found accommodation in Nektar rather than Meli."

"The Drin and Agnesa move into the same place as that Jeronimo," Guzim said.

"Jeronimo?"

"That make the bad job of clean the window."

"You mean Theo, the lapsed Jehovah's Witness?" I clarified.

"That's what I said. The Jeronimo, he to tell me the Agnesa lose big the temper when she to hear the rich foreign woman make much the cleaning work. The Agnesa complain she is poor and it is not right that the rich foreign woman to take the cleaning job that should rightfully be hers."

"What rich foreign woman?" I asked. It was the first I'd heard of a rich foreigner charring.

"The Mrs Burke."

"Mrs Burke isn't rich," I spluttered. "What a ridiculous notion. Do you really think she would go out cleaning in her eightieth year if she was rich?"

Guzim looked so downcast that I almost felt sorry for him. Having always been terrified of Violet Burke, it seemed he now had another bolshie old harridan to contend with in this Agnesa person.

"Victor." Guzim visibly shrank before my eyes as Marigold yelled my name from an upstairs window. The poor sap really was intimidated when it came to strong women. "Victor, Vi's just been on the phone demanding you get over to the taverna pronto. She says it's urgent."

"I'm on my way now, my cherub," I called out.

"If I were you, I'd get your skates on. Your mother sounds like she has a bit of cob on," Marigold advised. From the slight slur of her words, I hazarded a guess that Marigold and Doreen had cracked open the Mastic Tears.

"I have to go," I told Maria and Guzim. Presuming their argument would continue once I'd gone, I'd put money on Maria making mincemeat out of the shed dweller.

As I strode back across the garden, Guzim chased after me. Grabbing hold of my shirt, he cried, "I have something the important I must tell you."

"Not now, Guzim," I said, shaking him off. "I'm already late and there'll be hell to pay if I keep Mrs Burke waiting."

"But…I must tell you."

"Not now, Guzim."

Chapter 23

The Battle of the Chars

Leaving Guzim and Kyria Maria to duel things out in the garden, I set off towards the taverna to see why Violet Burke had summoned me with such urgency. Since stopping off in the garden had delayed my departure, I winced at the thought of the dressing down I was likely to receive from my mother for my tardiness. She was sure to have a strop on by now. I might be a grown man in my sixth decade, but Violet Burke in full harridan mode could, on occasion, still make me tremble.

"*Ela, Victor, o filos mou.*" Spotting my good

friend Spiros rushing across the street towards me, my mood immediately lifted, Spiros' company always a tonic.

"*Pos eisai, Spiro*," I greeted the undertaker.

"I come to drink the *ouzo* with you," Spiros said. Throwing an arm across my shoulder, he tried to steer me back to my house.

"I'm sorry, Spiro. No can do. I have to meet my mother in the taverna urgently."

"The Violet can to wait. *Ela*, invite me in for the *ouzo* and we to make the latch."

"The latch?"

"The latch. How you say, the latch-up?"

"Ah, catch-up. I wish I could, Spiro, but I'm already late. Anyway, Doreen's upstairs with Marigold…"

"Say no the more." Spiros grimaced, before changing direction and steering me away from the house. "Forget the *ouzo*. I not have the head space to listen to the Doreen bend the ear about the great love story with the Manolis again…"

"I know what you mean. Doreen's like a broken record where her new boyfriend is concerned…"

"I not to hear that before. He is one of those idiots?"

Momentarily confused as to why Spiros would refer to his good friend Manolis as an idiot, I belatedly caught his drift.

BUCKET TO GREECE (VOL.14)

"I think the word you're after for broken record is idiom, not idiot."

Slapping his forehead, Spiros tried out the word for size, stressing each syllable. "Idioms, I should to remember. You go on about them so the much, you to sound like the broken record." Spiros released a hearty chuckle, pleased with himself for turning the idiom around on me.

"I really must go..." I said apologetically. I would much prefer to share an *ouzo* with Spiros than leap to Violet Burke's bidding.

"*Ela*, I walk with you to the taverna. We drink the *ouzo* there, Victor. I must to say, you look the frizzy..."

"Frizzy?" I queried, touching my hair to see if some random electrical spark had frizzed up my coiffure. Feeling my hair was in neat and smooth order, I ventured, "I think you mean frazzled. That's down to Guzim."

"Ah, the Sampaguita tell to me that the Guzim to lose the Marigold's cat and make much the big trouble."

"How on earth did Sampaguita get wind of it? You must swear her to secrecy. There'll be hell to pay if word of the cat going missing gets back to Marigold."

"I not understand. It was the Marigold who tell to the Sampaguita that the Guzim to lose the cat..."

"What? That makes no sense." Flabbergasted, I stopped abruptly, sending Spiros crashing into me. "Marigold had no clue that the cat was missing. Are you sure that Sampaguita heard about it from my wife?"

"*Sigura.*" Spiros' confirmation that he was sure sent my head in a spin. I must be living in some sort of parallel universe. Surely, if Marigold had discovered that Catastrophe had been missing, she would have had my guts for garters when I returned home from work, yet she had carried on as though everything was perfectly normal. I considered that perchance she may have been reluctant to rip into me with Doreen present, before discounting the idea: after all, the presence of her trusty sidekick hadn't stopped my wife from laying into me before. I was at a complete loss. Recalling that Guzim had been desperate to impart some seemingly important news as I'd fled the garden, it occurred to me that he may have confessed to Marigold that he'd locked the cat in the wardrobe. I may have to tentatively broach the subject with my wife on my return, without of course implicating myself.

"The walk he is the good healthy, yes?" Spiros said as we continued strolling to the taverna.

"Indeed, walking is excellent for one's health. Back in England, I led a much more sedentary life. Since moving to Greece, Marigold and I make a point of enjoying a daily walk as often as we can. We really feel that the exercise, along with the healthy Greek diet, has helped to keep us fit and improved our health."

"Enjoying and walk, I not to put together," Spiros said.

"Well, it's certainly not like you to willingly walk anywhere," I said. It had only just dawned on me that Spiros hadn't insisted we hop in the hearse to cover the short distance we could walk in five minutes as he usually did. Most of my Greek neighbours preferred to drive even the shortest of distances, rather than walk. Walking for exercise was considered a somewhat strange foreign habit by most of the Greek locals. Although many of the local ladies walked in the fields, foraging for *horta*, they dismissed the idea that such activity counted as exercise, not wanting to be seen as engaging in strange foreign habits.

"I must to lose the lard," Spiros proclaimed, patting his visibly growing paunch.

"Has my mother been insulting you?" I quipped, amused by Spiros' choice of lard instead of fat to describe his recent noticeable weight gain. His extra kilos came from the contentment he felt being married to Sampaguita. No doubt her excellent cooking had something to do with it too.

"Can we to rest the minute?" Spiros asked,

shooing a cat off a stone wall as he took a pew. "If I to tell to you the reason for the walk, you must to promise to not tell the Sampaguita?"

"You can trust me to keep shtum," I assured him. "Mum's the word."

"I have much the pain in the leg for long the time. I go the doctor in town and he make many the test. He say to me, the *artiria*…"

"Artery," I guessed.

"The artery in my leg, he is the clog," Spiros said, slapping his leg in case I wasn't sure where it was.

"That doesn't sound good."

"He say to me, I must to walk the three kilometre every the day to make the blood circulate the good. If I not to make the walk, he must to make the operate."

"Well, I'm very glad to see that you are following doctor's orders and walking," I said.

"I take the doctor very the serious. I not to want any the operation." Spiros shuddered as he spoke.

"But you've kept Sampaguita in the dark?"

Spiros stared blankly at me. "She have many the light in the house. They turn them off when I forget to pay the bill but now we are the reconnect."

"I mean you haven't told her about your blocked artery and the doctor's warning."

"It is not good to burden the Sampaguita with

the worry."

"I don't think you should keep it from her…I'm sure she'd rather know."

"I tell her that I walk to lose the lard." Spiros patted his paunch again before lighting a cigarette. "I think I will be even more the sexy when I to lose this the gut."

"Undoubtedly," I said wryly, Spiros' conceit never failing to amuse me. "Smoking can't be good for your blocked artery."

"I will to walk the ten kilometre the every the day if it let me to keep the cigarette. The doctor, he not to know the everything."

Reading between the lines, I guessed that the doctor had advised Spiros to knock the cigarettes on the head. Still, it wasn't my place to nag my friend about quitting his filthy habit. I reflected that giving up smoking in Greece was no easy matter since most of the Greek population seemed to have a cigarette permanently clamped between their lips. Moreover, even in official government buildings, ashtrays were always readily available, conveniently placed directly under the No Smoking signs.

"You have the good time with the Bill?" Spiros asked, a light breeze carrying the scent of embalming fluid my way.

"An excellent time. Bill and Vasiliki were wonderful hosts. I'm delighted that you facilitated our meeting."

"I miss much the Bill. He the very good friend of long time."

"I very much enjoyed his tales of the two of you in your youth."

"We have many the good time. The Bill, he to tell you about his first the car?"

"No, he didn't mention that. Do tell," I encouraged. Little did Spiros know, but I considered his amusing anecdotes to be perfect fodder for filling the pages of my book about moving to Greece, imbuing our story with plenty of local colour and anecdotes. I felt no qualms about stealing his material since Spiros would never pick up a book written in English. If he had any clue what I was up to, I felt sure he would give me his blessing.

"It was in the last year the Bill live here, when we were the seventeen. The Bill persuade me to go to the Athens with him, it not so quick to get there at that time. By the time we get there, he was the time to come home again," Spiros said. "The Bill want to go the Athens to buy the car from the cousin. Not many the people had the car back then, the car the big novelty in the Meli. When the Bill buy the car, it was the first car in the village." Spiros' tone was filled with pride, as though he was speaking of his own very first automobile.

"It must have been hard to get around back

then," I said, calculating that Spiros must be referring to the early seventies.

"We have the foot and the donkey...so, we get back to the Meli in the Bill's new car. It was the time for the olive harvest. Much the work to move between the olive grove with all the, how to say, carpets?"

"Nets."

"*Nai* nets. And back then, we not have the green light net, we have the heavy black type..."

"I know the ones, like heavy oilskin tarps."

"They difficult to move, very bulky. The Bill say to his mama, '*Ela*, we must to put the net in the car to make the easy work.' The mama refuse to get in the car with the Bill, she think he crazy. She tell the Bill he not know how to drive and the car dangerous...she cry he will kill them the both."

"Hold on, Spiro. If no one in the village had a car, how did Bill learn to drive?"

"On the Panos' tractor..."

"So, he used Panos' tractor for his driving test?"

Spiros broke out in hearty laughter. "Victor, back then, no one to think of the drive test, only in the town they make such the nonsense. There was no the police to stop the car to ask the paper. The Bill, he to make the test later, when he move to the Patras. In the city, the police to stop for the paper."

"I'm not surprised that Bill's mother refused to

get in the car with him," I said. I would never dream of taking such a risk with someone that hadn't passed their driving test. No doubt, Bill hadn't even bothered to tax and insure the vehicle.

"She more the used to the donkey. The Bill tell her, the donkey not so fast like the car," Spiros said.

"So, she preferred to ride between the olive groves on the donkey rather than get in the car?"

"No. She to put the nets on the donkey and walk behind it."

I could just picture it. Oftentimes, on the long drive to town during the olive picking season, I had seen little old ladies in mountain villages, laden down under the weight of olive branches, walking behind their donkeys rather than riding them. I imagined it was a tradition that was dying out. Soon, the remaining donkeys would be replaced with less aesthetically pleasing pickups, belching exhaust rather than dropping random piles of excellent fertiliser in their wake.

"The Bill's father say to the wife, 'Why you not to get in the car to make the work the easier?' She say, "The Bill will to kill himself.' The father he to say, 'If the Bill to kill himself in the car, your the life would not be worth the living any the more. If the Bill to die in the car, you would to throw yourself in the grave with your the son.' He say, 'If you think the Bill to be kill, it is better to be kill with him than to suffer his loss. Without our the son, our life would be over.' So, the Bill's father go in the car with the Bill and no one to dead."

Spiros' tale certainly highlighted the way Greek parents put their offspring on a pedestal.

"When no one the dead, the next day the Bill's mother go in the car with the son and the husband. She to say, 'The Bill the wonderful driver, he not to kill himself or the father.'

"I love her logic," I said.

"The Bill's parent still alive and to live in the Patras. They tell the Bill, they want me to make the bury in Meli when they to dead."

Lending Spiros a hand to pull him up, I reminded him, "Well, you'd better follow doctor's orders and keep up the walking if you want to avoid an early grave."

"Not to worry, Victor. I will to walk everywhere in the village and save the hearse for going the town and the funeral. The doctor, he say, the more I walk, the less the leg will pain me."

"It sounds like a win-win then. Your leg will improve, you get to avoid being operated on, and you might lose some of that lard from around your middle."

As we entered the taverna, Violet Burke was busy slopping her mop over the taverna floor, pausing

V.D. BUCKET

only to tenderly pat Dina's shoulder. Slumped in a seat at one of the tables, Dina's lovely face was visibly tear-stained. Even though I rather suspected she'd been blowing her nose in the tea-towel discarded on the table, I hadn't the heart to give her a lecture on her disgustingly unhygienic habits.

"About time." Violet Burke slammed the mop in the bucket with such force that the water splashed over the sides. Looking around, I noticed the taverna was as clean and tidy as I'd ever seen it, not a cobweb in sight. It was a far cry from the dusty neglected state it had been in when we first moved to Meli. "What kept you?"

"In case it escaped your notice, Mother, I was working on Pegasus today," I countered.

"It's all right for some, swanning about in Vasos' yacht. He's a good one, that Vasos. If I was thirty years younger, I'd have snapped him up by now." I thanked my lucky stars for Vasos' relative youth.

"So, what was so urgent?" I asked as Spiros dug out a bottle of *ouzo*, topping up four glasses of the clear spirit with water, turning the drinks a milky-white colour, before taking a seat next to Dina.

"Some Albanian woman is trying to muscle in on my cleaning jobs. I want to know what you're going to do about it, lad."

"Nothing. I've had a long day."

BUCKET TO GREECE (VOL.14)

Ignoring my protestation, Violet Burke continued to bark her orders. "For a start, I expect you to have words with that fella that lives with Maria. Can you believe he had the nerve to get this woman in to clean in Maria's place?"

"I take it you are referring to Maria's son, Papas Andreas?" It never failed to amaze me that Violet Burke always spoke of Maria's son with such disrespect, seemingly taking umbrage with his position in the Orthodox Church, even though it was in no way affiliated with the Methodist clan that had disowned her. "Don't worry, Andreas won't be employing the Albanian woman again. Maria made it quite clear to him that she wasn't happy about it."

"You mean you knew about it and didn't say owt..."

"We were away at the time. For some inexplicable reason, Papas Andreas didn't consider it necessary to telephone me on my second honeymoon to ask my permission before he got someone in to clean."

"It's the start of a slippery slope, lad. The pushy woman was in here earlier when Dina was on her lonesome, trying to muscle in on my cleaning job, haranguing and bullying Dina to get rid of me and give her some work. Dina got that upset." Placing a comforting arm around Dina's shoulder, Vi mangled a couple of words of Greek.

V.D. BUCKET

Sending Vi an affectionate look, Dina weepily confirmed that the Albanian woman had demanded, "*I Alvanida eipe dose mou douleia. Dose mou douleia,*" meaning, 'Give me a job, give me work.'

Violet Burke and Dina had grown close during the months Vi had been scrubbing and peeling at the taverna. Managing to communicate with simple words and the help of Nikos' translation skills, they had forged a genuine, if unlikely, friendship. Recognising Dina's sweet nature, Vi had become very protective of her friend. It was always wise to have the formidable Violet Burke on one's side than to make an enemy of her.

"Dina reckons she had a right mouthy gob on her. It wouldn't surprise me to find this woman is the Albanian equivalent of that common as muck, low life, Edna Billings."

"Haddock on Friday," I quipped, my mind immediately conjuring a vivid image of my mother's vulgar next-door neighbour back on the Warrington council estate.

"If I'd have been here, I'd have sorted her out." Vi clenched her fists menacingly as she spoke. "The flaming nerve of the cheeky mare, shouting at Dina who wouldn't hurt a fly. Dina asked her to leave. The woman spoke hardly any Greek but she made it clear she'd be returning at seven o'clock with backup. Dina got herself all worked up, she got herself in a right old tizzy. I reckoned if this Albanian cow is coming back with backup, you ought to be here as backup for Dina, Victor."

The very notion that I would be backup in the face of a posse of pushy Albanians, made me shake in my boat shoes.

"Isn't Nikos here?"

"He's not back from the fields yet. That's why I told Marigold to send you over. We need you to translate, lad. Like I said, this Albanian woman hardly speaks any Greek beyond 'give me a job' and she doesn't know a word of English."

"You want me to translate. You do realise that I don't speak a word of Albanian?"

"You must have picked up a bit, lad. You're always hanging around with that gormless gardener of yours."

"In case it's escaped your notice, Guzim speaks Greek," I pointed out.

Picking the mop up, Vi pointed it at Spiros, wagging the head in his face. "What about you, Spiros. How's your Albanian?"

"I not to know any. If you want the someone to translate, you should to ask the Guzim."

As Spiros mentioned Guzim's name, it occurred to me that the Albanian woman that had upset Dina must be Agnesa, the same woman who had been trying to brainwash Guzim with ridiculous notions that he was entitled to extras on top of his wages. I couldn't see Guzim willingly trotting over to translate after he had just declared he hated her. I felt greatly relieved that Spiros had come along to the taverna with me. If Violet Burke expected me to stand up to the nasty person that had upset Dina, at least I had Spiros to stand behind. I do loathe physical confrontation.

"The Tina tell me that an Albanian woman demanded work cleaning the shop but the Despina threw her," Spiros said.

"What did I say, she's going all round trying to muscle in on my jobs," Vi said. "Dina, is this her, here now?"

Although Dina doesn't speak any English, she caught Violet Burke's drift, shaking her head in agreement that the woman approaching the taverna was indeed the woman who had threatened to return with backup. Fortunately, the imagined posse of irate Albanians backing up Agnesa appeared to consist of nothing more than one man, and a pretty unassuming one at that.

Having heard so much about Agnesa, I focused my attention on her as she marched into the taverna, what I presumed to be her husband, trailing behind her. Aware of how many feathers she had already managed to ruffle in such a short time, I was quite surprised to see at first glance that she appeared to be a pretty nondescript woman, displaying no typical characteristics of the stroppy and entitled harridan I had conjured in my mind. Nevertheless, I felt a wave of relief when Spiros and Violet Burke each took a place by my side, the three of us forming a protective barrier between the Albanian couple and the anxious Dina who had started weeping into the tea-towel again. Wary that things may kick off at any moment, I was relieved to see that both the Albanians were as scrawny as Guzim; Spiros and Vi ought to be able to handle the pair of them if things got physical.

I would hazard a guess that the couple were in their forties, though the weatherworn wrinkles creasing their faces may have made them appear older than their years. Clad in a plain, dour serviceable skirt and blouse, limp brown hair escaping from a drab green headscarf tied beneath her chin, Agnesa exuded frumpiness. She looked too workaday ordinary to be the sort to have caused such a rumpus in the village or to be capable of upsetting Dina. Standing beside his wife in tattered and dirty work clothes, Drin's hangdog expression gave the impression of a henpecked husband who had been dragged along to the taverna against his will. As Drin shuffled uncomfortably next to his wife, he swayed drunkenly.

Planting herself firmly in front of us, Agnesa

fired off some indecipherable Albanian at Drin, exposing her near toothless gums in the process. Catching my eye, Spiros winked, mouthing "I think she to tell him what to say."

Focusing his eyes on the floor, Drin addressed us, nearly flooring us with his beery breath when he opened his mouth. Speaking in simple, ungrammatical Greek, Drin gestured with his thumb towards Agnesa, saying, "She want work."

Stepping forward, Spiros told Drin that there was no work for his wife at the taverna. Pointing at Vi, Spiros said that she cleaned the taverna and they weren't taking on additional staff. Drin duly translated.

"Spiros, tell that fella to tell her that she's got some nerve trying to muscle into my territory," Vi interjected. "I don't know how that woman has got the brass neck to call herself a cleaner. She did a right lazy job at Maria's, never heard of elbow grease or bleach. Then to top it all, she went and upset Maria by demanding the blankets off her bed."

Taking a step backwards, Drin gestured towards Violet Burke with his thumb, saying "*Anglika*," before firing a torrent of Albanian at his wife. Agnesa grew visibly angry, spewing a torrent of Albanian back at Drin.

"Agnesa say it not right to hire the rich English to clean. The Agnesa is the poor Albanian and need work. You must to give the work to Agnesa."

"What's he saying," Vi demanded as Spiros stepped in, translating Drin's inadequate Greek into English.

"Who's she calling rich?" Vi shouted as though the four-letter word was a choice expletive. "And tell her that if she's got any ideas about stealing my expats, then she can expect a good clobbering."

Agnesa was practically steaming as she waited for Spiros to translate Vi's words into Greek for Drin, before Drin redelivered them in Albanian. Clearly incensed by whatever Drin told her, Agnesa started yelling at Drin like a thing possessed, Drin immediately giving as good as he got. I must confess, I was able to recognise a few of the words as some of the expletives that Guzim was fond of hurling around when he lost his temper in his native language. However, I was as taken aback as the others when the argument between the couple turned physical. Drin, puce in the face, yelled at Agnesa, his spittle flying around in a most unhygienic way. Squaring her shoulders, Agnesa landed a punch on Drin with such force that it floored him.

Spiros was the first to react, rushing forward to frogmarch Agnesa outside. "*Arketa. Fyge apo edo*," Spiros shouted, telling them, 'That's enough. Get out of here.' Grabbing hold of a table leg, Drin pulled himself upright before scuttling off after his wife.

"Good riddance to mouthy riff-raff," Vi spat. "He'll have a right shiner tomorrow."

"We not want the people like that in the Meli," Spiros pronounced, grabbing the *ouzo* and topping up the drinks. "I to think it not the first time that the Agnesa knock the Drin. You to smell the beer on him, Victor?"

"It was hard to miss."

"To think that I moved to Greece to get away from undesirables like that," Vi grumbled.

"They're certainly few and far between in these parts," I reassured my mother.

"If no one gives them work, they must to leave the village," Spiros reasoned.

"Let's hope so."

"Victor, look." Grabbing me by the arm, the undertaker pulled me towards the taverna door.

"What are the odds?" I exclaimed, watching in open-mouthed amusement as Yiota trotted by on a donkey.

"It not even the olive harvest time," Spiros said.

"Perhaps the youngsters are turning back to the old ways," I suggested. "At least Yiota is riding the donkey, rather than walking behind it."

Chapter 24

Blat's Humble Home

"Victor, 'appen you should use your key to pop into mine and see if that emaciated little kitty is still clinging onto life," Vi instructed as I left the taverna.

Tempted though I was to linger in the taverna to eat with Spiros, I had other plans. When I told Spiros, I must leave, he invited Violet Burke to join him when she'd finished peeling the potatoes, telling me in an aside that it would be good for the still shaken Dina to have Violet around. I had promised Marigold that I would call in at Blat's place to see if Blerta was up to the challenge of a humongous pile of Bucket ironing in return for my giving Tonibler another English lesson. I must confess that I had rather embraced the village custom of bartering skills and fresh produce rather than handing over cash: saying that, when I had helped Spiros out with the Stranges' purchase of old Leo's house, I had turned down Spiros' decidedly morbid offer of a free burial at some unknown date in the future, rather than a cash commission.

I was quite keen to touch base with Tonibler again, the child having impressed me no end. Despite the schools being closed for the long thirteen-weeks school holidays, Tonibler struck me as the sort of studious child that wouldn't let the small matter of the annual break stand in the way of him getting stuck into his lessons.

Recalling that Blerta had arrived bearing gifts of some eggs and a mangled carrot when she first visited the Bucket household, I was delighted to be able to turn up with a fish, an attractive, freshly caught *barmpouni* at that, along with a bag of nectarines I had picked from the garden. It wouldn't do to arrive empty-handed since Blerta had displayed such generosity despite the family's obvious poverty.

The apartment that Blat rented was located in part of a rundown old stone house owned by a Greek family now living in Athens. The house, having been divided over thirty years earlier to provide separate accommodation for the different generations, had been allowed to fall into rack and ruin since the owners had long since stopped making the journey from the capital. Blat had mentioned to me that whilst his accommodation was pretty basic, the cheap rent appealed to him, his priority being to save up a nest egg to give them a good start once their hero, Tony Blair, stepped up to the plate and arranged their move to England. Despite there being zero evidence that the British prime minister had any plans to relocate the Kosovan family to Great Britain, Blat stubbornly held onto his dream.

Blat's apartment was accessed via a steep and mossy narrow stone staircase. Climbing the stairs, I was confronted with two doors, one directly facing the stairs and one to the right. Unsure which was Blat's front door, I knocked on the one straight ahead.

"*Eimai stin touleta.*" The familiar voice of young Tonibler announced he was on the toilet. Realising the door that I had selected was actually the door to the bathroom, I rapped on the other, pondering the thought that the family must have to step outdoors to access the bathroom. I shuddered at the chilling thought of needing the loo on a cold winter's night, though of course Blat, being much younger than I, might be able to manage a whole night without any inconvenient, prostate driven, nocturnal visits to the lav.

"Mr Victor, what the great honour for you to visit us," Blat pronounced, throwing the door open wide and practically dragging me inside. As he switched to speaking in Albanian, I hazarded a guess that he was pointing out the patently obvious to his wife, that Mr Victor was visiting. Whilst Blat barked at Blerta in his native language, I took the opportunity to surreptitiously glance around their accommodation, drawing the conclusion that Blat's description of it as pretty basic had been an understatement.

Their home comprised one long narrow room, with evidence of damp visible in the paint bubbling and peeling from the plastered walls, and in the fusty smell permeating the room. A makeshift kitchen lacking any natural light graced one end of the room; peering through the murky shadows, I spotted a double hotplate fuelled by a large gas bottle and a quartet of mismatched chairs surrounding a spindly table. The only light penetrating the gloom came from the shadows cast by the evening sun through a pair of glass doors at the opposite end of the room to the kitchen, leading out to a rickety looking balcony, rugs airing over the rails. The only access to the glass doors was via a narrow space between two dated wooden sofas spewing their stuffing. Heaped high with blankets, the sofas clearly doubled up as beds.

Despite their very basic living conditions, an effort had undoubtedly been made to make the space more homely. As my eyes adjusted to the dingy lighting, I could see that the walls were covered, not with the usual family photographs, but with images of Tony Blair, cut out of glossy magazines and black and white newspapers, then Sellotaped in place. No matter which direction I turned, I was confronted with a gruesome image of the British prime minister, grinning at me with his signature messianic smile. The original letter from Tony Blair, a copy of which Blat had shown me during our first meeting, took pride of place in an actual picture frame. Narrowing my eyes to better see in the fading light, it dawned on me that the candle stubs scattered throughout the room weren't there to offer romantic lighting in Blat's humble family dwelling; rather they served as a substitute for the lack of essential electricity.

"We are very the honour that you visit, Mr Victor. Please to sit and take the glass of *shliva*," Blat invited, ushering me towards one of the sofas.

"*Shliva*?"

"He is the plum *raki*," Blat explained as Blerta pressed an old chipped cup into my hand. I suppressed an involuntary snort as I clocked that the mug was emblazoned with Tony Blair's ugly mug. As Blat topped the lethal smelling contents up with water, turning the clear liquid a milky white, Blerta rushed over with a cushion for my back. I can't say that it came as too much of a surprise when I ended up leaning on a plumped-up image of Tony Blair. I hazarded a guess that if money was no object, the whole place would be set up as a shrine to the British prime minister.

It struck me that Blat's home might benefit from Marigold and Doreen's decorative touch; the pair of them could do amazing things with bits of repurposed fabric as they had already demonstrated in the pink palace of love. Perchance they could creatively hang some fabric to cover some of the damp spots on the wall. Reflecting that even one of their infamous makeovers might do little to compensate for the lack of electricity, I realised that they may just raise a spark if they made liberal use of Marigold's collection of old brushed nylon.

"Try the *shliva*," Blat urged.

Not wishing to appear rude, I took a tentative sip of the strong spirit, though I must confess that I found it quite unnerving to press my lips up against Blair's perpetually smug visage.

"We are the celebrate," Blat announced. "This week the Mr Vangelis and the Mr Barry ask me to work for them full time. They have much the building work on."

"That's excellent news," I said, raising my mug in a celebratory toast, pleased to hear that Blat would be spared lining up with the other day labourers down on the coast, jockeying against the competition to be picked for a hard day's graft. A steady job would offer stability along with a regular wage packet.

"The first job is in Meli for an English man. This will be good to try more my English," Blat said. Presuming he was speaking about the work on John Macey's place, I imagined that Macey would insist on trying out his Greek on Blat.

"I popped over to see if you'd like me to tutor Tonibler in English again." Omitting all mention of ironing, I managed to get my words out in between bouts of coughing induced by the powerful fruit *raki*.

"Tonibler has talk of nothing else. He very much like to learn more the English. He have been to practising the great language you speak," Blat replied as young Tonibler entered the room. Despite the school having already broken up for the long summer holiday, the child was still kitted out in his bizarre school uniform, a small kitten peeping out of his blazer pocket. I was delighted to note that the plaster covering one lens of Tonibler's spectacles had been upgraded to a superior blue one that complied with food hygiene regulations. The boy had obviously taken onboard the crucial lesson regarding the danger of lost plasters presenting a choking hazard if dropped into vast pans of curry or other food stuffs.

Watching the child stroke the kitten poking out of his blazer pocket, I asked him, "What's the name of your kitten?"

"She is called Clinton," Tonibler replied.

"After the great American President, Bill Clinton, who came to the aid of my country in the war," Blat added.

"And is Clinton spelled with a Kosovar twist in the same way that Tony Blair has morphed into Tonibler?" I asked.

"The Clinton start with the K," Blat revealed.

"Ah, so the kitten is named Klinton," I said with a smile, even though the two words sounded identical. "Make sure you give your hands a thorough scrub after handling the kitten, Tonibler. It may be harbouring zoonotic germs."

"What are zoonotic germs?" Tonibler queried.

"It refers to the type of germs that animals harbour. There is a risk that they can be transferred from animals to humans," I clarified.

"Mr Victor, I would like for you to teach me more about germs. Ever since I dropped the plaster in the pan of curry, I have been interested in the idea of foreign contaminants. I was fascinate when you told me about bacteria." As Tonibler spoke, Blat beamed on proudly.

"Fascinated," I corrected. "I'd be happy to do that," I agreed, beyond impressed not only with the child's precocious intelligence but his quick mastery of almost flawless English. "I'm certainly impressed that you wish to study English during the school holidays."

"The English they teach at the school is too easy," the child modestly replied. "I need my English to be good enough for the great Great Britain."

"Ah, yes, where you have aspirations of one day becoming mayor of London," I recalled.

"Mr Victor, does the newt have germs?"

"I must confess that I'm not too familiar with newts, Tonibler, but I do believe they can harbour salmonella germs."

"Salmonella?" he queried.

"Yes, it's a bacterium that can give you a nasty dose of food poisoning."

Scratching his head in confusion, Tonibler questioned, "The newt won't poison me if I don't eat it?"

"We certainly don't eat newts in England."

"Do you have the advice to teach the Tonibler how to become the great mayor of the great London?" Blat's question reminded me of his determination that Tonibler would follow in the steps of Ken Livingstone, newt and all.

"Whilst I am sure that aiming to be the mayor of London is a laudable ambition, I think Tonibler should concentrate on establishing a career before venturing into politics. I don't think he'd be able to bag the top job straight after finishing his studies. A career in politics may be chancy since there's always the possibility of being voted out. It would be sensible to have a solid career to fall back on."

"I think I would like to be the public health inspector like Mr Bucket," Tonibler trilled with enthusiasm. I considered this to be a much more realistic ambition than the usual childish dreams of becoming an astronaut or a famous footballer. Moreover, I was terribly flattered to think that I could perhaps shape the destiny of the future Tonibler by nurturing his interest in germs and bacteria. Of course, if Blat's family never managed to emigrate to Great Britain, I wasn't sure if Tonibler would be able to make a career out of inspecting dirty kitchens in Greece. In my experience, public health inspectors appeared to be pretty thin on the ground in my adopted homeland. Still, I reasoned, we did live out in the sticks. For all I knew, Athens may well be teaming with a veritable army of public health inspectors.

Translating on behalf of his mother, Tonibler

said, "Mama asks me to thank you for the fish and the fruit." It was clear that the child had attempted to emulate my own English accent, his words carrying not a trace of the Gheg Albanian dialect.

"We eat now. You must to eat with us," Blat dictated, his tone brooking no argument. Having no desire to deprive the family of any of their essential victuals, naturally I protested, my cries falling on deaf ears. It was clearly a matter of personal pride to Blat that he was able to demonstrate his hospitality by sharing the family meal with their uninvited guest, even if it meant that Blerta must eke out their meagre portions.

"Blerta will to cook the fish to serve with the traditional Kosovan dish of the stuffed eggplant," Blat said, directing me towards the kitchen table.

"Now, if you want to improve your English, you'll need to drop that particular Americanism," I said. "The English word is aubergine, not eggplant."

"I planted an egg in the dirt to see if he would grow into an eggplant..." Tonibler confided.

"Aubergines are fruits that grow from seeds," I schooled him.

"The aubergines," Blat tentatively sounded out the new word. "He is stuff with the..." Blat's words tailed off as he looked to Blerta to fill him in on the stuffing.

V.D. BUCKET

"Mama says the aubergine should be the stuff with the egg, the cheese and the curd, but today it is only stuff with the egg…she doesn't have any cheese and curd," Tonibler translated for Blerta.

"What a relief. Marigold says that too much cheese and curd play havoc with my cholesterol levels," I hastily replied so that Blerta could save face.

Taking a seat at the spindly table, I watched in fascination as Blerta made quick work of preparing the *barmpouni* I had contributed to the meal. After scaling and gutting the fish with natural aptitude as though born to it, Blerta sprinkled the fish with salt before dousing it in flour and flinging it into a frying pan of hot oil. Removing the sizzling fish from the pan, Blerta plonked it on a piece of kitchen roll to absorb the excess oil. Placing the fish on a platter, she squeezed the juice of a lemon over it before dividing it into four unequal pieces, garnishing the side of the platter with slices of cucumber.

Although I felt a tad embarrassed that the fish which I had brought along was a bit on the small side, clearly inadequate to feed four people, Blat and Blerta both expressed their gratitude and appreciation for the *barmpouni*. Blat told me that since fresh fish was a luxury they could not afford, just a small taste of it was a wonderful treat. Blerta presented me, as their guest, with the largest serving of fish, Blat and Tonibler receiving the remainder of the lion's share, Blerta placing only the tiniest sliver of fish on her own plate.

Although the fish looked and smelled wonderful, I could not imagine enjoying it. My own pleasure in the food would be ruined by the thought of Blerta going without. Switching the plates around, I put my own in front of Blerta, assuring the family that I was a carnitarian. Three blank faces stared back at me. Fortunately, as I had my handy English to Greek dictionary in my pocket, I was able to leaf through the pages and tell them I was a *karnitis*. Even in Greek, the word meant nothing to them, so I explained that I didn't eat fish on ecological grounds. Admittedly, I fibbed, but it was all in a good cause. I would derive far more satisfaction from watching the family of three enjoying the fish than I would have done eating it myself; I was, after all, in the privileged position of being able to enjoy fish whenever Marigold picked some up from Thomas' fish van.

As Blerta served the traditional Kosovan dish of stuffed aubergine, I noticed her embarrassment at offering me an authentic dish lacking half the customary ingredients. Even with the fish to eke out the aubergine, there was barely enough food on the table to feed the three of them, without stretching it to four. I made a mental note to pop round tomorrow and leave a discreet offering of some of my fresh garden produce.

"Does this dish originate from the part of Yugoslavia you hail from?"

"Blerta learn to cook it in Kukes…"

"Ah, yes, that's the part of north east Albania you moved to…I really know nothing about that area beyond the little I've read."

In truth, my knowledge about Albania had been woefully lacking until we moved to Greece and my interest in the neighbouring country had been sparked through interacting with Guzim. Despite recently reading up on the history of Albania, I had neglected to keep pace with the complex and convoluted news about the war in Yugoslavia which preceded our move to Greece, the war that had resulted in Blat's family becoming refugees. Tentatively broaching the topic, I was immediately shut down by Blat emphatically stating that it was a subject he did not want to talk about. I ought to have realised it was liable to be a sensitive topic.

Instead, Blat shared some information about Kukes, the Albanian town the family had taken refuge in.

"Kukes is the small town in the Accursed Mountains… you know the Albania build many the concrete bunker?"

"Indeed, I read that the communist dictator,

BUCKET TO GREECE (VOL.14)

Enver Hoxha, fearful of an invasion, decreed a concrete bunker be built for every citizen…"

"In Kukes, they go more, they build a network of tunnels under the ground…"

"Fascinating. I must read up about it," I said, thinking a network of subterranean tunnels wouldn't be such a blot on the landscape as a proliferation of hideously unsightly concrete bunkers. Finding the subject quite intriguing, I wondered if Marigold might be persuaded to take a road trip to Albania at some point in the future. Somehow though, I rather doubted that exploring concrete bunkers and subterranean tunnels would appeal to my wife.

Tucking into aubergine stuffed with eggs, I raised the subject of Blerta doing the Bucket ironing again, mentioning that Marigold had a pile of frocks that needed a good pressing from our recent holiday. I decided to leave it to Marigold to broach the topic of giving their humble home a makeover. She and Doreen would be over the moon to have another challenging decorating project that would likely rival their transformation of Guzim's hovel into the pink palace of love. I would have a word with Marigold later and see if she could utilise any of the soft furnishings that she had earmarked for the jumble sale. I decided it would probably be best if I didn't mention to Marigold that she'd have to decorate around Tony Blair. I couldn't see Blat approving of any decorative touches that papered over his hero.

Blerta consulted with Blat in their native language before Blat spoke on his wife's behalf in English. "Blerta says that Mrs Bucket has been so kind, recommending Blerta's ironing services to her friends. She is happy to do Mrs Bucket's ironing again but she cannot to do it tomorrow, she has another job. One of the great British lady that Blerta has begin the ironing for, asked her to cook an authentic Albanian meal for tomorrow evening."

"For how many people?" I asked, my interest piqued. Surely it couldn't be coincidental that Sherry was hosting the expat dinner party the next evening, a gathering where the host was supposed to cook a meal of foreign provenance. Albanian food would surely fit the bill.

"She think for the ten but the lady ask her to cook more, just in case."

"Is the lady named Sherry by any chance?" I asked nonchalantly.

"Yes, Sherry," Blat confirmed.

Although not a gambling man, I would put good money on Sherry passing off Blerta's cooking as her own the next evening.

Tucking into my stuffed aubergine, I reflected that although it was missing a few key ingredients, it was still most excellent fare. The imminent expat dinner party might not be so dire on the food front as our usual gatherings. Since Blerta was clearly a talented cook, I wouldn't have to suffer through the usual slop served up by the culinary challenged Brits in Meli.

Chapter 25

For a Good Cause

"Why on earth do you need me to come along to the jumble sale? It's not as though I'm in need of any second-hand tat," I complained, determined to resist Marigold's nagging. "You surely don't expect me to waste good money buying up our old curtains from Manchester."

"Really, Victor. It is for a good cause, after all," Marigold said in a blasé fashion. My wife was barely paying attention to me, more intent on checking her frock at every angle in the grand salon mirror. Quite why she felt the need to dress up for a noontime jumble eluded me.

"What good cause? It's the first I've heard about any good cause."

"I sometimes think that you never listen to a word that I say, Victor. I must have told you a thousand times that we're donating the proceeds to help to beautify the cemetery..."

"That doesn't sound very charitable. Your group will likely squander the cash on coffee and cakes to indulge in when you've finished your monthly bout of weeding. Or perchance you have more noble intentions like blowing it all on weed killer and gardening gloves."

"There's no need to be sarcastic," Marigold chided. "Oh, super, here's Doreen now. We're going over together to get everything set up before we throw open the doors to the villagers."

"I thought you were holding it outside."

"There's no need to be so pedantic," Marigold snapped. "We're expecting quite the crowd. Lots of Greeks have promised to turn up for their first jumble."

"Cooee, ready for the jumble. Isn't it exciting?" Doreen trilled, her face falling flat when she realised Marigold had dressed up for the occasion whilst she had dressed down in slacks and a pair of Crocs. Doreen's attire was certainly more suitable for lugging boxes of junk about. Perchance Marigold had no intention of humping boxes, preferring to delegate that task to me. I was having none of it.

"Doreen, can you believe that Victor is moaning about coming along to help?" Marigold griped.

"You don't want me getting under your feet. If I don't come along, there'll be more room in the Punto for you two and all your junk," I said.

"Jumble, not junk, Victor," Doreen insisted.

"I was just telling Victor that it's all in a good cause," Marigold said.

"That's right, Victor. We've decided to donate all the proceeds to the local strays," Doreen beamed.

"You can't just go around giving money to random cats. They aren't exactly equipped with the wherewithal to spend it wisely," I pointed out. "Or will it only go to the local strays that litter the cemetery?"

"Must you always speak in riddles, Victor?" Doreen snapped impatiently.

"Well, Marigold has just been telling me that the proceeds are going to be used towards beautifying the cemetery, and then you waltz in and say it's going to the cats. Which is it?"

"The cemetery," Marigold said.

"No, it's the cats. Don't you remember we decided the cats were a worthier cause?" Doreen reminded my wife.

BUCKET TO GREECE (VOL.14)

"Would that be after the pair of you downed the rest of that bottle of Mastic Tears last night by any chance?" I reflected it was a good job I'd dined with Blat and his family. By the time I got home, Marigold had been far too squiffy to sling the salad together.

"Oh, yes, it's all coming back to me now. We decided the strays are a worthier cause," Marigold backtracked.

"And it's all down to you, Victor," Doreen said.

"Don't go blaming me. You can leave me out of it," I protested.

"Doreen means that it's down to you that we decided the strays are a worthier cause than the cemetery."

"You've lost me. How on earth did I factor into your decision?"

"Well, it's because of that dirty little stray you took pity on. We thought we could establish an emergency fund for the village ferals," Marigold said.

"In case any of them need to be seen by a vet," Doreen added.

"I suppose it would be sensible to have an emergency fund to get them seen to so they don't go around reproducing willy-nilly." I considered it would be money well spent if it cut back on the number of local strays bestrewing the streets and

V.D. BUCKET

getting under the villagers' feet. There was far too much feral competition when it came to ferreting for food in the bins. "But don't expect me to be driving them up to the veterinarian and back."

"Cynthia will never go along with that." Marigold's plans had hit an obstacle. "You know how she feels about neutering. She says it is desperately cruel to deprive a cat of the chance of becoming a mother."

"I can't see what it's got to do with Cynthia," I argued. "You're the ones organising the jumble. Anyway, there wouldn't be so many strays in the first place if Cynthia would get that vile mutant of hers fixed. Kouneli is a total menace, responsible for fathering no end of strays with no end of reluctant felines."

"You know that Cynthia won't hear of it," Marigold insisted.

"You still haven't explained why you need to take any notice of what Cynthia wants…she won't even be there today. She's working."

"Well, she has made a sizeable donation to the jumble. She discovered a job lot of tinned food shoved in the back of their basement. It must have been left by Harold and Joan," Marigold said.

"I'm guessing they're British tins since Harold and Joan weren't into Greek food. How long do you suppose they've been down there?" I asked.

BUCKET TO GREECE (VOL.14)

Marigold evaded the question. "Tinned food has a long expiration date."

"I'm surprised Barry didn't claim them. What are they, beans and spaghetti hoops, I suppose?"

"It's quite the collection. There's at least half a case of tinned prunes..."

"Why on earth would Harold waste good money importing tinned prunes from England when Tina sells them in the shop?"

"I expect he wanted to make sure they were British prunes and not Greek ones," Marigold said.

"I don't believe I've ever seen a prune tree," Doreen said. It never ceased to amaze me that she had never quite got the hang of thinking before opening her mouth.

"You do realise that prunes are dried plums?"

"Really? I never had any reason to think about it. I never touch prunes, nasty things. Norman puts them on his porridge to keep him regular."

"Fancy that..." I began. Marigold fired a warning look at me. "What?"

Interpreting Marigold's look as a warning not to share with Doreen that I considered Norman to be as interesting as a bowl of congealed porridge, I changed tack, asking what other tins of British food Harold had squirrelled away in his basement.

"There are some tinned beefburgers...let me think, oh yes, some duck comfit and some Spam,"

Marigold revealed.

"My mother will want first dibs on the Spam," I said.

"I'll put them to one side for her," Marigold offered. "One of the perks of running the jumble is getting first dibs on all the best stuff. Do you suppose Vi will want the tins of all-day breakfast too?"

"Say what? All-day breakfast in a tin. I've never heard of such insanity in my life." I was genuinely flummoxed at the thought, my mind filled with images of runny egg yolks and soggy fried bread congealing in a sodden lump on top of a serving of cornflakes. "What on earth is in them?"

Marigold's expression curdled as she rattled off the list of ingredients. "Beans, sausages, mushrooms, and egg and bacon nuggets."

"Thank goodness we opt for a healthy breakfast of Greek yoghurt with honey and fruit," I said. "I knew Harold's taste was vulgar, but tinned all-day breakfasts take the biscuit. Perhaps you should offer a bottle of Gaviscon with every purchase."

"I'll put them aside for your mother," Marigold said decisively. "She might fancy them in a toastie."

"Garnished with mucky fat," I quipped. "Moving onto less stomach-churning topics, I called in at Blat's place last night. I have to say their living quarters are in a bit of a desperate state. Can you believe they have to muddle along without any electricity?

BUCKET TO GREECE (VOL.14)

I thought you two might like the challenge of giving the place a makeover like you did with Guzim's hovel."

The two women could barely conceal their excitement.

"Oh, we just love a good makeover," Doreen trilled.

"Oh, we do," Marigold agreed. "Doreen, perhaps we should have a good rummage through the jumble before we open the doors to the general public. We might be able to salvage some things to put aside to make their place more homely."

"What a good idea. It's lucky we have first dibs." Doreen clapped her hands with excitement.

"Is there anything in particular that you felt their home was lacking?" Marigold asked.

"If you can find any in the jumble, I think photo frames would go down quite well," I suggested, thinking of all the unframed pictures of Tony Blair adorning Blat's walls. Recalling the chipped Tony Blair mug my Kosovan *raki* had been served in, I added, "And perhaps some crockery and glassware might come in handy. Not to mention any candles you can get your hands on. Scented ones would be best to help cover the aroma of damp."

"Did Blerta agree to pop over and do the ironing?" Marigold asked.

"She'll be round tomorrow. She had another job

on today." I decided to keep shtum about Blerta cooking the food for Sherry's dinner party. I would derive much more enjoyment watching Sherry pretend that she was suddenly competent in the kitchen, before I let the cat out of the bag that Blerta had done the cooking. It would be most amusing to watch Sherry squirm her way out of that one. "Blerta was most appreciative of you recommending her ironing services. She's got quite a few clients from it."

"Oh, I am glad. They seem like such a nice family."

"I must confess to having a soft spot for young Tonibler. Thanks to my influence, he has ambitions to become a public health inspector. I will be teaching him all about germs and hygiene."

"Good grief, Victor. He's only six."

"But he's very keen to learn all about bacteria."

"Don't say you've finally found someone to share your interest? Has the poor child any idea what he's letting himself in for?"

"He's a very intelligent child. It is much more practical for him to aspire to a career in food hygiene than for Blat to fill his head with unrealistic dreams about becoming the mayor of London. They might never get the necessary visas to even make the move to England."

"We had it easy when you think about it,"

BUCKET TO GREECE (VOL.14)

Marigold said. "It was just a case of packing up when we decided to move to Greece."

"That's because we're part of the European community. Albania might be in Europe, but it isn't part of the club."

"We really should be making tracks, Marigold," Doreen urged.

"Are you sure we can't persuade you to join us?" Marigold wheedled.

"I've things to be getting on with at home this morning. I'll pop along to your jumble in a couple of hours to see how it's going," I relented. Catastrophe ambled over and started rubbing her body against my leg, a feline sign I interpreted as a demand for more food. Picking the cat up, I examined her. It didn't appear that she was any the worse for wear from being locked in the wardrobe.

Looking at me through narrowed eyes, Marigold said, "Tell me, Victor. Were you ever going to let on that you lost Catastrophe? You may as well come clean. Guzim told me everything, he couldn't bear to have it on his conscience. I swear he was practically weeping when he confessed."

"Come clean? I wasn't even here when your precious Catastrophe went on the missing list. I was with you in Arcadia; that makes you my cast iron alibi."

"But you knew all about it?" Marigold accused.

V.D. BUCKET

There was no point in denying it. Guzim had landed me in it when he made his, no doubt, grovelling confession.

"I didn't keep it from you to be deceitful, but to spare you any pain. You couldn't have done anything about it while we were away. Anyway, I thought it might find its own way home eventually, like Kouneli did."

"You're just lucky that the poor darling didn't have far to go, only a wardrobe door standing between her and the spare bedroom."

"I wasn't even here. It was all down to Guzim," I protested.

"There's no point in you trying to wriggle out of it, Victor. You were the one who decided that Guzim was competent enough to be left in charge of the cats. Hardly your most rational decision…"

"That gardener of yours hasn't even got the sense to realise how ridiculous he looks prancing around outside in those frumpy slippers," Doreen butted in. Marigold's side kick was so tone deaf that she failed to realise that the Crocs on her feet came in a close second to Guzim's *tsarouchia* in the frumpy stakes.

"I chose Guzim's shoes myself, Doreen." Marigold instantly transferred her annoyance to Doreen, letting me off the hook, for now at least.

"Come on, Catastrophe," I said to the cat. "Let's

see if there's a tin of luxury cat food with your name on it, squirrelled away at the back of the cupboard."

Basking in the bliss of some well-deserved alone time, I reflected it seemed ages since I'd enjoyed having the house to myself, able to revel in the musical delight of some light opera without Marigold calling me pretentious. With Puccini playing in the background, I settled at the desk in my office, losing myself in the exercises laid out in the touch-typing manual.

To my surprise, I seemed to have a natural bent for it. I determined to keep at it until I had mastered the art of typing with ten digits without looking at my keyboard. Once I had the skill of touch typing under my belt, I would be able to speedily crank out the corrected manuscript of Bucket to Greece, replacing all the words that old Scrapes had scrawled were too pompous and highfalutin. I certainly had my work cut out to make my style less affected.

Catastrophe sought me out as I typed, finding a comfy spot on my lap. At least the cat didn't appear to hold me responsible for her wardrobe ordeal.

Tempted though I was to ignore the phone when Marigold's name popped up as the caller, I dutifully answered. As expected, my wife was calling to nag me to get myself along to the jumble sale, now in full swing outside the taverna. About to fob

Marigold off with an excuse, she got in before me with a persuasive argument.

"Victor, you really ought to show your face. I know how much you want to impress the mayor, darling, and he's just popped in to the jumble. He says we're doing a wonderful job raising money for a worthy cause."

"The mayor's there now? I'm on my way," I promised. Grabbing my folder of notes on improving bin sanitation, I skedaddled down to the Punto, burning rubber in my haste to reach the taverna.

Chapter 26

Almost Full Circle

Leaping out of the Punto, I took a moment to compose myself. It wouldn't do to appear flustered or too eager in front of the mayor, or, perish the thought, greet him with damp, sweaty hands. If I expected him to take my proposals on bin sanitation seriously, it was imperative that I make a good impression. Adjusting the knot in my tie and smoothing my hair, I glanced around the taverna courtyard.

I had to give credit to Marigold and Doreen for their organisational skills. The place certainly looked inviting. Taverna tables standing in as stalls were dotted around the perimeter of the place, piled high with goods, colourful balloons flying above the stalls. Nikos had rigged up the old sheeting he had used at Barry and Cynthia's wedding to provide protection from the sun. Recalling how Nikos had confused his canapés with a canopy, I smiled at the memory of the linguistic mix up. Thankfully, Cynthia's mother, Anne Trout, hadn't been in attendance to complain about the lack of vol-au-vents and other assorted savoury pastry bites.

Marigold had used her considerable charm to rope in some of the Greek ladies from her beautifying the cemetery group to voluntarily man the stalls; judging from their smiling faces, they had happily thrown themselves into the jumble. Peering through the bustle of villagers milling around, I spotted a stall heaped high with fabric, other tables full of paperback books and CDs, clothes and assorted household junk. I saw that Doreen had made a petty move against Norman, lining up his traffic cones for sale. I expected she would have to sneak them back later as I couldn't see her getting any takers. It would be beyond sane comprehension if anyone else in the village shared Norman's tedious hobby.

I had to question my wife's judgement since it appeared she had left Kyria Maria in charge of the baked goods stall, hardly the most hygienic choice given our elderly neighbour's proclivity for sticking her fingers in food. Spotting Violet Burke at Maria's side, I hoped she could keep her friend's roving fingers in check.

In charge of one of the clothes stalls, Athena was helping an elderly gent try on a suit jacket that looked somewhat familiar. It suddenly came to me that Panos had been wearing it when he came to collect Violet Burke for a date. My mother had mentioned that Yiota had generously donated her grandfather's clothes to the jumble. I made a mental note to check with Athena if Panos' wellies were up for sale. If they were, I might well snap them up. Although they wouldn't be of any practical use to me since Panos had much smaller feet than I, they would have sentimental value. Marigold wouldn't have a leg to stand on if she complained about my frittering good money on wellies since I could counter it was in aid of a worthy cause.

"Victor." Waving back at Marigold, I picked my way towards her, failing to spot the mayor anywhere. My attention distracted by the very last thing I'd expected to see at the jumble, I felt a surge of annoyance.

"I don't believe it!" I exclaimed. I honestly thought I'd seen the last of the grotesque giant stuffed rabbit that I'd palmed off on Guzim. Taking up most of a table, the bunny attracted bemused stares from the locals.

"I know, quite magnificent, isn't it?" Doreen trilled, rushing over to my side. "That funny little Albanian of yours donated it. His generosity rather took me back. Marigold always makes out that he's on the scrounge, yet there he was, making such an altruistic gesture."

"He learnt his altruism from me. I gave the rabbit to Guzim to give to his baby boy, Victor Mabel. Fancy the ungrateful wretch offloading it."

"Well, it is for a good cause, Victor. All it needed was a good wash and a stitch up. It was quite filthy and some of its stuffing was coming out."

"Cynthia's vile cat got its claws into it."

"Well, thank goodness Kouneli couldn't get this one pregnant. Did you know that rabbit babies are known as kittens?"

"Of course. With Guzim being a tad rabbit obsessed, I know rather more about their mating habits than I'd like to. I'm surprised the bunny cleaned up so well after its trip on the Punto's roof. Marigold said it was too large to stuff in the washing machine."

"Oh, I give it a good dunking in my bathtub and sewed a patch over the hole where its stuffing was sticking out."

BUCKET TO GREECE (VOL.14)

"I never knew you had a bathtub," I said peevishly. "We've only got a shower."

"I remember from when I stayed with you," Doreen said. "There's nothing like a good soak. Do feel free to pop over to mine anytime with your rubber duck. Of course, I can't guarantee that Norman won't have left a tidemark behind him. He seems to have lost that young fellow he had round to clean. I can't blame the lad for jacking it in. Norman's a very difficult man to put up with and he completely fails to understand the concept of tidying up before the cleaner arrives."

Making my excuses, I ditched Doreen and joined Marigold. "I'm afraid you just missed the mayor, darling, but he did hand over five euros for my home-made lemon drizzle. It was only three euros but he told me to keep the change as it's for a worthy cause."

"You need to up your prices, darling. Three euros is practically giving a lemon drizzle away."

"I had to reduce the price because Kyria Maria had been poking at it."

"So, the mayor's left already?"

"He's a busy man. I told you that you should have come along earlier," Marigold said.

"I should have listened to you," I admitted, resigning myself to having missed another opportunity to ingratiate myself with the mayor. "How are your sales going?"

"It's been a roaring success so far. The villagers are loving it. I've got rid of most of that surplus courgette chutney you made but there isn't much call for second hand books."

"Well, if your buyers are primarily Greek, they won't want English books," I pointed out.

"I can't understand why we've ended up with more autographed copies of 'Delicious Desire' than we started with. I think everyone that passes has dropped in to offload their copy. I do believe that Milton's porn is the most popular donated item, but not a buyer in sight. I suppose you could always take them for mulch, darling."

"I don't want to risk corrupting my vegetables," I quipped. "It looks like Litsa may need some help. She's having a good rummage through your curtains."

"Those old curtains have been a hit with some of the older Greek ladies." Marigold's eyes twinkled with amusement. "They've been buying them up to fashion the fabric into new dresses."

"You mean they plan to turn our old curtains into frocks," I said, sharing Marigold's amusement. "Well, I can't imagine that you've got any blackout curtains in there that will do for Litsa."

Gordon Strange wandered over to join us, Waffles in tow. Gordon told us that he'd be flying solo at the expat dinner that evening because Moira had flown back to England to model her ears. "She's a bit despondent that the only offers her ears are getting these days are for hearing aids."

"It's a pity you haven't got Geraldine over at the moment," I said to Marigold. "Sherry's dinner party is going to be top heavy with unattached men that you could have dangled in front of her."

"I may be going alone but I'm still attached," Gordon objected.

"What unattached men?" Marigold snapped. "It's no wonder Doreen says you talk in riddles."

"Well, John Macey for one. And Norman. Don't forget that for all intents and purposes, Norman is single now, even if he is still lumbered with Doreen. I thought you'd be in your element at the potential for more matchmaking."

Sighing heavily, Marigold said, "I suppose you're to blame for John Macey coming along to Sherry's dinner. Really, Victor, you should have consulted me before inviting him along."

"It was nothing to do with me," I assured her. "Macey ran into Sherry in the shop and she extended an invitation. Perchance Sherry has Macey in her sights as her next boyfriend."

"I do hope not. I would hate to have to put up with him socially..."

"Perhaps he will pal up with Norman," I said

hopefully. "I'm all for new blood at the expat dinner parties if it means there's less chance of my being seated next to Norman."

"Would you look at this?" Gordon Strange said, holding up a video cassette labelled 'Prisoner Cell Block H'. I wonder what sad sap sat through this drivel."

"That would be my wife," I hissed as Marigold flounced off in a huff to join Doreen. Gordon followed in short order, Waffles dragging him off in the direction of the giant stuffed rabbit. I hoped that Waffles didn't follow Kouneli's example of attempting to mate with the bunny. Some of the elderly Greek ladies in attendance might have a fit of the vapours at such indecorous antics.

From the corner of my eye, I saw Norman approaching. Before I could make my escape, he had a damp grip on my arm. "Victor, just the man. A favour if I may? I don't suppose you could have a word with your mother for me."

"Well, she's around here somewhere, so why not speak to her yourself?"

"I find her a bit intimidating, to be honest."

"Don't be such a wuss, Norman. My mother is a harmless pensioner," I fibbed. "I believe you will find her over there at the baked goods stall. Since she appears to be tucking into what looks like flapjacks, you should manage to get a word in edgeways whilst her mouth is otherwise occupied."

"It's a bit awkward. I think it would be better coming from you," Norman persisted. "I've been having Theo in to clean but he's packed up and gone...left me in the lurch."

"Gone as in left the area? That's the first I've heard of it."

"Something about too much competition. Apparently, a new cleaner has moved into the area. And his window cleaning round never took off."

"Yes, he struggled with that. As well as being a tad clumsy, he never really got the hang of using a squeegee. And then many of the local orthodox weren't too keen on the idea of a Jehovah's Witness doing their windows, even a lapsed one."

Since Theo had been the youngest adult in both Meli and Nektar, I for one would feel the loss of his young blood. At this rate, we would have to wait until Anastasia and Nikoleta grew up before we had young adults in the village again.

"Anyway," Norman tentatively began. "I was wondering if you'd ask your mother if she could see her way to coming back to clean for me again..."

"I'm afraid you'll have to do your own dirty work, Norman." He certainly had a cheek. Without so much as a by-your-leave, he had dispensed with Violet Burke's cleaning services and replaced her with Theo. Now, Theo had done a disappearing act and Norman expected me to intervene on his behalf. "You'll have to speak to her yourself, Norman. I would recommend a lot of grovelling and a substantial pay rise."

"I suppose…I…what on earth? Those are my traffic cones…" Norman scampered off towards his treasured collection as though someone had stuck a rocket up his backside.

Relieved to be rid of Norman, I strolled around the stalls, perturbed to notice that Litsa and Kyria Kompogiannopoulou appeared to be engaged in a very heated argument. Each woman had hold of one end of the giant stuffed bunny, the rabbit the apparent victim of a tug of war.

"*Kyries,*" I intervened, stepping in before things became more heated.

"*Eida an proto.*" Tugging on the rabbit's ears, Litsa shouted that she saw it first. Litsa was demonstrating a side I had never seen before. She usually came across as such a sweet old dear.

"*To thelo gia ton engono mou.*" Kyria Kompogiannopoulou retorted that she wanted it for her grandson.

"*Thelo na to agoraso gia to moro tou Barry, ti mikri Anastasia,*" Litsa cried, saying she wanted to buy it for Barry's baby, little Anastasia.

Taking Litsa's arm, I pleaded with her to let Kyria Kompogiannopoulou have the rabbit.

BUCKET TO GREECE (VOL.14)

"Parakalo, afiste tin Kyria Sophia na echei to kouneli."

"Giati?" Litsa asked why. Leaning in close to Litsa so the other woman couldn't hear, I told Litsa that Anastasia was terrified of the rabbit and Barry would be distraught if it upset his baby girl again.

Dropping the rabbit's ears as though they were hot coals, Litsa told Sophia to have it, the other woman scuttling off to pay for it before Litsa could change her mind.

Smiling sweetly, Litsa told me that she didn't know what had come over her, getting so het up over a stuffed toy.

Making my way back to Marigold, I reflected on the irony of the grotesque bunny almost travelling full circle back to its intended recipient. I was delighted that my timely intervention had prevented Anastasia from being presented with the horror again. Since Sophia's grandson was a little older than my niece, he wasn't as likely to be as traumatised by it as Ana had been. If I spotted the boy, I would recommend that he use the bunny as target practice for his toy foam blaster gun.

Looking on the bright side, at least I wouldn't have to shell out the cash to buy the rabbit a bus ticket to Albania.

Chapter 27

An Edible Expat Dinner

"Victor, tell me that you're not seriously planning to wear those scruffy old wellies to Sherry's dinner party. You know that I'm not one to dictate your fashion style, but really. You'll be such an embarrassment to be seen with."

"I might be tempted if I could get my feet into them," I retorted, amused that Marigold had so easily fallen for my wind up. Naturally, I would never dream of turning up to a social event in wellies.

"Why on earth did you waste good money on them if they're too small?"

"Consider them my financial contribution to a

worthy cause. I had to buy something at the jumble and it was a toss-up between Panos' old wellies or another copy of Milton's porn. Actually, I thought of getting Guzim to bung these wellies on the scarecrow. I thought it might be the sort of fitting memorial that Panos would appreciate. The old fellow had a great sense of humour."

"I think your mother misses him dearly but she puts a brave face on. I must say, I'm delighted with the amount the jumble raised. It really went down quite well with the Greeks. We must make it an annual event. Now, do you want me to make you a quick sandwich before we leave for Sherry's?"

"I'll give it a miss this time."

"Are you sure? It's no bother, dear."

"No, really."

"It's not like you to miss doing a Scarlett," Marigold teased. "You don't want to be seen gobbling like a hog in company."

My wife wasn't confusing me with Scarlett Bottom, the pseudonym Milton used for his porn. Instead, her reference had become a running joke between us of late, Marigold comparing me to Scarlett O'Hara forcing some southern biscuits down before being laced into a waist-cinching corset prior to the barbecue at Twelve Oaks. Of course, Scarlett O'Hara had eaten before the barbecue to create the illusion she was a grand lady with the appetite of a bird. It wouldn't have been seemly for her to gobble like a hog in front of her myriad of charmed admirers. Emulating Scarlett's example, I had recently acquired the habit of having something to eat before attending the expat dinner parties since the standard of food served could only be described as inedible slop, best left on one's plate. It wasn't easy declaring one had enjoyed an ample sufficiency after barely consuming a bite, whilst one's stomach rumbled to the contrary.

On this occasion, knowing that Blerta would be taking charge of the cooking, I looked forward to tucking in and filling my boots; not to confuse my boots with Panos' wellies. Even though the ingredients had been somewhat limited, Blerta's cooking the previous evening had been of a very high standard. Marigold tolerated my little habit quite well without feeling the need to share it, happy enough to eat whatever came out of her friends' kitchens. Of course, after years of working as a pet food taster, Marigold's tastebuds were less sensitive than mine.

"I can't believe how chipper you are this evening, Victor. Usually, I have to drag you along kicking and screaming to these expat dos."

"For some inexplicable reason, I'm quite looking forward to it. Any idea which country's food Sherry will be cooking?" Already knowing the answer, I played the innocent.

"She's promised an Albanian feast. I just hope she hasn't bribed Guzim to give her a hand in the kitchen. I haven't spotted him taking a hosepipe shower since we returned from Arcadia. He's much too grubby to be let loose near the food."

Knowing that Blerta was in the kitchen, I felt confident that Sherry wouldn't have roped Guzim in to help as well.

"Shall we make tracks? We need to knock on for my mother."

"I think it's very considerate of Sherry to include Vi in her invites."

"Are we meeting Barry at Sherry's?"

"I'm afraid you'll have to manage without Barry this evening. He and Cynthia made some lame excuse...you know how irritating he finds Sherry. But Sherry did invite them, she's got over any qualms about inviting her builder to social occasions," Marigold said. "Can you imagine if we were back in England? There's not many that would be happy to sit down to dine with their builder and cleaner."

"There's no point in standing on ceremony over here. It's so much more relaxed living in Greece."

I wasn't the only one in a good mood. Violet Burke appeared full of the joys of spring and had clearly made an effort to tart herself up for the evening. Dispensing with her usual flats, she'd forced her swollen feet into a pair of bright orange kitten heels that clashed with the olive-green tweed number she'd forced her sizeable bulk into, the tweed so tight that I was surprised my mother could even draw breath. A full face of slap and back-combed hair completed the picture.

Ushering us into the *apothiki* to check up on the kitten's progress, my mother fairly brimmed with the news that Maria had snapped up a candlewick bedspread at the jumble and was planning to fashion it into a frock for Vi.

"It might turn out a bit shapeless." Marigold's observation oozed tact. She might just as well admit the plain truth that no one in their right mind would be seen in public in a candlewick frock. Vi would be well advised to stick to her usual tweed.

Sprawled on the sofa, the stray kitten I had rescued and palmed off on my mother until it received the all clear on the communicable diseases front, looked a sight healthier than it had just a couple of days earlier. It was certainly cleaner; perchance Violet Burke had given it a good bottoming. Sensing it was the focus of our attention, the kitten raised its head in a quite perky manner, pinning its little pink ears back. Without any gunk suppurating out of its eye, it was able to see clearly. If I hadn't been surrounded by women with a tendency to mock, I may well have taken the opportunity to formally introduce myself to the kitten as its saviour. It gladdened my heart to see the kitten looking as though it stood a fighting chance of surviving.

"The poor little mite's growing on me," Vi admitted. "I was that sick to see its backbone through its fur. I reckon some nasty beggar had mistreated it."

"Perhaps Victor could dig another kitten out of the bins for you, Vi, since he's set his heart on keeping this one," Marigold suggested.

"There were dozens of the beggars out there earlier when I bicycled over to the bins with my rubbish. Breeding like rabbits they are. I reckon it might be company to have a pet but a kitten can be a bit too skittish for my taste. 'Appen I could get a fish. It would give me something to watch when there's nowt on the telly."

"Don't tell me you've got through all those Coronation Street videos already," I said.

"Nay, lad, I've years to catch up with after working all them nights in the chippy, but Corries no good when the leccy goes off."

"Well, I'm sure a goldfish could give Vera Duckworth a run for her money in the entertainment stakes," I quipped.

"There's an idea, lad. You could call that kitten

V.D. BUCKET

Vera."

"Fancy you coming up with a Greek word for the kitten, Vi," Marigold said.

"There's nowt Greek about Vera Duckworth, you daft lass."

"No, but *vera* is the Greek word for wedding ring," Marigold countered.

"I'll think on it," I said.

"You could call it Vera with a Greek accent," Marigold persisted. "Just remember to put the *tonos* over the first syllable."

"I'd have a job getting a tuna fish into a goldfish bowl." Vi had got the wrong end of the stick.

"*Tonos* is the Greek word for the stress accent," Marigold enlightened her.

"I could swear Maria said a *tonos* was a tuna fish," Vi argued.

"It's both," I said.

"This Greek language business can be right confusing. Fancy having the same word for two different things," Vi grumbled.

"The English language is full of homonyms too," I schooled her.

"You what?"

"Well, off the top of my head there's bat and bat, and fine and fine."

"You don't half love the sound of your own voice, lad," Vi tutted dismissively.

BUCKET TO GREECE (VOL.14)

Satisfied that the kitten no longer appeared at death's door, the three of us piled into the Punto to head to Sherry's house. Whilst it would have been pleasant to stroll through the village on such a balmy evening, my mother complained her swollen feet would never make it up the steep hill to Sherry's place without exploding.

"Jolly good to see you all. Do come through, I'd almost given up on you," Sherry gushed in greeting, spraying kisses around indiscriminately. "I'm so glad to see you Mrs Burke, Marigold. I was beginning to feel outnumbered by the men."

"Sorry we're so late," I apologised, glaring at my mother. Violet Burke had made us unfashionably late, due to an unforeseen wardrobe malfunction. Straining to squeeze herself into the Punto, the too tight tweed had rebelled, an unsightly rip splitting her skirt from hem to waistband. It was beyond safety-pinning. It had taken my mother an age to prise herself out of the outfit and pour her bulk into another one with a bit more give.

"It's such a lovely evening, I've set the table in the garden. Do come through."

All the better to put some distance between her guests and the kitchen, I thought to myself, knowing Sherry would try to keep Blerta well out of sight and claim personal credit for the food. I was looking forward to winding her up by posing questions about her culinary methods that I knew she would be incapable of answering.

Making our way to the garden, Marigold praised, "The garden looks lovely, Sherry. The roses are exquisite. You've certainly got green fingers."

"I do enjoy a spot of gardening, such jolly good fun," Sherry brayed.

The garden was indeed looking blooming beautiful, flowers of every variety and hue trailing up trellises and sprouting from ceramic pots. It was clear that Sherry focused her attention on a floral oasis, not giving any space over to the cultivation of practical things such as vegetables or chickens. I supposed there would be little point growing veggies if one was clueless what to do with them in the kitchen.

"Who's already here?" Marigold asked.

"John's just over there tying that dog to a tree. It's been quite the menace, roaming about and watering my flower beds." Throwing her head back and braying with laughter, Sherry exposed her horsey teeth.

"John Macey? He never mentioned he had a dog," I said. Looking across the garden, I spotted a Labrador that looked a tad familiar. I was certain I'd crossed paths with it before.

BUCKET TO GREECE (VOL.14)

Striding over to join us, Macey said, "I'm dog sitting Percy Bysshe Shelley for the week while my friend Penny jets back to England."

"And you thought it appropriate to bring it along to a dinner party?" I chided, recalling with a sinking feeling that it was the very same Labrador that had found my leg so attractive on the beach. I could only hope Macey kept it in check. I had no desire to be humped by the creature again.

"I say in all modesty, I have experience in keeping dogs under control. Anyway, Shirley said it would be fine to bring him along as we're dining outside."

"Sherry," I corrected him.

"I don't mind if I do," he replied, making a grab for the bottle of Lidl wine we'd brought along with us.

"No, Sherry is the name of our hostess," I reminded him.

"I told you they weren't suited," Marigold hissed. "He can't even be bothered to get her name right."

Introducing John Macey to Violet Burke, my mother blurted to his face, "Is this the fella what's always boasting he's been living in Greece for sixteen years?"

"I may on occasion have mentioned it in the most modest of ways," Macey said, doing that slug-like thing with his eyebrows again.

Nudging him sharply in the ribs and winking, Vi said, "'Appen you'll be needing my services when you move into your house."

"Services?" Macey looked horrified. Considering the amount of slap Violet Burke had trowelled on her face, I could forgive Macey for getting the wrong impression.

"Aye, my cleaning services, lad. But from the look on your face, I'd say you've got a right mucky mind. I'll have you know that me and my mop are in great demand round these parts."

"Well, it will be a couple of months before I'm able to move into the house," Macey said dismissively. "By the way, Vic…"

"It's Victor," Marigold corrected him with a haughty air.

"I ran into that pair of American tourists this morning, the ones that you seemed so obsessed with on Pegasus…"

"I wasn't obsessed…" I denied.

"You were," Marigold insisted. "You thought they were stalking you. I've never heard anything so ridiculous." One would think that Marigold would have taken my side against Macey since she had taken against him since their first meeting.

"Anyway, they told me they were heading to Athens tomorrow to fly home," Macey said.

BUCKET TO GREECE (VOL.14)

"They won't be able to stalk you from the states," Marigold chortled. "You do let your imagination run away from you sometimes, Victor."

"I say in all modesty, I had a stalker of my own back in Crete. Some desperate housewife type on the hunt for a husband," Macey shared.

"Well, you want to watch out. Those types can be everywhere," I said, gesturing towards Sherry who was trying to round everyone up to take their seats for dinner. After jollying Doreen, Manolis and Gordon Strange to the table, Sherry tripped back towards us, her sights apparently set on Macey. If she wasn't careful, she would catch the heels of her unsuitable shoes in the flowing kaftan she was wearing and land in a heap at Macey's feet. I imagined that if she took a fall, Macey would be claiming that in all modesty, women were forever throwing themselves at his feet.

"I can't believe that Doreen brought Manolis along," Sherry complained. "I didn't invite him, not with Norman coming. I couldn't leave Norman out, what with him being such a great pal of yours, Victor."

"Great pal of mine. What on earth gave you that idea?" I asked.

"Norman did," Sherry said. "I find it all terribly embarrassing having to choose sides. I mean, naturally I have to side with Doreen as one of the girls,

V.D. BUCKET

but what does one do with Norman? It all gets so jolly complicated when couples split up."

"Well, I can't imagine Doreen objecting if you take Norman off her hands now that she's with Manolis," I suggested.

"Victor, it's not like you to matchmake," Marigold said.

"Sorry, am I stepping on your toes, darling? It's just that Norman is single now...more or less. And he has mentioned trying out the dating scene."

As I sauntered over to the table, Gordon Strange greeted me with a wink. Pointing to the Goldendoodle slumbering by his feet, he asked, "Victor, will you be wanting to borrow Waffles while you eat?"

"Not this evening, thanks all the same," I replied. Whilst quite fond of Waffles, I would prefer not to have him anywhere near me in case he attracted the ardent attentions of Percy Bysshe Shelley. "I'm sure that Sherry's cooking will be to such a high standard that I'll have no need of a canine dustbin."

"Are you feeling quite yourself, dear?" Marigold asked.

"Top form. Don't forget that Sherry never missed one of my cookery classes."

"But you said she was the worst student you'd ever had."

BUCKET TO GREECE (VOL.14)

"How you exaggerate, darling. I'm sure I never said any such thing."

"Everyone, do please take your seats. I must start serving or the main course will be overdone. Everyone's here except Milton, Edna and Norman. We'll have to start without them. I can't think what's keeping them. Norman was supposed to pick them up from the hospital hours ago. It's jolly bad manners to keep us waiting," Sherry said.

That at least explained Norman's absence. I had assumed he was a no-show because he was sick of Doreen rubbing his nose in her loved-up bubble with Manolis.

"Just sit anywhere. I did put place cards out but they seem to have been tampered with." Sherry glared at Doreen before tripping off to the kitchen.

"Can you believe that Sherry had the cheek to put me at the opposite end of the table to Manolis *mou*?" Doreen chuntered, her seat so close to Manolis that she was in danger of sitting on his lap. "It was a bit tactless of her to expect me to sit next to Norman."

"Well, you are married to him," Gordon pointed out a tad prudishly.

"Sherry's rushing us a bit. We haven't even had a drink yet," Marigold griped, carefully assessing which seat to select. Before I could stake my own claim, Marigold plumped for the seat between

Doreen and Gordon Strange, leaving me to sit next to one of the three vacant chairs. By the law of averages, I had a one in three chance of being lumbered with Norman if he ever turned up.

"Well, I'm that starved I could down a raw Fray Bentos, tin and all," Vi said. "I've had nowt to eat since that tin of all-day breakfast I picked up at the jumble."

"Good to hear that Harold's old breakfasts went to a good home," I said, beginning to wonder if there was no end to the abysmal food my mother was prepared to eat whilst turning her nose up at excellent fresh Greek fare.

Macey leapt out of his seat to gallantly relieve Sherry of the large tray she was carrying, laden down with bread and some kind of dip. Impressed by his gentlemanly behaviour, Sherry fluttered her eyelashes at Macey before announcing that she was serving a typical Albanian starter of fergese.

"What's in it exactly," I asked, feeling sure Sherry would be clueless.

"Fegese is a warm curd cheese dip with tomatoes, eggs and peppers added," Sherry pronounced with surprising confidence. I hazarded a guess that Blerta had brought young Tonibler along to Sherry's kitchen so he could translate the ingredients to our hostess. "I'll just bob back and get the salad."

BUCKET TO GREECE (VOL.14)

"Let me help you," Macey offered.

"No, no, I wouldn't hear of it," Sherry cried, reinforcing my suspicion that Blerta was still holed up in the kitchen, well out of sight of Sherry's guests.

"Salad and some curd stuff. I might have known that Sherry wouldn't be up to cooking owt proper," my mother grumbled.

"It's surprisingly good," Doreen said through a mouthful of dip that Manolis had just fed her. The loved-up couple appeared oblivious that their mating habits were a tad nauseating to the rest of us. I was tempted to say 'get a room' but it was still a sore subject since Doreen was stuck living with Norman, and Manolis with his slimy brother, Christos.

"I'd rather have one of them cakes your husband makes," Vi said. Doreen bristled, clearly annoyed that Vi was bringing up her marital status in front of Manolis.

Everyone except Vi tucked into the fergese dip accompanied by a simple Albanian salad comprised of sliced tomatoes, onions and cucumber on a bed of shredded lettuce, dressed with balsamic vinegar and olive oil. Basking in the praise of her guests, Sherry avoided my eye, turning selectively deaf when I repeatedly asked her how she'd made the dip.

Keen to have my suspicions confirmed that

Sherry had Blerta stashed away in the kitchen, I waited until our hostess was deep in conversation with Macey before slipping away from the table and making my way to the house.

"Victor. Where are you going?" Sherry called after me.

"Just popping inside to powder my nose," I retorted, confident that even Sherry would think it would look a tad strange if she followed me into the bathroom.

Heading directly to the kitchen, I found Blerta lifting an enormous casserole dish out of the oven.

"Mr Victor, hello." The genuine smile on Blerta's face transformed her somewhat harassed expression. My mother had said countless times that Sherry never stopped hovering while she worked.

"Hello, Blerta. I thought I might find you here."

"I leave. I come back later to clean," Blerta said, gesturing that she would be returning later to deal with the washing up.

"Delicious food," I said, repeating my words in Greek in case she hadn't understood my meaning. *"Nostimo fagito."*

Blerta beamed with joy at my heartfelt compliment.

"And Tonibler?"

"He...go." Blerta made a shooing gesture,

indicating she had sent him home, telling me that earlier Tonibler had translated. "Before, Tonibler...*metafrase*."

"*O gios sou einai exypno agori*." Telling Blerta that her son was a clever boy, I passed her basket to her as she left. Wondering what time Sherry expected Blerta to return to clean up after her guests, I decided to persuade Marigold that we should make it an early night. It wouldn't do for Blerta to be so exhausted that she cried off from tackling the Bucket ironing the next day.

Returning to the table, I assumed a butter-wouldn't-melt expression as Sherry glanced at me suspiciously before she hurried off to the kitchen. I could picture her relief when she found it empty. I imagined she'd been keen to send Blerta packing when she'd finished cooking, reducing the risk of anyone discovering a foreign presence in the kitchen.

Sherry presented the main course, ladling it from the casserole dish onto the plates. "This is the national dish of Albania, tavi kosi. It is baked lamb and yoghurt with rice, with garlic and oregano."

There were surprised murmurs of delight all round as we all sampled the Albanian national dish. As I had expected, it was excellent.

"Sherry, the garlic in this dish is very subtle," I gushed. "Did you grate, chop or press it?"

Sherry's reply of "all three yes" attracted some puzzled looks from the odd expat familiar with a kitchen and a head of garlic.

"You've really done us proud this evening, Sherry. How did you manage to get the lamb so tender?" I pressed.

Sherry's relief was evident when the doorbell rang, sparing her from answering my probing culinary questions.

Chapter 28

Barricaded Out

Studiously avoiding his estranged wife, Norman made a beeline for the vacant seat beside me.

"I see that Milton and Edna pair aren't with him," Violet Burke remarked. "At least I'll be spared that lovesick dope, Milton, making cow's eyes at me all evening."

"Norman drove Milton and Edna here," Sherry said. "They're just freshening up in the bathroom before joining us."

"Together?" Doreen huffed under her breath. "Sherry flat out stopped Manolis from coming into the bathroom with me."

"Let me get you some tavi kosi, Norman," Sherry offered. "I'm afraid you're too late for the appetiser, worst luck."

As Sherry ladled more lamb stew for the new arrivals, Norman leaned in, practically attaching himself to my ear as he hissed, "No need to have that word with your mother after all."

"I wasn't going to. If you are too intimidated to speak to my mother, it's your loss."

"Well, I may have accidentally taken on another cleaner...can't say that I'm quite sure how it happened."

"Another cleaner?" I parroted, my antennae going off. I assumed he could only be referring to the Albanian woman, Agnesa, who had already tried to muscle in on a few of my mother's cleaning jobs, not to mention ruffled quite a few feathers in the village.

"This strange woman turned up on my doorstep. Before I knew what was happening, she was down on her hands and knees on the kitchen floor with a dustpan and brush. I didn't want to risk offending her, so I let her get on with it. I have to say though, she didn't make a grand job of it like your mother did, just a lick and a spit. Not to mention, I couldn't understand a word that she said..."

"Well, you're not exactly fluent in Greek or

BUCKET TO GREECE (VOL.14)

Albanian," I pointed out.

"And then she kept pointing at the towels in the bathroom. She got quite heated but I couldn't make head nor tail of what she was jabbering on about. In the end, I thought the best thing to do was just bung the towels in the washer and get Doreen to give them a good boil wash. Can't think what else she was getting at."

"I rather imagine she was demanding you gave her the towels on top of her wages," I said. "She has form."

"Give her the towels. Doreen would make my life even more of a misery than she already does if I started giving her towels away to all and sundry. Now this woman's going rate was a lot less than your mother charges, but if I'm expected to throw in towels on top, it would soon add up." Norman grabbed my arm. "Hang on, you said she has form?"

"She sounds like the Albanian woman, Agnesa. She thinks she is entitled to extras on top of her wages. You want to be careful. She gave her husband a right shiner yesterday evening. I can't believe that you're so naïve you would take a complete stranger on without references."

"I never thought. Oh my, she could be a serial killer for all I know...I think I may have been a bit rash." Norman visibly gulped as it dawned on him that he may have taken on a violent cleaner he knew nothing about. "How on earth will I get rid of her if she comes back?"

"You could brush up on the Albanian for 'get lost'," I suggested.

"Perhaps you could have that word with your mother after all…"

"You'll have to man up and do it yourself," I retorted. "I'm not one to insert myself in my mother's business."

Sighing heavily, Norman changed the subject. "Have you heard about Doreen's latest trick? She only tried to sell off my traffic cones at the jumble sale…"

"Norman, let me introduce you to John Macey," I interrupted, gesturing for Macey to come over before Norman could start prattling on about his painfully boring hobby. "I have a feeling that John will be absolutely fascinated to hear all about your traffic cones."

Before Macey could jump to my bidding, Milton and Edna made their entrance, Milton supporting his wife as much as his dodgy hip allowed. As they shuffled slowly across the garden, Violet Burke cackled, "You look like a pirate, lass. All you need is a parrot."

A tear trickled out beneath the eye patch Edna was sporting, no doubt prescribed by the ophthalmologist that had performed Edna's cataract surgery. Pausing to pull a hankie out from the sleeve of her cardie, Edna sniffed loudly before burying her nose in the soggy rag.

"I didn't mean to set you off, it was just a joke." Vi rolled her eyes. "You'd think you'd have a sense of humour, lass, what with being married to that daft Milton."

Jumping up, Doreen rushed to Edna's side, helping the elderly lady across to the table. Once the pair of impoverished pensioners were seated, I noticed something seemed amiss.

"Milton, you're looking very glum," I said. He hadn't once gazed at Violet Burke with his usual adoration. "How did it go at the hospital?"

"Edna's operation went well, old chap. Yes, very well. The old girl should be able to see well enough to avoid tripping over the cats from now on, what."

"Oh, Milton. The cats," Edna wailed, sobbing pathetically.

Patting his wife's arm, Milton stretched in his seat. "The old hip's a bit creaky, what. Darned uncomfortable sleeping in a chair next to Edna's hospital bed for two nights."

"Two nights? Were there complications?"

"Nothing like that, old chap, just they rather take their own sweet time with these things. Edna

V.D. BUCKET

had a day of tests, then the op the next day. The doctor, wonderful chap, said she should stay another night after the op so he could check out the old vision this morning. Took all day, what, before he discharged her."

"Well, at least it sounds thorough. But if it all went well, why so glum?"

"Something terrible has happened…"

Everyone's attention was now focused on Milton, eager to find out what terrible thing had occurred.

"What's going on, Milton?" I pressed. "Don't say you've been duped by another unscrupulous scammer?"

"I'm ashamed to admit that I've gone and made rather a botch of things. All my own fault, what. We can't get into the house, old chap. We're at an absolute loss what to do," Milton said.

"What do you mean, you can't get into your house?"

"Well, when Norman drove us home from the hospital, Kyriakos refused to let us into our house. You remember Kyriakos? He moved in to cat sit for us while we were up at the hospital but when we got home, he flatly refused to let us in."

"He refused to let you into your own home. Why?"

"And he's thrown the cats out," Edna sniffed.

BUCKET TO GREECE (VOL.14)

"The garden was full of the poor things, they looked so lost."

"Got to admit, we're at our wits end, old chap. Never expected to be barricaded out of our own house. Of course, it's all my fault, inviting him to stay in the first place. I should have realised he was quite barking mad when he thought he could fly off his balcony, what. It's just horrid to think that my actions have resulted in Edna and the cats being made homeless."

Everyone offered their two penn'orth worth on the situation, shocked by the turn of events.

"So, Norman was with you when you tried to get in the house?" I questioned, wondering why Norman hadn't intervened on behalf of the old couple or tried to force his way in.

"Yes, but there was nothing he could do. When we tried to talk with Kyriakos, he'd clean forgotten all his English and none of us speak Greek."

"Rather convenient of Kyriakos, I must say. He was speaking English perfectly well just a couple of nights ago," I said, smelling a rat. "He invited us in to look for Marigold's missing cat. Barry thought Edna might have taken it in."

"Really, Victor," Marigold piped up. "Do you mean to say my own brother knew Catastrophe was missing and kept it from me?"

"He didn't want to worry you," I said.

V.D. BUCKET

"Well, there was nowt wrong with that Kyriakos' English this afternoon," Violet Burke interjected. "I was round there after the jumble. He paid a good whack to have me give the place a right good bottoming. He reckoned all them cat hairs were bringing him out in a rash."

"So, you cleaned the place earlier…"

"I thought that Greek fella was wanting it all clean for when Edna got home from hospital."

"So, the place wasn't barricaded when you were there earlier, Violet, what?"

"Course not. Do I look like I'm in the habit of breaking into houses to clean them, you muppet?"

"I have to say, Kyriakos seemed to find the abundance of felines littering the living room a tad irritating," I said, remembering how he had complained about the multitude of cats in the Hancocks' house. I thought it best not to mention that Kyriakos had shooed a dying kitten off the doorstep in case Edna had a total meltdown.

Turning to Norman, I gave him a piece of my mind. "I must say, I think it was very irresponsible of you to bring Milton and Edna here when this mess needs sorting out. You sat down at the table as though nothing was amiss, griping about your problems with your char, never once mentioning anything about the Hancocks' dire situation."

"But…" Norman looked suitably shamefaced

to have received a dressing down. "The Greek bloke in the house was bigger than me and he was waving a big stick out of the window."

"I would imagine that was one of his crutches. This fellow might be bigger that you but he's rather incapacitated on account of having recently broken both his legs."

Doreen couldn't resist the opportunity to get a dig in. "What can you expect from Norman? He's always been a snivelling coward."

"Any ideas what we can do, old chap? I'm at my wits end," Milton said.

"I think that you and I should get down there, Milton. We need to sort this out pronto before the situation escalates. Let me just make a quick call."

"I'd rather you didn't involve the police, old chap," Milton said.

"Only as a last resort," I promised.

Waffles tagged along beside me as I strode across the garden to find a private spot to make the call. As I waited for Spiros to answer his phone, I searched my pockets for any treats to offer the Goldendoodle. Coming up empty, Waffles had to settle for a friendly pat on his curls.

Spiros took an age to answer the phone. Dispensing with the usual pleasantries, I rushed right in. "Spiro, I need your help. Can you meet me outside Milton's house in ten minutes?"

"Milton?"

"The old fellow that writes the porn."

"Ah, yes, I know," Spiros chuckled. "Is it the important? I was to watch the *romantikos* movie with the Sampaguita."

"We have a situation," I said, filling Spiros in on recent events that culminated in Kyriakos barricading himself inside the Hancocks' house and refusing to let them in.

"This is not the good for the international relations between the Greek and the British. I meet you there, my friend," Spiros promised. "I hope very much we not to need the riot police."

Returning to the table, I said, "Come on, Milton. We need to get down there and try to talk some sense into Kyriakos and get this situation resolved. Best if Edna stays here with the others until we've worked things out."

Glancing around the table, I wondered if any of the other men present would volunteer to come along as backup. Noticing how they all squirmed shiftily in their seats and avoided my eyes, I decided that Violet Burke's assessment that the British contingent of males in Meli were a collective bunch of big girl's blouses, was spot on.

Making my way to the Punto with Milton, Marigold rushed to my side. "Darling, I think it would be best if you wait here for me," I urged.

BUCKET TO GREECE (VOL.14)

Leaning in close, Marigold whispered, "I've no intention of coming along. I just wanted to warn you not to go getting any chivalrous ideas about offering the Hancocks our spare bedroom; he does write porn, after all. And don't go offering to take in any of Edna's mangy stray cats. Our pedigrees just aren't up to mixing."

Chapter 29

A Suicidal Cat Sitter

Driving down to Milton's house, I felt a stab of disappointment that I hadn't managed to milk anywhere near the full mileage out of Sherry passing Blerta's Albanian cooking off as her own. Perchance I had teased the situation enough that the others might eventually cotton on, but the likes of Doreen and Norman were hardly the brightest bulbs in the box. Having been fellow students of Sherry in my cookery classes, I would have expected them to realise how absurd it was to imagine that Sherry would be capable of turning out the excellent lamb and rice main. One could say that Norman had turned out to be the star of my classes, though he had spurned my Greek recipes in favour of perfecting his gooey range of French fancies.

Parking up the Punto, Milton and I picked our path to the door, fighting our way through an obstacle course of cats, dozens of the things littering the small garden. It was apparent that Kyriakos had indeed banished the felines he was supposed to be cat sitting, in addition to the house's rightful residents.

Banging on the front door, I called out to Kyriakos, hoping he was downstairs. It could turn into a long evening if I needed to wait for the stairlift to deposit him on my level.

"Kyriakos. It's Victor Bucket here. Why are you refusing to let Milton into his own home?" I bellowed.

After I'd wasted another couple of minutes hammering on the door, Kyriakos threw open an upstairs window. Leaning out, he shouted down. *"Den boreis na beis."*

"What's he saying, old chap?" Milton asked.

"He says we can't come in."

In no mood to act as a translator between Milton and his stubborn cat sitter, I called up, "Speak in English, Kyriako."

"I not coming out and no one to come in,"

Kyriakos shouted down.

"Come on, be reasonable, Kyriako. This is Milton's home; you can't just keep him out."

"It is my the home now. The Milton, he ask me to live here…"

"He asked you to stay there to look after the cats…since you appear to have chucked them out, you have hardly lived up to your side of the bargain."

"I not leave. It is so nice and peace here, no the wife and the mother fighting the day and night. I cannot to go home. I cannot. I cannot." His tone grew ever more strident as he repeated himself. It was clear that the poor fellow had got himself in quite the state but it was no excuse for his behaviour.

"Look, you can't just barricade yourself in and keep Milton and Edna out. There must be Greek laws about trespassing."

"If you to make me leave, I will throw myself off the balcony," Kyriakos threatened dramatically, extending his arms through the window and flapping them in a poor imitation of a bird.

"You'll have a job. The house doesn't have a balcony," I snapped, losing patience with his theatrics. It was hardly fitting for me to engage in a shouting match on the street. I might end up with a reputation for being as vulgar as Edna Billings.

BUCKET TO GREECE (VOL.14)

Kyriakos was perfectly capable of gliding down to the door on the stairlift so that we might conduct our business in the manner of civilised gents.

"Then I will throw myself out the window or off the roof."

"I say, old chap, don't do it," Milton cried. "You don't want to have to go through all that rehab again if you break your legs for a second time."

"This time, I will to kill myself," Kyriakos threatened.

Clutching my arm, Milton pointed towards the street, his voice quivering as he said, "I say, old chap. Isn't that the undertaker fellow? It's a bit rich of him to show his face, premature of him, what. Kyriakos has only just threatened to kill himself. Seems a bit keen for business, what."

"I asked Spiros to join us. I hoped he might have a better chance of talking some sense into Kyriakos since he knows him well."

"Ah, got you, old chap. Stupid of me to think he was coming to plan the funeral before Kyriakos jumps."

"Victor. You speak with the Kyriakos?" Spiros asked, rubbing his fingertips over his bushy eyebrows.

Before I could reply, Milton told Spiros in a panicked tone, "Kyriakos is refusing to let us in, what. He's threatening to jump out of the window or off the roof. He says he'll kill himself if we make him leave."

"We may need to tread carefully, Spiro," I advised. "It appears we now have a suicidal cat sitter on our hands. Hopefully, he's just bluffing."

"Did he to take the *chapia*?" Spiros asked.

"He doesn't look happy to me, old chap. Can't think that a happy chap would threaten to throw himself from a second storey window, what."

"Spiros wants to know if Kyriakos has been taking pills again. *Chapia*, are pills, Milton. You said it was the pills that made him think he could fly the last time he hurled himself off a balcony."

"No clue if he's been guzzling pills, old chap."

"Let me to speak to the Kyriakos and talk some the sense to him. I know him all my life but since he make the retire, he much the change. He cannot to cope with the endless fighting in the home, it much depresses him. Victor, you to know the mother of the Kyriakos?"

"I can't say I've had the pleasure," I replied.

"He is not the pleasure." Spiros emphasised his point by running his finger across his throat. "The mother, he is the terrible woman, he would to try the patience of the saint. I not to blame the Kyriakos for leaving the home."

Switching to Greek, Spiros engaged in a long conversation with Kyriakos who was hanging precariously out of the upstairs window, in danger of losing his grip. If he fell, he would probably have a soft landing since the garden was practically carpeted in cats, but the cats wouldn't thank him for being squashed into oblivion.

I must confess that I was only able to understand snippets of the conversation because Spiros and Kyriakos spoke at great speed. Moreover, my slightly more than rudimentary Greek didn't incorporate the necessary vocabulary for dealing with suicidal cat sitters barricading themselves in someone else's home. It was hardly an everyday sort of situation. As Spiros and Kyriakos verbally sparred, I reassured Milton that we would hammer out a solution so that he would be able to sleep in his own bed that night. I was with Marigold one hundred percent in not wanting the Hancocks cluttering up our guest bedroom.

After five minutes of incomprehensible back and forth Greek between Spiros and Kyriakos, Spiros turned to address Milton. "The Kyriakos say you ask him to move into your the home."

"Yes, to look after the cats while we were at the hospital."

"So, you were the happy he to live here? He say, you to know he have the very difficult time with the wife and the mother."

"I thought if old Kyriakos stayed here, it would

give him the opportunity to have a break from his family, what. It certainly sounded as though he needed some time away."

"So, you would be the happy for the Kyriakos to live here for the short time, not to look after the cat but to pay you the rent money? It would be the good, yes."

"You mean have him stay here as a lodger?"

"*Ti?*"

"*Enas enoikiastis*," I said, offering Spiros the Greek translation of lodger. "That sounds like an ideal solution, Milton. You could certainly do with the money."

"Hmm, take Kyriakos in as our lodger. I must say, we got on swimmingly until he barricaded me out …"

"But he only to do that from the desperation," Spiros assured Milton. "He think the death the better than to return to the intolerable home. You know the much famous motto of the Greece, Milton? We to say, '*Eleftheria i thanatos*.' It to mean freedom or death. If the Kyriakos to stay with the you, it will to give him some the freedom. He say he would rather to jump to the death than to return to the own home and suffer the slow death from nagging."

"And he promises that he won't throw himself out of the window…or off the roof, if I let him stay as a lodger? I can't have Edna getting herself all in a tizzy, what. She's only just out of the hospital."

Spiros conferred with Kyriakos again before the suicidal cat sitter pulled himself back in the house. A moment later, we heard the electrical whirr of the stairlift starting up.

"The Kyriakos promise he not to throw himself or make to fly. He to give his the word to be the good tenant and to pay the good cash. In return, he only ask that you not to let the cat into his the bedroom. If you let him to stay for the short while, he will, how you say, take stock, and think of how to resolve the intolerable living at his house. Away from the house, he could to try to respark the *romantikos* with the wife."

"Putting some distance between them whilst courting his wife sounds eminently sensible," I said. "Milton, do you think Edna will go along with having Kyriakos as a lodger?"

"I should say so, what. If we have some rent money coming in, Edna will be able to splurge on the good cat food."

With the seemingly impossible situation amicably resolved, Kyriakos removed the barricades and threw the front door open.

"You were the hero of the hour, darling." Marigold nestled up close to me as we perched on the outside stairs, the silvery light from the moon casting shadows over the kitten I'd saved, curled up in the shoebox by our feet.

"Nonsense. It was Spiros who saved the day. It was a stroke of genius to suggest the suicidal cat sitter move in as the lodger to help the Hancocks out on the cash front."

"Is it really true that Sherry had Blerta do the cooking this evening? I can't believe she cheated; it goes against the whole ethos of the expat dining club."

"Doesn't your beautifying the cemetery group have rules against passing off shop bought biscuits and cakes as home-made? I'm all for a bit of expat cheating if it means we get to eat something actually edible at those dreadful dos."

"You know you enjoy them really."

"Only because you are there with me."

Resting her head on my shoulder, Marigold's Titian locks teased my chin. "This evening has brought home to me how lucky we are, Victor. One would imagine that everyone living in such a Greek paradise lives a contented life, but things aren't always what they seem behind closed doors. Imagine, that poor man was so desperately unhappy that he thought that moving in with Milton and Edna was an improvement on his home life."

"I dread to think how he'll cope with all those cats. Kyriakos seemed to have a low tolerance."

BUCKET TO GREECE (VOL.14)

"Speaking of cats..."

"Don't spoil the mood by bringing up that business about Catastrophe," I pleaded.

"I was going to suggest that we get little Vera checked out at the vet tomorrow so that we can bring her home properly, if she gets the all clear. It makes me nervous to think of Vera being in your mother's care. The kitten is a bit delicate for Vi to be practising her mothering on. What if she accidentally sat on the poor little mite? It doesn't bear thinking about."

A light breeze gently wafted over us, releasing the intoxicating scent of the potted geraniums and jasmine lining the stairs. The kitten stirred in the shoebox, blinking rapidly as she woke. Scooping her out of the box, I settled her on my lap, feeling the pulse of her tiny heart beating beneath her patchy fur as she purred in contentment.

"You're going soppy, Victor," Marigold teased. "Fancy risking a dose of some unhygienic nasty just to enjoy a feline cuddle."

A Note from Victor

I hope you enjoyed the latest volume of the Bucket saga.

All Amazon reviews gratefully received, even a word or two is most welcome

Please feel free to drop me a line if you would like information on the release date of future volumes in the Bucket to Greece series at
vdbucket@gmail.com
or via Vic Bucket on Facebook.

I am always delighted to hear from happy readers.

Printed in Great Britain
by Amazon